The Gossamer Thread is the memo:
psychotherapist, telling the story of hi. ~~progression from a hard~~
nosed behaviour therapist with a strong commitment to science to
a psychodynamic therapist with an interest in narrative. Along the
way it illustrates the way the main schools of psychotherapy (behavioural, cognitive, psychodynamic) work, using case material from
his professional practice. It shows the mistakes made and the lessons eventually learned from patients. The focus on clinical cases
enables the reader to see psychotherapy in operation and get drawn
into the ups and downs of trying to help some fascinating and often
tricky people who rarely conform to what is expected of them.

This book is free of jargon and can be enjoyed without any prior
knowledge of psychology or psychotherapy. It is designed to entertain and inform the reader about the mysterious world of psychotherapy and what goes on behind the consulting room door. It will
be of particular interest to the increasing number of people who
encounter psychotherapy either through their own experience of
seeking help; the experiences of family and friends; or through the
reading of popular books on the subject. It should also prove invaluable for those interested in training as a clinical psychologist, counsellor or psychotherapist.

John Marzillier is a clinical psychologist and psychotherapist. He
worked as a therapist for thirty-seven years in various clinical set-
tings including psychiatric hospitals, GP practices, a university clinic
and in private practice before retiring from his professional practice
in 2006. He now works as a writer. For more information visit John's
website www.johnmarzillier.com

THE GOSSAMER THREAD

THE GOSSAMER THREAD
My Life as a Psychotherapist

John Marzillier

KARNAC

First published in 2010 by
Karnac Books Ltd
118 Finchley Road
London NW3 5HT

British Library Cataloguing in Publication Data

A C.I.P. for this book is available from the British Library

ISBN-13: 978-1-85575-802-5

Typeset by Vikatan Publishing Solutions (P) Ltd., Chennai, India

Printed in Great Britain

www.karnacbooks.com

To Mary, Kate and Sarah, with love

Certain things I remember exactly as they were. They are merely discoloured a bit by time, like coins in the pocket of a forgotten suit. Most of the details, though, have long since been transformed or rearranged to bring others of them forward. Some, in fact, are obviously counterfeit; they are no less important. One alters the past to form the future.

—*James Salter*, A Sport and A Pastime

The past is what you remember, imagine you remember, convince yourself you remember or pretend you remember.

—*Harold Pinter*, Old Times

CONTENTS

AUTHOR'S NOTE

This book is based on the events of my life as a psychotherapist. It is, in one sense, factual: these are the experiences I went through over almost four decades in three different cities. But it is, in another sense, a work of fiction. To preserve client confidentiality, I have carefully and systematically changed many aspects of the people I treated. The events I describe happened but not necessarily in the way they are portrayed in the book.

—John Marzillier

"That's the typical guff you psychologists spout!" Kevin glares at me across the low table that divides us. I'm startled. What have I said? Kevin is convinced that the person in the flat above him stomps noisily across the floor whenever Kevin switches on his television. It's a deliberate act of provocation according to him.

"Are you sure?" I'd said, unwisely I now realize.
Kevin snorted. Of course he was. The man hated him.
"Might it not have been a coincidence?" I enquired. Tactfully, I thought.
Kevin shook his head angrily at my stupidity. "I *know* he does it."

It was then that I spouted my typical psychological guff. What I'd said was that Kevin could test out the hypothesis by keeping careful records of when the stomping occurred and if it did coincide with his switching on the TV, then he would be proved right. If not, it would be a coincidence. Kevin is a scientist so I thought he'd appreciate the idea. But he was having none of it.

"I *know* he does it," he repeats, contempt oozing from his voice. "You psychologists know nothing."

Suddenly I am feeling *very* angry. I just stop myself saying, "So why the hell do you come to see me?", my contempt a match for his own. Anyway, Kevin's not listening. He is going off on another rant about some bloke he'd met in the pub who completely misunderstood quantum physics and wouldn't listen when Kevin wanted to put him right.

I glance surreptitiously at the clock. Oh dear, 20 minutes to go.

***

Emma bustles into my consulting room, her eyes shining bright. "It's been a good week," she says as she throws herself down in the chair. With Emma there are good weeks and bad weeks. She has been coming to see me for 18 months. She is at last making progress but it has been a roller-coaster ride. On her lap she has a Sainsbury's shopping bag. She dives into it and pulls out a transparent plastic box in which nestles a bunch of bright red tomatoes, still on the vine.

"Not from Mr Sainsbury," she says archly. "Oh no. Home grown. First of the crop. They're for you." She hands them over proudly. I take them automatically and then place them on the low table between us.

"I'm sorry, Emma, you know I can't accept gifts." I say it rather sadly as though not accepting the tomatoes was a supreme sacrifice on my part. Emma recoils as though I have slapped her in the face.

"Why ever not? Such *stupid* rules. They're only tomatoes. They won't bite you."

No, I'm supposed to bite them. My facetious thought masks my anxiety. I know Emma desperately wants me to take them. *What harm can the gift of a few tomatoes do?*

"I'm sorry," I say inadequately. The tomatoes sit accusingly between us in the silence that follows.

"Shit and fuck," says Emma. She grabs the box and stuffs it back into the bag and then dumps the bag carelessly on the floor. She turns and stares out of the window. After a while she says, "I suppose your wife grows wonderful tomatoes, but then that's another rule, isn't? You won't tell me that either."

It's not going to be an easy session.

***

We are in the Underground on the Circle Line. There are three of us. Me, a fully fledged behaviour therapist, Jason, my trainee who is here to learn from me, and Stu who is an agoraphobic and petrified of going anywhere, especially on the tube. To say Stu is panicking would be an understatement. He is sitting next to Jason, wedged against the window, shaking all over and moaning to himself, his head buried in his arms. The woman opposite does not give him a second glance. When I had told Stu that we were going on the tube as part of the flooding treatment for his agoraphobia, he had come up with every conceivable excuse including that he would panic and the other passengers would stare at him. I assured him that, panic as much as he liked, the latter would definitely not happen. At least I am proved right on that. You could strip stark naked on the tube and you would be lucky if anyone looked up from their magazine.

"Concentrate on your breathing," says Jason quietly. "In-out. In-out. And don't worry. You'll feel better over time. That's the way it works."

I admire his certainty, but then it's what I had told him will happen. We are going to go all the way round the Circle Line, which should allow enough time for Stu's anxiety to decrease. Theoretically, at least. I have never done this before. Cleverly, I have bought the cheapest tickets for all of us, the cost of going one stop. We will end up back where we started.

The tube train jerks to a halt. The doors screech open. I notice a lot of people are suddenly rushing out. Having travelled on the tube to school in my youth, mostly without a ticket, I am attuned to the subtleties of passenger behaviour. The inspectors! Sure enough, there are two of them at the far end of the carriage, starting to check everyone's tickets. The doors slam closed. Shit!

Jason has seen them too. "What're we going to do," he says?

"Hold tight. I'll think of something."

But what can we do? If I tell the inspectors that Stu is a psychiatric patient and we're treating him, it would be breaching confidence. And it does not explain why we did not buy full fare tickets anyway. I am beginning to panic myself.

Stu's seen them now. They are moving inexorably up the carriage towards us. He looks up at me. "Inspectors?" he says. I nod. For some reason their appearance seems to calm him. I have a momentary fantasy that he is going to demand that they rescue him from the evil clutches of his psychologist captors.

One of the inspectors is now upon us, demanding to see our tickets. I freeze. I hear Stu's voice saying. "Sorry, inspector, we're from the Maudsley Hospital. We're doing a treatment for agoraphobia. We only got tickets for one stop 'cos we going back to where we started." He shows them his ticket. Meekly, Jason and I do the same.

The inspector looks at the tickets, looks at Jason, looks at me and turns back to Stu. "Okay, doctor," he says. "Don't worry about it."

***

Belinda and I face each other in silence. She is looking down and to the right, not at anything in particular, but caught up in her thoughts. I am watching her, waiting patiently. It is only our fifth session. I am intrigued by her, by the mixture of bravado and anxiety she has shown in the sessions, by her singular and at times chaotic life. She lifts her head and looks at me.

"I was at the National Gallery on Saturday," she says, emphasizing every word as she is wont to do. "Do you know Titian's picture, *The Death of Actaeon?*"

I don't say anything. Belinda continues as though I have.

"It's a tremendous picture. You know the story of course, how Actaeon was out hunting and chanced upon Diana and her nymphs bathing in a pool. She was naked. Horror of horrors."

I cannot tell if the exclamation is meant to be ironic.

"Diana punishes him by turning him into a stag. His own dogs tear him to bits. Titian shows the moment he's been set upon. Diana, very beautiful, is shown holding a bow on the left of the picture. On the right Actaeon, with a stag's head and a man's body, is being savaged."

Belinda stops. Why is she telling me this? I am tempted to ask her but hold back. I surmise that it is a coded message about us. Men who see women naked are likely to get torn to bits. Hmm. Does she see psychotherapy as a way of stripping her naked? In which case I am in mortal danger. On the other hand, there is an erotic charge to the picture or so it feels though I have not actually seen it. Is this transference? What am I feeling at this very moment? I like Belinda. I look forward to seeing her. It feels like she is *special*. Bloody difficult this psychotherapy, I think, veering away from the transference implications which, for the moment, I am not sure how to handle.

"I wonder why you're telling me this," I say, non-committally. "I suspect it's a reference to your being here, in therapy. But what are your thoughts?"

A cop-out on my part? Or a way of letting Belinda do the work, which is supposed to be the golden rule, if there is a golden rule.

Belinda smiles. "All men turn into beasts in the end, don't they?" She says it sweetly, a definite irony in her tone this time. Yet I know, and she knows I know, that in her life men did indeed become beasts and very nasty ones at that.

***

These fragments of my experience have been culled from 37 years of working as a psychotherapist in which I changed from a bumptious behaviour therapist, a fervent believer in rationalism and science, through various transformations to what might be called a psychodynamic narrative therapist—but that for me is just the way I found psychotherapy worked best. In this book I show this transformation in detail, mixing casework with theory, and bringing out the personal reality of being a psychotherapist, sometimes painful, often startling, occasionally boring, but for the most part exhilarating as I am allowed privileged access to other people's lives in a way that few others are. Having stopped my psychotherapy work, I wanted to write this account to show *what it is really like*. Of course, that is ridiculous. My take on psychotherapy is as subjective and partial as the next person's. If I have learned anything from a lifetime career as a psychotherapist, it is that there is no universal truth, that everyone is different and that you, the reader, should take what I or anyone else tells you about psychotherapy with a large pinch of salt.

But if there is no universal or absolute truth, there is still truth. The events I describe in the book happened and the people I portray are based upon real people and real events. I have written "based upon" because I have changed significant details of my patients' stories and, often, significant aspects of their characters and their lives. I have occasionally constructed a mélange where I have brought in bits of several cases and created one composite case. I have largely invented dialogue drawing upon how I thought the exchanges might have happened. Given that many conversations occurred years or sometimes decades ago, I have had to do that. Even where I still had detailed notes, they rarely consisted of transcriptions of an actual conversation. My overriding concern was to protect the anonymity of my patients. I could not ask their permission as most had long disappeared from my life and I had no means of contacting them.

I made a decision to begin with the reality, with the person and the therapy, and create a disguise, a fiction from the raw material of fact. In this way the people who became Peter or Naomi or Cordelia or Matthew are all real but the account I give of them and of their therapy has been fictionalized. Their stories have been changed in order to create a disguise. But, despite this, I have strived to be honest. I have not changed the outcome of the therapy, for example. I have not distorted the truth in order to make myself appear in a better light. That would defeat the object of the book. Psychotherapists, like anyone else, are imperfect. Their privileged position may make them appear wiser and better than they actually are. I have known many psychotherapists and not one of them was free from fault, including me. We are all human beings beneath the persona.

Therefore, to any of my former patients who, in horror or fascination, pick up this book, wondering if you appear and how I might describe you, I sincerely hope that you will be disappointed. However, a few of you may recognize something, an event or conversation or problem that seems familiar perhaps, or realize that the case I am describing is based, at least in part, upon your therapy even if the biographical details have been changed and the therapy is not quite as you remember it. I trust my elaboration and invention have provided the necessary disguise so that you will not be recognized. Above all, I hope you do not feel that I have diminished you or your story by writing this book. That has been my main worry throughout its gestation.

A patient once said to me, wondering what this strange business of psychotherapy was about, that it was a highly unusual form of personal relationship, intensely intimate yet at the same time detached from normal life. An image of a gossamer thread came into my mind, delicate, shimmering, evanescent, and sometimes seeming to disappear altogether, but always there in the background. I have taken the metaphor of the gossamer thread for the title of my memoir. I did not always think of psychotherapy in this way. For a long time I saw it in very different terms and it was only later in my professional career that I understood how important the personal relationship was, the thread that bound patient and therapist together. But that is to get ahead of myself. My journey starts, like all good journeys, at a crossroads, a point when everything seemed to lie ahead of me and all I needed to do was to take the first step.

SECTION I

GETTING MY HANDS DIRTY

CHAPTER ONE

Beginnings

A blond, curly-haired, slightly chubby 17-year-old boy sits by a squat, black telephone staring out of the top-floor latticed window of a grand house on the Berkshire/Surrey borders. The telephone is the old-fashioned sort with a circular chrome dial that has letters on it as well as numbers and requires a hard tug to make it move. The phone does not ring and the boy appears not to be interested in it. In fact, the vacancy of his gaze, his casual, slumped posture, the occasional, irregular drumming of his fingers on the window-seat, suggest that he is entirely caught up with his internal world and that the external world is, for the moment, lost to him. Were he to take in what is in his immediate vision, he would see a square, gravel forecourt below, temporarily empty of cars, leading to a drive that bifurcates in front of what, in the summer, is a sumptuous rose-garden but is now a long parcel of dark earth. There is a small cottage beyond and, everywhere to his left and right, stands the gaunt tracery of trees and bushes that make up the extensive grounds. If he were to open the window, lean out and look to his left, he would just see the top of a tennis court. And if he were to look to the right, he might catch a glimpse of Rosie, his brother's foul-tempered horse, in the field beyond the hedge. And if he had been looking out of a window on the other side of the house, he would see manicured lawns, neat, cultivated flower-beds, a rectangular swimming pool dormant under a grey plastic cover, and an expansive view across fields and woods unimpeded by another house or building. It would remind him, if he needed reminding, that he was a privileged child, the son of rich and successful parents, on the brink of what he hopes will be a glittering career.

This is a memory. And I am the boy. The year is 1963 and I am in that time between leaving school and university, now called a gap year though in my day it was just a gap, a yawning chasm of boredom and inactivity, as I waited for my new and wonderful life to start. My recollection is an example of what psychologists call *autobiographical memory*, the way we gather together events in our past lives to help make sense of ourselves and our world. This is in essence what my book is about. But how accurate is autobiographical memory? One of my clients told me how, throughout her childhood, she lived in continual fear of her father who had a terrible temper. She believed this contributed to her high anxiety as an adult. This is not a memory of a specific event but a generalization or abstraction about her past. It is a summation of many events over many years. It is true in the sense that it is clearly what she remembers. I accepted it without question though it is in fact a perception, a way of looking at her past, and will exclude alternative views of the same events. But it is *her* perception and that is important.

Another of my clients recalled a fragmentary memory of a frightening, smiling face coming closer and closer to her. She thought it might be a very early memory from when she was still in a cot. When she watched a television programme on child abuse, the memory seared into her consciousness and terrified her. This is sometimes called a *flashbulb memory* because of its vividness and emotional intensity. Is my client remembering actual abuse by her stepfather? She might be, for in many ways he was a nasty man. But I did not know and nor did she. It would have been easy to reconstruct the experience in therapy, to flesh it out, perhaps rather too appropriate a term in this context. But there would be a real danger of creating a false memory out of this fragment, that is, one that comes to be firmly believed by the client not because it is true but because it makes sense.

My memory of my 17-year-old self is inevitably a reconstruction. In my mind's eye, I can see the top floor of my parents' house as though I have just left the landing and gone down the stairs five minutes ago. I sat by that old-fashioned telephone many times. But what I most remember is the feeling of dissatisfaction and frustration at that time of my life. I was an adolescent and, like all adolescents, my moods were mercurial. One moment full of energy, the next inert as a beanbag. I knew I was not happy but I did not know how to describe what I was feeling. Imagine that I mentally search a thesaurus for the words to describe my state of mind. *Disconsolate, dispirited, despondent, dejected, downcast, fed-up, frustrated, gloomy, glum, moody, melancholic, morose.* But there is one adjective I deliberately avoid: DEPRESSED. As I stare unseeingly out of the window into my hazy future, I know I could not possibly be depressed. I am absolutely sure of this for the following reasons:

1. Depression is a form of mental illness and I am not mad.
2. My parents are rich and we live in a grand house with its own tennis court and swimming pool. I am about to go to Oxford. How could a privileged boy like me be depressed?

Later, when I became a psychotherapist, I realized that anyone can be depressed. It did not matter how rich or successful or clever or secure or loved you were. Depression could swiftly descend like Sylvia Plath's bell jar and the world become horribly muffled and distorted. But in 1963 I knew nothing about depression. In truth, I knew nothing of any importance having been educated in a good public school that had as its main, and it seemed to me at times only, tenet the urgent desire to ensure that we boys knew nothing whatsoever about girls, so much so that, although there was a girls' school somewhere nearby, in my six years at the City of London School for Boys I never found out where the City of London School for Girls was. Apart from the annual debating society when the girls took on the boys and wiped the floor with them, I never so much as saw a girl.

However, although convinced I was not depressed, I was interested in depression. This was because of a boy called Bradshaw and Albert Camus.

In the 6th form we were encouraged to have debates and discussions, a way of sharpening our brains, preparing ourselves for what the masters believed to be the cut-and-thrust of Oxford or Cambridge tutorials. This showed how little our masters knew about Oxbridge tutorials, which proved to be much more like an alien landscape pitted with unexploded mines that you had somehow to find a way of carefully avoiding. Bradshaw, a quiet, lanky boy with an interest in art, had stated in one debate that one could only be a true artist if one had suffered. Suffering was, he averred, the basis of all creativity. This was vigorously opposed by almost all the class for we took ourselves for true artists and none of us middle-class kids had remotely suffered. But Bradshaw was unrepentant. Depression was the dynamism that led to great works. All great artists were depressed. Look at Van Gogh and Virginia Woolf. Rubbish, we cried. But the thought stayed with me, burrowed itself in my mind like a parasitic worm: to be the great writer I was destined to be, I had to be depressed. But, annoyingly, I was not depressed. Sitting by the squat ugly phone staring out of the window I then became depressed because I was not depressed. *Why* couldn't I be depressed? Why couldn't *I* have a deprived and miserable childhood like everyone else? It was simply not fair. (This is the rich boy's *crie-de-coeur*. I imagine it cuts very little ice on council estates or in the communities that Irving Welsh writes about in his novels).

As for Albert Camus, he was the 1960s' existentialist hero. His novel, *The Outsider,* or *L' Étranger* as we snobbishly preferred to call it, was the book we all professed to be profoundly moved by, so much so that some of us had even read it. I have to say that my novel reading up to that point had been limited, consisting mainly of *Lady Chatterley's Lover*, the seminal parts of it so to speak. Camus's depiction of the gloomy introverted *Meursault* inspired us. We all wanted to be like *Meursault* and patrol a beach in France thinking about our dead mothers. That was truly living. That or having Pernod with the sexy, all black-clad Juliette Greco in a café in the Bld Saint Germain. After all, this was 1963, the year that Larkin was to fete so memorably, before the Swinging Sixties got underway and a good five years before the Parisian students took to the barricades to support the bemused car workers. Existentialist angst was in the air and I desperately wanted to be a part of it. These thoughts occupied my mind as I wasted hours staring out of the window, adding to my listlessness and unrecognized depression.

Jump to 1993, 30 years later. I am lying on my psychotherapist's couch in her consulting room in Oxford. I talk about this gap year, the gap in my life, and how I now realized why I was depressed. Six years earlier the whole family had been uprooted from Whitehaven, a town in the north of England where up to then I had spent all my life, to come to the stockbroker belt around London. My father had sold his successful chemicals business and become a millionaire, having started the business from scratch with £10 borrowed from his partner's uncle. In Whitehaven I had friends, I had begun at the grammar school, I was playing football, I was beginning to see the attraction of girls particularly when playing Postman's Knock. In Surrey the nearest house to us belonged to Lady Chobham, someone we never ever met. I had no friends and the nearest place to us, Sunningdale, was six miles across the common. My brother and I travelled to school in London by train and tube along with the sweaty press of commuters, taking an hour and a half to get to our destination. In the evenings and at the weekend we were marooned in our large house and garden, cut off from the life-blood of all adolescents, other adolescents. Then my brother left to go to university. No wonder I became depressed.

Angrily, from the couch I berate my parents for their failure to look after us properly, for not having the foresight to stay in the North-West so that I might grow up to be another Melvyn Bragg with a strong Cumbrian identity instead of the rootless person I think myself to be. My therapist listens and when I eventually run out of steam, she gently wonders if the whole family had not been depressed. For had my father not been forced out of the chemicals business he had set up from scratch and had my mother not lost her best friend, the wife of my father's business partner, who had been culpable in my father's expulsion? And, as immigrants to this country, coming from Germany as they did, would they have not found it difficult to make another move, not quite as drastic as the one that took them to England in 1930, but still another uprooting? I am stunned. I had never thought of this. Instantly, I know it to be true. I feel ashamed of my adolescent narcissistic anger. I see my parents, both dead, in a different light and feel a sadness that had up to then eluded me.

This is psychotherapy or at least one way of doing it. A comment is made that unexpectedly transforms an experience. A way of looking at the world is changed, releasing a hidden feeling, sadness in this case. It is possible then to think rather than feel or react. How does the therapist do this? That is one of the matters I address in this book. It is not a straightforward thing to do. Nor is this the only way of doing psychotherapy. But I am grateful to my therapist for enabling me to see that that time in my life when I was 17 and depressed was not all about me. Moreover, as I think more about her comment, I realize that while I was very soon to escape, to leave home, my parents had no option but to stay.

How depressed was I in 1963? Not very is the honest answer. I doubt if even the most biologically inclined psychiatrist would have diagnosed me as clinically depressed. I was a moody adolescent, unhappy, at a loose end, unsure of myself, frustrated, not least sexually. I was in a temporary state of low mood that should be lifted once circumstances changed. I needed to get out of the impasse I was in and, sure enough, when in October 1964 I started as a student at Oxford, my depression vanished. Ignorantly, I had equated depression with mental illness or madness and to my untutored mind madness seemed something arcane and frightening, a state of otherness that reduced the person to a gibbering wreck or, like Dr. Jekyll's other persona, Mr. Hyde, released dark and murderous impulses. Surely I was sane. That I could be sane and depressed did not occur to me though it is obvious to me now. Most people who are depressed are quite sane. Lurking beneath this deceptively simple statement is a more fundamental one about mental health and mental illness, a question that was to dog me all my professional life. What does it mean to be anxious or depressed? Are these experiences illnesses? If you find yourself checking whether you have left the gas on before you go out, are you just being a bit obsessive or do you suffer from obsessive-compulsive disorder? If you follow a diet that strictly limits what you allow yourself to eat, are you an anorexic? If you occasionally hear voices in your head, are you psychotic? The line between normality and mental illness is not easy to draw. And it shifts, influenced by changes within society, not just the advancement of scientific knowledge but also by fashion and morality. Among the first patients I treated as a clinical psychologist were homosexual men. I used a form of behaviour therapy known as electrical aversion therapy, its goal being to make them "normal" (i.e., heterosexual). Not surprisingly, this did not work and when I mention this to friends, they look at me with a mixture of pity and horror. But at the time I thought I was being helpful. Some years later, in 1980, the American Psychiatric Association *voted* the diagnosis of homosexuality out of its diagnostic classification, one of the strongest indications of the way political factors influence what constitutes mental illness.

In 1963 I knew I could not be depressed for quite the wrong reasons. But I was interested in mental states like depression. I was puzzled by the way people behaved, why they did or said certain things, and by this strange entity, if entity was the right term, the mind. This was one reason I decided, against the advice of my teachers and to the surprise of my parents, to study psychology at university. I thought it would tell me about the mind and enable me to understand myself and other people. I was to be rudely disillusioned.

In 2006, the year I am writing, psychology was among the top choices of academic subjects among British university applicants. Rightly so. It is a rich, diverse, challenging, exciting, and enjoyable subject. Students are exposed to many and varied ways of understanding the human experience, from tightly controlled laboratory experiments to naturalistic observations, from computer simulations to clinical case studies. They get to know about the mind, and are introduced to memory, attention, perception, appraisal, emotion, intellect—all the mental functions I had hoped to find out about when I came up to Oxford for interview in December 1963. It was not always thus.

The Oxford college I applied to, Queen's, did not yet have a psychology tutor. It turned out that among the group of applicants to the college I was the only candidate to apply to read psychology. I cast my mind back to that time long ago and, if this were a film, the screen would start to dissolve and music play... .

I am sitting at the long refectory table in the college's dark panelled main hall waiting for my interview along with the other candidates. I know no one and surround myself with a cocoon of my own thoughts. My reverie is broken by a disdainful voice booming out across the room: "Who is this person who wants to read psychology?", as though this was the sort of choice only the very stupid or mad might make. I gingerly put up my hand and scrabble to my feet making my way to the front of the hall under the pitying gaze of my fellow applicants. I am hauled away to a tiny room where I am introduced to two ancient men (they seem ancient to me anyway) who cheerfully tell me they are philosophy dons and they know nothing about psychology. Would I mind, they graciously inquire, if we talked about something else, philosophy perhaps? Not at all, I say, secretly relieved for I had read only one psychology book, Frieda Fordham's *Introduction to C.G. Jung* and, quite frankly, I had understood very little of it. In the week before my interview I had begun reading Bertrand Russell's *History of Western Philosophy* and had a vague grasp of some philosophical schools. But I do not need Russell's help, for all the questions I am politely and courteously asked are entirely hypothetical, requiring me simply to think on my feet.

"Suppose, Mr. Marzillier," one of the dons says, "you were to see a man strike down and kill another man in front of you in the street, could you say with absolute certainty if that man was guilty of the deed?"

I know enough about the world to think that the answer could not be yes. I frantically search my mind for alternative explanations.

"Not necessarily. I might have been having a dream. A nightmare I guess! Or I might be a mad man and be having some sort of mental fit."

The two dons say nothing but look at me in what I fondly imagine is an encouraging way.

"Or I might be under the influence of LSD or another drug. But," I add hastily, "I have never taken such a drug", in case they take me for a hardened drug addict.

"Then can we never know the absolute truth?"

Having occasionally listened to the Brains Trust, I latch onto Dr. Joad's characteristic way of handling difficult questions.

"It depends on what you mean by *absolute truth*," I say enigmatically.

This occasions knowing smiles. We go on to talk in a civilized way about different forms of truth until the two dons tell me, apologetically, that they have to see some other applicants otherwise I get the impression they would have been delighted to converse with me for hours about such interesting matters.

When I am accepted into the college to read PPP (psychology with either philosophy or physiology as a second subject), naturally I choose philosophy as it seemed to me that it did not require anything more than the ability to talk in a general way about absolutely anything.

In October 1964 when I arrive at Oxford, Queen's has a psychology tutor, David Vowles. To be accurate, he is a zoologist. Very few of the early academic psychologists studied psychology as their first degree simply because few degree courses existed outside the USA. For my first essay Vowles asks me to read *A Study of Instinct* by Nico Tinbergen and kindly lends me his copy of the book. I am to write an essay on something called *innate releasing mechanisms*. I leaf through the book and discover this to be Tinbergen's idea about how instinctive behaviour is translated into action. He conducted an experiment with male sticklebacks, which in typical male fashion tend to attack each other furiously when they meet. By using a dummy stickleback and manipulating various characteristics of its appearance, Tinbergen discovered it was the red colouring of the fish that elicited the aggression. There must be an innate releasing mechanism attached to the stimulus red, he claimed. This is all very interesting but what has it to do with the workings of the mind? I read on but only find more observations and experiments on animal behaviour. Nothing about the mind. Humans are scarcely mentioned. I am stumped. It then dawns on me that academic psychology, far from enlightening me about the mysteries of human existence, is about understanding some basic biological processes, ones shared by humans and animals. I struggle all week and write an indifferent essay consisting of a précis of the book's main findings. Well, I still have philosophy to fall back on, I say to myself.

Dr. Vowles was kind to me and gradually I learned how to put together a scientific essay that went beyond a simple summary. But the subject matter of academic psychology depressed me. The academic movement that had dominated psychology since the 1900s was behaviourism. J.B. Watson, the founder of the movement, eschewed any mention of mental processes. We must stick to what can be observed and measured, he thundered. No speculation. No untestable hypotheses. No airy-fairy ideas about mental processes. How different from philosophy where reality seemed not to be important at all. Psychology was about data and laboratory experimentation, a grim adherence to controlled investigation of the behaviour of rats, pigeons, and other animals in mazes, boxes, and cages. Later I realized that Tinbergen and the other ethologists whom Dr. Vowles introduced me to were seen as renegades from this artificial approach because they worked not in a laboratory but in the natural world. Had they been studying human behaviour as later they were to go on to do, their precise and careful observations would have been of much more interest than the artificial behaviour of rats in mazes or pigeons in a Skinner box. Another zoologist-turned-psychologist, Desmond Morris, was to make a small fortune from realizing how entertaining this approach could be to the general public.

I completed my degree in 1967, gaining an undistinguished 2nd. In the course of my studies I discovered that the biological basis of psychology could be fascinating and that philosophy was not as simple as I had first thought. But in the three years of the course I had been set only one essay on anything to do with what had driven me to psychology in the first place, the workings of the mind. I had to write an essay to show why Freud was wrong. This was not difficult since almost every academic psychologist disparaged Freud and was keen to point out the many deficiencies in his work. I did not even have to read any Freud to come to the right conclusions.

Like many graduates in the 1960s I was unconcerned about finding myself a career. There seemed no pressure to do so and it was not in tune with the spirit of the times to search too hard. A job would fall into one's lap sooner or later. I took temporary jobs, completed an English language teaching course, spent a few weeks in Heidelberg ostensibly to learn German but more to have fun, applied to an advertising agency but was rejected as overqualified and then, at a loose end, I contacted David Vowles to see if my psychology degree might lead to something a little more permanent. He suggested clinical psychology and told me that there was a master's course at the Maudsley Hospital in South-East London. He knew very little about it, he said apologetically, except that the Maudsley course was *scientific*, stressing the word as though generally clinical psychology was something a little *outré*, a bit like some people might regard reflexology these days. I contacted the Maudsley and filled in the application form they sent me. I asked when I'd hear about an interview date only to be told that they didn't interview candidates since there was no scientific evidence that interviewing added anything to the selection process. I would hear in due course whether they would offer me a place. This was my first experience of the application of psychological science to actual practice. It struck me as rather surprising. After all, surely you would want to meet the people you were to train as clinicians to screen out the oddballs?[1]

I decided I had better apply to another course. This was now the height of the Swinging Sixties and London was the place to be. There was only one other London-based clinical psychology course, at the Tavistock Clinic in Belsize Park. At that time I had no idea that the Tavistock Clinic was the renowned centre for UK psychoanalysis and that the course trained psychologists to be psychoanalytic therapists. The Tavistock either did not know or did not care about the scientific evidence on interviewing and I was invited to attend two days of interviews, IQ tests, personality assessments, clinical case studies and group exercises. Two days! I went along with some trepidation and found myself one of 20 applicants, mostly women and many older and far more experienced than I was. I soon discovered the psychoanalytic orientation of the course. At the end of my first interview with a charming elderly woman whose grey hair was pulled back severely into a bun, I bumptiously asked what she thought of Eysenck's recent, well-publicized critique of psychoanalysis, claiming that it wasn't scientific and the method didn't actually work. She smiled and told me I had to have faith. Faith! Was psychoanalysis the new religion? What if I did not have faith? What if it was all hocus-pocus? Then and there I decided I did not want to go to the Tavistock. I would hope to get a place at the Maudsley and become a proper scientist. But I still had more than a day and a half of assessments to go. I decided that I would carry on and see

---

[1] A few oddballs were selected on to the Maudsley course but that did not mean they were necessarily unsuited to clinical psychology. One of the best trainees I supervised was a depressed, withdrawn woman who spoke hardly above a whisper and always wore black. Around her neck a large metal chain hung, its symbolism scarcely more obvious than if she attached a message saying "life's a bitch". The more troubled patients loved her and, more to the point, she had an incredible ability to help them. Maybe the Maudsley was right.

if I could get them to offer me a place even if I only turned it down later.

One of the personality assessments was called the Thematic Apperception Test or TAT. It consists of a series of shadowy black-and-white pictures of human shapes in various ambiguous situations about each of which the person taking the test had to tell a short story. I cheerfully scribbled a few lines for each picture, enjoying making up little stories about the characters. What it had to do with my personality I had no idea. Nor did I care. My next formal interview was with the chief psychologist at the Tavistock, Herbert Phillipson, who, I later discovered, pioneered the use of the TAT in the UK.

When I enter the small office, I see a man in his fifties sitting behind a desk, smoking a pipe. He is wearing a grey suit with a grey cardigan beneath the jacket, a crisp white shirt and what looks like a red and black striped regimental tie. He carefully puts the pipe down and with a welcoming smile beckons me to sit in a chair to the side of the desk. His hair is black, short and sleeked back. His face is nondescript except for his eyes which are deep and dark brown and fixed attentively on me. He asks me a few undemanding questions in an amiable sort of way. He compliments me on how well I did in the IQ test and says that he is impressed by my academic ability. He asks me about Oxford and what I liked about the place. It all feels like a cosy chat with a friendly uncle. Then putting on his glasses, he looks at the stories I wrote for the TAT.

"Hmm," he says slowly, "I noticed in several of your stories you wrote about romantic relationships breaking up." He looks up at me. "Could that be something that has just happened or might happen to you?"

I sit frozen in the chair. I have just broken up with my girlfriend, having met a French girl in Heidelberg whom I have now got involved with. It had been painful breaking the news to my former girlfriend and I still feel guilty about it.

"No," I lie brazenly. "Sorry, no."

"Hmm," he says again, picking up his pipe and taking a few puffs. He asks me some more questions that I answer as best I can. I am in confusion, shocked by the way this test seemed to reveal an aspect of myself I did not want known. The interview ends. I get up to leave.

Dr. Phillipson is just as unperturbed as he was when I entered the room. I hesitate, standing in the doorway. I decide I cannot leave without confessing the truth and somewhere in the back of my mind is the knowledge that to do so would go in my favour.

"Actually," I say, "you were right. The pictures. The TAT. I have just broken up with my girlfriend. I just didn't want to admit it."

Phillipson nods his head. "Thank you for telling me," he says with a quiet smile as though he knew it already.

A week or so after the interviews a letter came offering me a place on the Tavistock course. I politely wrote back turning it down. I explained that I was waiting for an offer from the Maudsley and when that finally arrived, I accepted it. Such are the turning points in one's life. Had I gone to the Tavistock I would have been trained in the psychoanalytical tradition and become a psychoanalytical therapist. Instead, at the Maudsley I joined the Psychology Department where H.J. Eysenck was the head, Freud was regarded as little better than a conman and science was the god at whose feet everyone worshipped.

CHAPTER TWO

A suitable case for treatment

I am sitting at one of the long tables in the Institute of Psychiatry canteen along with my fellow students on the Maudsley course. It is a coffee break between lectures. I am struggling to understand why I am here, why I want to be a clinical psychologist. For the most part the lectures are about psychometric tests, tests of intelligence, personality, aptitude, attainments. Intelligence tests like the Wechsler Adult Intelligence Scale (WAIS). Tests of reading and spelling. Tests of fine and gross motor skills. Tests that supposedly give rise to personality profiles and tests that somehow suggest what jobs suit people best. This is what clinical psychologists do, what I am being trained for, and I am seriously wondering if I should have done something different. Perhaps I should have gone into advertising after all.

We are being lectured about the scientific basis of these tests. Our lecturers are searingly critical of almost everything to do with them, their construction, their standardization, their theoretical basis, their fairness. It seems the tests are of uncertain reliability, doubtful validity, and limited utility. Oddly enough, we still have to give them to the patients and, more to the point, pass out on their administration rather like passing a driving test. This disparity between theory and practice is one I am destined to come across many times in my career.

I have been assigned to a child placement, which means, when I am not being lectured to or reading, I follow a clinical psychologist around hoping to learn about the unique contribution psychologists make to children in an inpatient psychiatric unit. I am struggling here too because, as the youngest in my family, I have had virtually no contact with children. Moreover, I have taken little interest in child development, managing to miss most of the lectures at Oxford. When my supervisor asks me what is abnormal about a possibly autistic child's behaviour, frankly I do not have a clue. I know he does not speak any proper words and he is five years old. *I think* five-year-olds should be speaking more than repetitive, nonsense sounds but I don't really know. The child is called Tommy and I shall be spending quite a lot of time with him, but that is, as they say, another story.

I drink my coffee and listen to the chat. I feel out of place and out of sorts. Then, without a warning, there is a voice in my ear, asking if I could spare a few minutes to talk about something. The voice is soft with a South African accent. "I need a male therapist," the man says, "to take over a therapy client. I wondered whether you might want to do this." I am startled for the request comes from Dr. Rachman, a man I have already begun to admire, whose book I have been reading, not just reading, but assiduously taking notes on. Jack Rachman is a pioneer of a new form of psychological treatment, behaviour therapy, and his lectures are the ones, perhaps the only ones, that grab my attention. And here he is offering me a chance to carry out some therapy. I quickly stammer my acquiescence and follow him to his office.

***

In the 1960s most psychological therapies were variants of the psychoanalytic method Freud pioneered, what is generally called the *psychodynamic approach*. The focus was on talking and uncovering the intrapsychic, unconscious conflicts that were presumed to underlie neurotic behaviour. Only by getting to the unconscious conflicts could the symptoms be properly resolved. Most treatments were lengthy and, if the critics were to be believed, spectacularly unsuccessful. Behaviour therapy on the other hand was a brief, pragmatic therapy based, so it was asserted, on scientific psychology. When he had been in South Africa, Dr. Rachman had been a colleague and collaborator of one of the main proponents of the approach, Dr. Joseph Wolpe. Wolpe had published several articles and two major books in which he described how to do behaviour therapy. He claimed a staggering 90% success with neurotic patients though this figure was later disputed by the psychologist, Arnold Lazarus, who had worked with Wolpe on their early cases. Lazarus claimed that when he had followed up the apparent successes, many had relapsed. Wolpe was so angry that he excised Lazarus's name from the second edition of his books. Pioneers tend to be rather prickly if their claims are disputed. Freud, for example, expelled several colleagues from his magic circle when their ideas challenged his psychoanalytic orthodoxy.

In Dr. Rachman's office was a psychologist who had just graduated from the course. He had one remaining unfinished therapy case. If I was willing, I would take it over, be handed the reins and with a few flourishes, or so I saw it, complete a successful cure. Dr. Rachman explained why he wanted a male therapist. The patient, whom I will call Peter, had a rather unusual phobia. It was a fear of using public toilets. It would be embarrassing to him to talk about this to a female psychologist. I listened eagerly to a resumé of the case. Peter was 23—my age! He was training to be a solicitor. His phobia meant that when he tried to use a public toilet, he would get so anxious that he could not pee. It was particularly bad if a man came in and used a urinal, especially one next to him. It had got to such a point that Peter would avoid using public loos altogether. This had become a major problem for him. He worried that his fellow solicitors would find out and think him odd. He had a restricted social life because, if he was out and about and the need to pee came upon him, he would have to go back to his flat rather than use a public loo. Almost safer not to go out at all.

Thinking about Peter now, I realize how little the form or origin of this odd phobia was commented on. Why did Peter have this fear? Did it have any wider meaning? Why if he had had it for several years was he seeking help now? Was it masking other problems? Some psychotherapists would have wondered whether there was a latent fear of homosexuality, a fear that in a public toilet, where in the 1960s gay people would secretly meet for illicit sex, Peter might be perceived as homosexual or even that his own hidden homosexual impulses might be revealed or acted out. But this was too psychodynamic, too much the stuff of Freud and his ilk to cut any ice with Dr. Rachman. And, in my naivety and ignorance, I confess I never even thought about it.

Peter was in the middle of a behavioural treatment called *systematic desensitization*. The method was straightforward. I had read about it in Wolpe's books. Peter would be helped to overcome his phobia by undertaking a graduated programme of activities that brought him nearer to the object of his fear. His fear would be overcome by tackling the problem when his anxiety was low and while relaxed. He would then move on to the next item in a hierarchy of increasingly feared situations until he finally confronted the most difficult fear, which was using a public toilet when a man comes and pees in the urinal next to him. Peter had been taught relaxation and was working through a hierarchy that he and his therapist had constructed. I say, "working through" yet this was not done in reality but in imagination. Peter, thoroughly relaxed, would imagine a scene—say, approaching a public loo, maintain the image, and then relax. This would be repeated four or five times before moving on to the next scene. Strange, you might think, for a *behavioural* therapy to use imagination rather than actual behaviour. But then Wolpe, the founder of this approach, had used imaginal scenes arguing that the learning would simply transfer to real life. Of course, it is much easier for a busy doctor like Wolpe with a large outpatient clinic to do all the therapy in his office. Much more time-consuming to take clients out. And if it works as well, then there are no problems. Except of course there were.

I cannot remember clearly the first time I met Peter. I have a generic picture of a slight, diffident youth with a quiet manner, serious, somewhat detached, anxious to do the right thing. I remember him being angry at the way the psychologist he had first been referred to had treated him, injecting him with a diuretic and forcing him to go to the public toilets until he peed. Peter had felt degraded, humiliated. I could not help but agree. I thought how I might feel if I'd been treated in that crass way. We progressed through the hierarchy, with me diligently following the rituals of the technique and Peter, eyes closed, imagining hypothetical scenes involving men in public lavatories. Now it seems a surreal scenario but then it was entirely credible. But the problem was that there was no change outside therapy. We set specific tasks, homework assignments, but either Peter failed to do them or they did not work in the way they should have. I consulted Dr. Rachman who suggested we build real-life tasks into the therapy. There was a small loo at the end of the corridor. What I needed was a male accomplice who would be in the loo when Peter entered or would come into the loo while he was in there peeing. My friend and fellow trainee, Bill, steadfastly did this on two or three occasions and indeed Peter's anxiety about using public toilets lessened a little.

But—and in therapy there is almost always a "but"—Peter did not seem happy. In the interstices of the desensitization, the beginnings and ends of the sessions, which I was later to realize were so important, Peter and I chatted. Somehow he discovered that I lived in Camden Town, a long trek across London to Denmark Hill where the Maudsley is located. His flat was in West Kilburn. Couldn't we meet somewhere nearer to both of us, he suggested? Ever keen to please, I readily agreed. But where? What about a pub after work, one of us suggested? I think it was Peter but then I might like to think that, not wanting to be seen as the sort of therapist who had no notion of boundaries. But the truth was I had no idea there might be problems in carrying out therapy in a pub. In fact, I remember thinking with some delight that Peter could have a couple of pints of beer and after that he would have to use the loo. So in fact a pub was the ideal place for us to do the therapy. We settled on a large pub off the Tottenham Court Road, a stone's throw from Peter's work.

Peter is already there when I arrive, seated at a small round table with a half of bitter in front of him. He smiles at me slightly self-consciously and I smile back. The pub is a more relaxed place than the claustrophobic treatment room at the Institute.

"What'll you have?" he says, making a move to stand up.

"No, sit down. I'll get the drinks. I can claim this back on expenses." I have no idea if I can but it does not feel right that Peter should pay. "Anyway," I say, as I move to the bar, "you need a pint."

I come back with two pints and sit opposite him. The pub is filling up with people after work. There is a buzz of several conversations going on at once, occasional bursts of loud laughter, the stuttering noise of the fruit machine as it pays out.

"What if any of your friends comes here? One of your fellow lawyers perhaps? We ought to have a story, something to tell them." This has the air of a conspiracy, a lark.

Peter shakes his head. "They won't. Anyway, I don't have many friends."

He says it factually, not with any sense of wishing it to be otherwise. We each take a sip of our drinks.

"We need to stay here at least 45 minutes, maybe more, for the beer to work," I say. "Then when you're ready, just go to the loo." He looks a bit uncertain but nods. There is a silence and I wonder what to say.

"Are you married?" Peter suddenly asks.

"No. I live with my girlfriend, G." I find myself telling him about G, how she is French and how her parents thinks she is flat-sharing in Earls Court whereas she is living with me. I make it sound like something more than it is, something I tend to do anyway, to make a story out of my own experiences often making me into the main player, the hero. Peter listens, seemingly genuinely interested. At a pause I ask: "What about you? Do you have a girlfriend?" He tells me about a girl he likes but has not plucked up the courage to ask out.

"Is she a lawyer?"

"She's a drama student. She's part of my film group."

"Film group?"

Suddenly, Peter is animated. He tells me about his amateur film group, how they shoot films around London. It turns out he is the director, this quiet, introverted youth and I begin to see a different side of him, a more steely, determined, artistic side. We talk about films. This is the 60s: the films of Godard and Truffaut, Bergman at the height of his powers and the Antonioni film, *Blow-Up*, which we both love. Time passes. I get two more pints. Eventually, Peter gets up. With a slightly nervous laugh, he says, "I guess I should try it. I had almost forgotten why we were here."

"Sure," I say nonchalantly, "if you feel up to it."

"I'll give it a go," he says, and heads for the stairs down to the toilets. A few minutes later Peter reappears, a big grin on his face. "I did it," he says triumphantly, as he sits down opposite me. "A man came in just as I was finishing, but I was okay."

"Great," I say. "Let's drink to that." We lift our pints in a salute, eyes shining. Our conspiracy has been successful.

After that, I met Peter four or five times in the pub near his work. We drank beer, talked, used the loo, talked some more. He never had any problems in the pub but outside it still remained a concern to him. One day when Peter arrives, he seems more excited than usual.

"I've got something to tell you," he says, a wide grin on his face. "I'm going to India."

"India?" I'm flabbergasted.

"Yeah, filming. I've wangled a six-month sabbatical from chambers. I've always wanted to go to India. If I like it, I might stay, give up the law, take up filming seriously."

Peter had already told me how he found his studies stultifying. His father is a solicitor and had always wanted his son to follow in his footsteps. He had dutifully done so. Now it seems he was rebelling. Peter talks on eagerly about his plans. He has applied for a visa. He wants to start in Bombay and later move to southern India. It is clear he has been planning this for some time, but it is the first I have heard of it.

I feel somewhat miffed at his not having discussed it with me first. I cannot help pouring cold water over this highly romantic notion. "You know in India, people don't use public loos. They pee and crap in the street. Doesn't that bother you?" (I am totally unaware of my latent envy of his sudden break with his studies, his ability to just take off and leave everything behind.) Peter in his enthusiasm pays my feelings scant attention. After all, I am only his therapist, a stepping-stone to something else, something he has now managed to do.

"I'm sure I'll be okay," Peter says airily.

His indifference to what had previously been a major anxiety takes my breath away. I do not know what to say.

"I have a lot to do," Peter goes on, "so I think this should be our last session." He looks me in the eye, confident, happy, relaxed. He holds out his hand. "Thanks, John. You've been terrific. A great therapist." I shake his hand. I could not feel less like a great therapist. In fact, I feel a failure. I have an obscure feeling that I have missed something important but I cannot for the life of me think what it is.

Curiously, that was not the last time I saw Peter. Two years later I was walking along Primrose Hill Road on a wintry Saturday morning. A car stopped suddenly in front of me. The car had four young men in it, one of whom quickly got out. "John," he shouted.

"How are you?" Amazingly, it was Peter. He brought me up to date, how he had been to India, had a great time, shot some good films, travelled around, made new friends. Then he had come back to London and resumed his legal studies. In a few weeks he would start his job as a qualified solicitor. He asked how I was getting on and I told him I was now on the staff at the Institute and how I was doing a PhD. Then there was a hoot from the car, and he started to move off.

"But," I said hastily, "what about ... you know ... the problem?"

A puzzled look came over his face replaced by sudden enlightenment as he understood what I meant.

"Oh, that. I still have it but it doesn't bother me any more."

My first psychotherapy case. Looking back on it now I see so many lessons that a beginning therapist might learn. The most obvious one was that what the client presents as a problem is not necessarily what matters most. Peter's peeing problem was his "ticket of entry" into therapy for something else. As I see it now it was his sense of being lost, unhappy, unsure about law as a career, a vague disturbance that even he may not have fully recognized. Our time in the pub meant that he could talk about these matters quite easily. The most important event in the therapy was Peter's decision to go to India. This was not ever discussed at our meetings but I like to think that's where he got the confidence to make this bold move and in doing so, he found a way out just as I did years before when I left home to go to Oxford.

Another lesson is that spontaneity can transform a routine treatment that may be stuck. Our spontaneous decision to meet in a pub meant we were no longer inhibited by the trappings of work. Our relationship changed. We were on a more equal footing, more relaxed. This allowed the conversation to flow and important issues to emerge, like Peter's unhappiness. Nowadays a trainee therapist who did this would be severely censured and darkly told about the need to maintain proper professional boundaries. But I knew no better and my supervisor was unconcerned as long as the behavioural treatment was being done. There is a fine line between spontaneity and chaotic, uncontrolled therapy. I believed what I was doing had a therapeutic rationale and, although in the end the behavioural programme was tangential to what Peter needed, it was still important. It provided us with the justification to carry on and was the frame that held our meetings together.[1]

And then of course there was our personal relationship. Peter and I were the same age, both training for a profession. We shared an interest in films. Because I knew no better I did not hide behind a professional façade but openly talked about myself, my girl-friend, my life at the Institute of Psychiatry, the films I had seen. Self-disclosure. It is drummed into therapists that they should not self-disclose, certainly not personal matters, but be "'professional" in their approach. This leads to the sort of exchanges that often infuriate clients. Client: *"Have you ever been depressed?"* Therapist: *"I am wondering why you want to know this, perhaps to be reassured that I understand how you feel."* The question is not answered and the client forced onto the back foot. I disclosed a lot about myself, almost certainly too much, but the effect was to make Peter feel like a human being.

These are some of the lessons I could have learned from Peter, but in fact I learned none of them. I attributed my success to behaviour therapy and threw myself into this approach with enthusiasm and vigour. And as a good behaviour therapist, I had to follow the cardinal rules. I was enjoined always to take what the client says is the problem at face value, not to pretend to know more than he or she did. I was only to use treatments that had been proved effective in proper research. I was to base my approach on the fundamental principles of scientific psychology. I was not to bother with any of the Freudian guff about the personal relationship or the unconscious or insight or what the client was thinking. Above all, I was to make the client better. The naïve simplicity of behaviour therapy entirely escaped me at the time. Some years later when I was less naïve, one of my behaviour therapy colleagues boasted that we were really just

---

[1]There has been a long dispute whether psychotherapies work because of the specific techniques or the non-specific factors that are common to all of them. The psychotherapist, Jerome Frank, argued that the *therapeutic ritual* was what mattered regardless of whether it was lying on a couch in psychoanalysis or going through a structured behaviour therapy programme. But the therapist must believe in what he or she is doing for the ritual to work, an ironic paradox since, according to Frank, the therapist's belief is misguided. Despite knowing nothing about behaviour therapy I believed in it avidly. Ignorance is often the most effective way of becoming convinced that something is vitally important.

like plumbers with a set of tools and established techniques. I bridled and objected. Not because I was snobbish about being compared to a plumber. Quite the opposite. A plumber could mend taps, replace washers, fix errant cisterns, repair washing machines, sort out noisy boilers etc. Human beings were more tricky to help.

But before that, like Don Quixote, I embarked on my mission, to be a successful behaviour therapist.

CHAPTER THREE

Getting my hands dirty

G ary and I are sitting on the uneven grass that passes for lawn in the Maudsley Hospital. Just in front of us is a flower-bed, a long thin rectangle of earth to which some straggly rose bushes cling hopefully. We are about 30 metres from the Villa, the euphemistically named locked ward in the Maudsley Hospital complex. It is July 1969 and the sun is shining, the beginning of a long warm spell. The patients in the Villa—the mad, the bad, and the *very* dangerous to know—are not allowed out of their "sanctu-ary" except under vigilant supervision. But they can see us from the windows of the patients' sitting room. What Gary and I are doing out there must have been very puzzling to these onlookers and, to some, must have appeared as mad as anything they had ever done themselves.

Gary is staring moodily at the ground while I prattle on. He is 26 years old and comes from a solid and supportive working-class family in Chipping Norton. He is an inpatient with a diagnosis of obsessive-compulsive disorder or OCD. Those with OCD fall into two categories: washers and checkers. Gary is a washer. His whole life is governed by the necessity of ensuring everything and everybody around him is free from contamination. He likes to wash his hands a lot. A lot means more than 30 times a day, scrubbing them with detergent repeatedly until he is satisfied they are properly clean. His hands—if you could see them for he is holding them across his chest and under his armpits—are red and raw.

"The thing is, Gary," I am saying with the blinding confidence that comes only from complete inexperience, "you have to make your hands dirty, really dirty, and then *not* wash them. Sure, you'll feel bad at first. Your anxiety will shoot up. But we *know*"—and I stress the word *know*—"it will come down over time. As long as you don't wash them or do anything that makes you feel better. Do you understand?"

Gary nods, barely. He does not look convinced and he is still holding his hands in his armpits.

"Here," I say. "Watch me." I plunge both my hands into the manky, dusty earth of the long untouched flower-bed. Luckily, it has not rained for several days and the soil is dry and crumbly, not the heavy wet clumps that stick everywhere. I rub my hands together while Gary looks on and then rub the traces of dirt into my face, my neck and my hair. Gary shudders but keeps looking at me with a mixture of horror and amazement. "There, not so difficult," I say, as though I am talking to an eight-year-old.

The truth is that it is not hard for me to do this. It is fun. But I know it will not be fun for Gary. I get him to take his right hand from under his armpit and place it over mine as though we are comparing hand sizes. His hand is large and red like a butcher's. I get him to shadow me as I bring my hand towards the flower-bed. He does it slowly, reluctantly. I bring my hand nearer and nearer until it is touching the soil. Then I take it away. Gary's hand hovers over the earth.

"Now touch the soil," I command. There's a long pause. "Come on, Gary, you can do it," I cajole.

And then it happens: he touches the soil, immediately pulling his hand away as though he had received an electric shock. I give a whoop and for the first time Gary smiles. We repeat these bizarre actions for the next 30 minutes: each time Gary does a bit more, until at the end he has done what I have, dirtied his hands and covered his face and neck with the traces of dirt. He draws the line at his hair and I know better than to push my luck any further.

This is behaviour therapy. What Gary and I are doing is essentially similar to the technique of *systematic desensitization* that I was carrying out with Peter. The difference is that rather than work with imaginary scenes, we are doing it in real life. It is Dr. Rachman's idea that we do this. I, the trainee therapist, take Gary to what he fears most, model the actions needed and get Gary to imitate me. Then I prevent him from doing anything that might undo the actions such as washing his hands. We proudly call this *modelling and response prevention*. So far no one has done this. Gary is our first case, our guinea pig. We are gambling that the technique will break the stranglehold of his obsessionality, that it will make him better. Theoretically, it should. By washing his hands to reduce his anxiety, Gary never learns that his anxiety has no foundation in reality. Stop him washing his hands, his anxiety will in the end dissipate of its own accord. And he will not be contaminated, the thing he fears most.

We have managed to persuade Gary's psychiatrists to try this new approach before they take the more radical step for which he was admitted. This is to be a lobotomy, that is, excising a small bit of his frontal lobe, which, if the American research is correct, should make him less anxious and therefore less bothered by his obsessions. Milos Forman's film of Ken Kesey's book, *One Flew over the Cuckoo's Nest*, has yet to be made. Even so a lobotomy is a risky thing to try. There is no going back once the bit of brain is removed, and the outcome is pretty uncertain. The doctors are happy for us to experiment.

Gary and I walk back to the ward, faces blacked up like SAS troopers. Who cares? We are excited. It has been a success. Gary's anxiety has virtually gone. The therapy has worked.

"'Now," I say firmly, as we reach the ward, "you are not to wash your hands or face or anything until 6 o'clock. The nurses know that so if you feel bad, you can talk to them. But I think you'll be okay."

"No washing till 6? Not even if I have some grub? Or go to the bog?"

"No," I say firmly. "6 o'clock. Then only enough to get them reasonably clean." I gloss over the hygiene issue in my mind.

"You're the boss," he says.

It is how I feel too. Like a boss. Is this what therapy is about? Being bossy. I can do that. I waltz off to the staff canteen for lunch. At the first men's loo I go in and scrub off the dirt from my face, neck, and hands. I do this guiltily, thinking about poor Gary but then mutter to myself: "I didn't say *I* would keep the dirt on till 6. I don't have OCD." This is the first of many such convenient rationalizations in my psychotherapy career.

Dr. Rachman, Ray Hodgson, his research assistant, and I saw Gary hour after hour, day after day, for a month. By the end of therapy he was totally free of his obsessional anxieties. He was never given the lobotomy. He was discharged home. At follow-up six months later, he was still fine. A success. We celebrated in the way all good academics do. We published a paper.

***

The behavioural treatment of obsessional patients is not that different today except for a few additions. At its simplest behaviour therapy means treating the *behaviour* rather than any hypothetical notions about underlying meanings or causes. Gary washed his hands repeatedly. Whatever the reasons may have been for this, this was an observable fact. We stopped him doing this. In fact, we went to the opposite extreme, contaminating Gary and his environment with dirt. At the end of therapy we knew he was better for we could see it. His washing behaviour changed. *Treat the behaviour. Don't make assumptions about underlying causes. The patient will improve.* The behaviour therapist's mantra. But this is deceptively simple. One of the reasons we adopted the *modelling and response prevention* approach was theoretical, based on the notion that Gary's anxiety about contamination was reinforced by his washing behaviour. Anxiety is a construct, the term derived from *Angst*, first introduced to psychotherapy by Freud, which is presumed to underlie and explain problem behaviour. Our therapeutic approach was based upon what we saw as maintaining Gary's problem, his anxiety. In other words, we made an assumption about what caused him to wash.

Changing a person's behaviour is not always enough on its own. This was made crystal clear to me by an inpatient I attempted to treat soon after I had qualified. She was an elderly woman who had a delusion that other people needed to speak so that she could speak back. She would annoy everyone on the ward by clutching at their arm or another part of their bodies, staring insistently at them and demanding repeatedly: "You speak, then I'll butt in." She had irritated the life out of the ward and had been assaulted by other patients. I started a behavioural programme whereby the nursing staff spoke to her only if she did not clutch at them. If she clutched and demanded they speak, they would turn away. At the same time I encouraged the nurses to talk to her more at other times rather than avoid her as they had been doing. Sure enough, the clutching, demanding behaviour was eliminated. I was very pleased. I had modified a persistent delusion by behaviour therapy. Wow! However, in the ward round when, having been complimented on her improvement, she was asked by the consultant psychiatrist whether she still believed that others had to speak before she could speak to them, she replied artlessly: "Oh, yes, but I can't say that on the ward any more." Her behaviour may have changed but not her underlying belief.

It took more than a decade for behaviour therapists to realize that what a patient believes is as important as what they do. Behaviour therapy was eventually transformed first into *cognitive behaviour therapy* and then simply *cognitive therapy*.[1] Techniques were incorporated that addressed what clients thought and believed as well as what they did. Cognitive therapists now grapple with anxious ruminations, negative thinking, dysfunctional beliefs, and even psychotic delusions. Cognitive therapy became the new and favoured psychotherapy, so much so that as I write this chapter, the Department of Health is being persuaded that it should be funded as the treatment of choice for depression, anxiety, and other common psychological states. But all this is in the future. In the 1970s the psychiatric establishment reacted with suspicion to the idea that clinical psychologists should carry out therapy of any sort. Our job was to administer psychometric tests and write long, detailed scientific reports that nobody actually read. Therapy was infringing onto their bailiwick. But if what we were doing could be justified as experimental research, firmly based on psychological principles and carefully controlled, then reluctantly we were allowed to proceed. This is one

---

[1]Despite their dismissive attitude to cognitions the early behaviour therapists used some cognitive techniques. Wolpe, for example, suggested thought stopping as a way of dealing with persistent anxious ruminations. The client would be encouraged to start ruminating and then without warning the therapist would bang the table hard and shout, STOP! The startled client would find their ruminations had been disrupted and probably their heart racing ten to the dozen. This would be done a few more times and the client then asked to do it on their own, initially out loud and then sub-vocally. The idea was to suppress ruminative thinking though I cannot help feeling this also symbolized Wolpe's general attitude to cognitions.

reason why behaviour therapy needed to be seen as scrupulously scientific.

Nothing succeeds like success. Behaviour therapy worked. Gary was just one of many cases where directly focussing on the problem behaviour paid huge dividends. Once I had completed my training, I threw myself into doing behaviour therapy. No matter what the problem was I believed the behavioural approach could tackle it. I was the boss and, after 13 months' training and half-a-dozen therapy cases, I knew what was what. In reality, I knew virtually nothing. But I concentrated on anxiety problems, phobias in particular. And here I got some spectacularly good results. Jackie is a case in point.

Jackie, a single mother of 29 with a six-year-old son, Martin, has been referred to the psychiatric outpatient department because she is pathologically frightened of dogs. Large dogs are the worst, Alsatians in particular, but the sight of any dog in the street causes her stomach to lurch, her heart to beat faster, her legs to tremble, and her body to break out in sweat. She panics and runs away. She is now so fearful of meeting dogs that she only leaves home when she has to go to the shops or take Martin to school. She does not have a car and so any journey is fraught with potential danger. She follows long, circuitous routes, carefully chosen to minimize the chance of meeting dogs. And of course trips to the park with Martin are out of the question.

I first meet Jackie in the waiting room. Everything about her is a dull brown, from her mousy hair to her shapeless, dark clothes, her scuffed flat shoes, and her large, battered shopping bag. Only her face, pale, almost ghost-like, stands out. Her nervousness shows in her eyes which flicker here and there restlessly. It is as though she is checking all the time, making sure no dog could suddenly appear from the shadows.

I introduce myself and explain that this is an assessment, a chance for her to tell me what's bothering her and see if I can help.

"I'm scared of dogs," she says directly when we have settled down in my office. "Terrified. Whenever I go out, which is not often, I'm always on the look-out for them. *I hate them,*" she says with a vehemence that startles me.

"Have you always been frightened of dogs?"

"No. Used to love them. My nan had a Staffordshire bull terrier, Rollo, he was called. Cuddly, sloppy dog. My brother and me used to play with him all the time. But that was when I was a kid."

"So when did you become frightened of dogs?"

"7th December, 1966." The exact date. Etched into her mind.

"What happened?'"

I see a bead of sweat on her forehead. Jackie has not taken off her coat. She is perched on the edge of the chair, her bag still clutched on her lap. Gradually, hesitantly, she tells me what happened on that day four years ago. I have already guessed, not that you need to be a psychologist to work it out. She was walking on her own back home from work when a large Alsatian bounded out of an alleyway right in front of her. It was a dark, filthy night, a strong wind blowing gusts of rain into her face. The dog stopped in its tracks and looked at her. In Jackie's eyes it appeared huge, a giant of a dog, even with its coat flattened by the driving rain. What particularly caught her attention was its long wolf-like face, the black snout, the bright pink sliver of tongue that appeared and disappeared as it panted and the occasional flash of white teeth. Jackie had also stopped, taken aback by the dog's unexpected appearance. There was no sign of an owner. She slowly started to move out on to the road, hoping to give the animal a wide berth. The dog stiffened. Its ears went back, its lips curled into a horrible rictus. There was a low snarling sound. Terror gripped Jackie and she panicked. She whipped round and tried to run back the way she had come but before she had moved more than a couple of paces, she felt the crushing weight of the dog on her back, the foul smell of its breath against her cheek and then a searing pain in her left arm. She collapsed on the hard, wet pavement, banging her head so that she momentarily lost consciousness. She fancied she heard a shout. Then, without warning, the weight was gone. A man was bending over her, asking if she was alright. He'd scared the dog off, he told her. "He wuz a devil, that dog," he said, "would have done for you if he'd had the chance, I reckon. You're a lucky girl."

Jackie pauses. She is trembling. Her eyes are glistening. Her hands clutch the bag tightly. Her account is as vivid as though the attack happened yesterday, not four years ago. Slowly, she tells me the rest, how an ambulance arrived and she was taken to hospital. The wound was only a flesh wound, nasty and painful but nothing worse. However, they kept her in for the night as a precaution because she had hit her head on the pavement. From that time on Jackie had been terrified of dogs.

One-trial learning. The attack was so traumatic that Jackie developed an immediate terror of dogs. Nowadays, psychologists talk about a post-traumatic stress reaction, but that notion was yet to be invented. Instead, I see it in my best scientific language as a conditioned emotional response that has generalized from one dog to all dogs. It has persisted for the common and expected theoretical reason, avoidance. Jackie has never really challenged the basis for her belief that all dogs are potential attackers, killers even. Every time she avoids dogs, she reinforces her belief. And in my mind the treatment would be simple. To reverse the process, put in place a behavioural programme, reintroducing Jackie to safe, unthreatening dogs so that she regains her confidence and loses her fear. I am about to explain this to Jackie, when she speaks again.

"I don't want the little one to get it. I don't want Martin to have the same fear of dogs as me. But it's beginning to happen. I've seen him get worried if there's a dog in the street. *Bad dog*, he says."

So here was the motivation, the reason why Jackie was seeking help now. And it was a powerful one, for what parent does not want the best for her kid? I tell Jackie about my behaviour therapy approach, outlining two ways of doing it. *Systematic desensitization*— a slow, gradual progress working through the fear first in imagination and then in reality. Or *flooding*—a newer, speeded-up version whereby we tackle the fear head-on in a few long sessions that could go on for two to three hours. I explain that in flooding, anxiety gets very high but comes down in the end. And that progress is quicker with this method. I have no doubt about this though I have never actually done any flooding. Only read about it in the academic journals. But I have the confidence of youth, an unwavering belief in behaviour therapy and an enthusiasm to try something new. I am delighted when Jackie opts for flooding.

A week later Jackie and I are in my office again. With us is Margaret, my trainee, who I have roped in to help with the treatment. And under my chair behind my desk, unbeknown to Jackie, is Flossie, a sweet, mongrel puppy, the size of a small spaniel. Flossie belongs to Margaret who assures me that her dog would not hurt a fly. I had been playing with Flossie before Jackie arrived and she is a typical friendly, lively puppy. She never once showed any aggression or tried to bite. Pretty important this as a colleague had just helpfully told me how he had tried flooding for a dog phobic woman and the dog had bitten her!

Now I have a dog, a helper and a plan. It is a basic plan in truth. It is to go down to the scrap of open area just outside the Institute main entrance and get Jackie and Flossie to, well, bond. Then, as I said to Margaret beforehand, we'll see what happens. Such is the skill of the budding behaviour therapist. But before we do this, I make a huge mistake.

"Jackie," I announce, "in a moment we'll all go outside. I haven't told you but underneath my chair is a small, playful puppy called Flossie who... ."

I do not finish. Jackie lets out a scream and jumps up from her seat. Flossie, terrified by the noise, barks surprisingly loudly for such a small dog. Margaret rushes round the desk to calm her dog down. I sit frozen in the chair. Meanwhile, Jackie is having a major panic attack right in front of me. Her breathing is shallow, fast, and urgent. She is standing up, leaning on the chair and saying, "No, no, no, no, please, no," while her face is now chalky white and her eyes wild with fear. Shit! This was not supposed to happen. I feel a complete idiot.

Margaret pulls Flossie from under the chair, cradling the little dog in her arms, talking soothingly to her. I feel I should do the same to Jackie. Not cradling her in my arms of course, but talking in what I hope is a soothing manner.

"There, you see, she's a very small dog. Nothing to be frightened of, Jackie. She's on a lead. And Margaret has her firmly in her arms. She can't hurt you." At that moment Flossie yawns and gives out a pathetic squeal. "See. She's more frightened of you than you of her."

"I don't think so," says Jackie. But she is looking at Flossie and she appears slightly calmer.

"Let's all go downstairs," I say, taking charge at last. "You and I first, Jackie, then Margaret with Flossie. You are totally safe. She's a delightful little puppy, no harm in her at all. We'll keep her under control all the time ... ." I witter away in this manner as we descend the stairs and head outside.

Forty minutes later I watch as Jackie calls out, "Flossie! Come here!" and the little puppy runs excitedly up to her and jumps into her arms where she snuggles down, licking Jackie's face. Jackie's eyes are shining, not with tears of fright this time, but sheer pleasure. Margaret and I are clucking away beside the two of them like proud parents. Forty minutes. That is all it took. I started with Margaret and Flossie on the lead standing about 30 metres away while Jackie came as near as she dared. Then Jackie and Margaret walked Flossie round the patch of grass, the puppy on the further side well away from Jackie. Then back to Jackie approaching Flossie, still on a tight lead, this time coming closer. More walking, with Margaret explaining about Flossie and dogs in general, how you can tell if they're friendly or not, how most dogs prefer to smell a stranger's hand before being touched. After a while I propose that Jackie should gently touch Flossie. A huge step forward and I try the same shadowing technique I used with Gary. Margaret holds Flossie tightly in her arms while I bring my hand nearer with Jackie hesitantly following suit. But Flossie struggles and yelps, not liking this bizarre human behaviour. It is Jackie who says to put her on the ground and that she will do it herself. And she does, slowly but determinedly. I see she is rapidly losing her fear of Flossie and so I leave Jackie to make the running, to decide what to do, how far to go, and that is how she ends up gambolling with Flossie, picking her up and making a fuss of her.

A success. And absolutely predictable from behavioural theory. One-trial learning brought on the phobia. One session of behaviour therapy cured it. QED. Okay, a small, friendly puppy is not the same as a large, ferocious Alsatian. Some dogs *are* dangerous. So we spent the next few sessions when we were not playing with Flossie talking about dogs and what was sensible and what was phobic avoidance. We agreed that it would be perfectly okay if Jackie never went near an Alsatian, a Doberman, a Rottweiler or a Bullmastiff. These were breeds to avoid even if the owners claimed they were totally harmless. But Jackie was to stop taking circuitous routes to avoid meeting dogs. She should not cross the street if she sees a dog on a lead. She would be positive about dogs to Martin with the same provisos. If she felt really confident about a dog, perhaps one belonging to a friend, then she should stroke it in the way that Margaret showed her. But she did not have to do that. She could choose how much she interacted with dogs, her choice dictated not by unreasonable fear but by common sense.

Making someone better is highly reinforcing. The patient is grateful and it is gratifying to see someone's life, up to now dominated by anxiety and fear, freed from unnecessary constraints. One's self-confidence as a therapist increases exponentially. It also shows that theory can be successfully translated into practice, the basis of behaviour therapy. Ah, if only it could be like that every time. I was soon to learn that the life of a behaviour therapist was not that simple.

CHAPTER FOUR

How many psychologists does it take to change a light bulb?

After just over a year's training I qualified as a clinical psychologist. I registered with Dr. Rachman for a research PhD intending to demonstrate in a scientific study how successful behaviour therapy was. A half-time clinical lectureship at the Institute came up. I was offered it and, this being the Maudsley, without so much as an interview. My main duties were to provide a clinical service to one of the wards and to do the odd lecture. The other half of my time I would do my doctorate. I had hoped to work on an adult ward and carry on my behaviour therapy work. But there was in fact only one job available and that was working on the psychogeriatric ward at the Bethlem Royal Hospital in Beckenham, Kent. I knew nothing about psychogeriatrics. I had never worked with elderly people. And, I thought gloomily, what prospects would there be for behaviour therapy? Were they not, well, too *old* for therapy? Such was my unabashed arrogance.

In the two years I was to work on the psychogeriatric ward, I spent most of my time administering psychometric tests, the purpose of which was to separate the dementing patients from the depressed. The tests took over an hour, sometimes longer, and almost all the elderly patients failed to answer most of the questions.

As I ploughed on, some became highly distressed. It seems I was creating psychological problems rather than solving them! Later, when I discovered that the psychiatrists took little notice of my detailed, carefully argued reports and, further, that within a few weeks it was pretty obvious who was dementing and who was depressed (the depressed patients began to recover, the dementing patients did not), I curtailed the testing and extrapolated the final results, something that was a sin in the psychometric lexicon but seemed to me the lesser of two evils.

There was indeed not much behaviour therapy to be had on the psychogeriatric wards, but I also attended a weekly psychiatric outpatient clinic at the Maudsley. Here, as the news about behaviour therapy's successes began to trickle through to GPs and others, referrals came wanting this new approach. There was a great deal of interest in the treatment of agoraphobics in particular, that is, women—and it was mainly women—who had a morbid fear of leaving the safety of their own home. Contrary to what most people think, agoraphobia is not primarily a fear of open spaces. If anything agoraphobics are more frightened of *enclosed* spaces. The term *agoraphobia* means a fear of the market place (from the Greek *agora* meaning market), a more accurate summary of what most patients fear, which is getting trapped where there are crowds of people, panicking and appearing a fool. Their worst nightmare is being in a busy shop or supermarket, queuing at the checkout and having a massive panic attack. Many have a dread that the ambulance will be called and they will be hauled off to A & E or admitted to the loony bin. Recent American research had shown that an *in vivo* behavioural programme in which agoraphobics are taken out to confront their fear, called rather sparely *exposure*, was proving very effective. Research trials were underway at the Maudsley, Oxford, and elsewhere to see if this method worked over here. This was a chance for me to do some behaviour therapy, to do what I wanted to do, to get people better. The behavioural treatment could be summed up starkly as, *get the person out and keep her out*. While going out would cause an immediate increase in anxiety, theoretically it should decline if the patient remained in the situation long enough. The therapist could also teach coping skills such as relaxation, distraction, and controlled breathing so the panic could be contained, though some behaviour therapists argued this was unnecessary.

If you had been around Camberwell in the 1970s you might well have seen some odd-looking couples walking slowly from the Maudsley outpatient department in Denmark Hill towards Camberwell Green. One, a bright, eager young man or woman, often with an A4 notepad and pen, the other, a reluctant, slow-moving, taciturn, and wary older woman. Every so often this odd couple would stop and the young person would be talking—encouraging, coaxing, cajoling, persuading—while the older woman, the agoraphobic patient, would be hesitating uncertainly, anxious to return to a place of safety. Then, after a short time, the pair would turn and head back to outpatients. I did this countless times. Later on in the programme my patient would be sent off on her own for 50 metres or so while I waited in view like a devoted parent, an unconscious re-enactment of the scene Bowlby describes in his book, *Separation*, the mother sitting on a park bench while her child explores the immediate environment, glancing often at her mum or returning fleetingly to her in order to feel safe. At the time I had not read any of Bowlby's works and it was only much later that I came to realize how relevant separation anxiety was for understanding agoraphobia.

Bowlby was a psychoanalyst who, unlike most analysts at the time, was more interested in actual relationships rather than fantasized ones, particularly the attachment between mother and infant. For most of his life he was, as a result, on the periphery of the psychoanalytic movement although, belatedly, he was recognized as a truly major figure. His idea of *a secure base* can be applied not just to agoraphobia but also to psychotherapy itself. A therapist who creates a sense of security for his or her clients provides the safety necessary for them to take risks. As a behaviour therapist I had no conscious notion of this, but my naïve confidence in the treatment, and in the wonders of science, could well have contributed to my clients feeling safe.

***

One day I received a referral from a GP saying that he had a patient, a chronic agoraphobic, Mrs. Hewittson, who lived on the Dog Kennel Hill estate in Peckham. She was totally stuck in her flat. Her grown-up daughter had heard of behaviour therapy and thought her mother would benefit from this new approach. Could I help? The GP gave me only the barest details but one thing stood out.

Mrs. Hewittson had been an agoraphobic for more than 30 years. Here was a chance to put things right, to turn this unfortunate lady's life around.

By this time I had trainee clinical psychologists of my own to supervise. I was keen to teach them the wonders of behaviour therapy. So it was with a young psychologist, Graham, that I went to meet Mrs. Hewittson in her flat on the Dog Kennel Hill estate. This part of the world was, and very likely still is, pretty grim. A large, soulless mass of redbrick, high-rise blocks. No amenities anywhere. No play areas or youth clubs or shops. Nothing. It was as though the planners had not thought any further than housing the inmates—that is what they seemed like—and then got bored. The one distinction of the Dog Kennel Hill estate was that the notorious criminals, the Krays, were brought up there.

I park my car on the road that borders the estate, thinking that the safer option. Graham and I walk down the hill seeking to locate Arlington House where Mrs. Hewittson lives. I am aware that we stand out, dressed in our smart, professional clothes, each carrying a leather briefcase. But no one bothers us and we find No. 7, a ground floor flat fortunately, so we do not have to negotiate what I imagine to be urine-smelling lifts or flights of bare concrete stairs. I ring the bell and wait.

I had briefed Graham beforehand. This is to be an assessment. Given that this is behaviour therapy, it would of course be a behavioural assessment. My plan was that flanked by the two of us, Mrs. Hewittson would come out of her flat. Then we would send her off on her own as far as she could go until she could not go any further. And I was going to be really scientific about this, for we would note down exactly how far she went, how long she took and how much anxiety she experienced on a scale of 0 to 100. This would be the baseline against which her recovery would be measured. In my mind, I fantasized Mrs. Hewittson going further and further each week until we had her travelling all over London.

The door is opened cautiously by a young girl, no more than nine. I explain that we are psychologists and that we have come from the Maudsley Hospital to see Mrs. Hewittson.

"Nan," she yells back into the flat, "there's two psychos from the hospital to see ya. Waddya want to do?"

We hear the sound of talking from inside the flat, two voices, one female sounding very tremulous. Graham and I exchange looks. The door opens wider. "'Nan says you can come in." The girl disappears into the gloom of the flat. When we get used to the darkness, for the curtains are drawn and the main lighting comes from a TV blaring away in the background, we see that the room is full of people. There are three girls, including the little girl who opened the door, playing around a Wendy house in one corner. A woman, barely in her teens, is seated at a table holding a baby who is guzzling milk from a bottle. A tiny, wizened man in an old grey suit sits on a huge settee, a cigarette dangling from his hand. And, in a rocking-chair in the centre of the room, there is a woman in her fifties, strands of mousy brown hair straggling down either side of a pale, thin face in which watery blue eyes stand out like on those odd goggle-eyed fish one sees in aquariums. She is staring at us unblinking. Mrs. Hewittson I presume.

It is an unnerving situation, not what I had expected. I had imagined Mrs. Hewittson stuck on her own, lonely perhaps, even pleased to have a bit of company. Not in the midst of a mêlée of people. But I am the professional. So I take charge.

"Mrs. Hewittson?" I say, addressing the lady in the rocking-chair. "We're psychologists from the Maudsley. We've come to help you get better."

The woman says nothing. She rocks forward and back in the chair. I am uncomfortably reminded of the Bates motel in *Psycho* and the skeletal mother in the basement.

"Your daughter," I press on, "arranged for us to come and help you."

"Did she now?" Mrs. Hewittson says. It's a rasping, throaty voice, the product no doubt of thousands of cigarettes smoked in the gloomy flat. "That was nifty of Jean."

Somehow I feel that being "nifty" is not something Mrs. Hewittson approves of. The tiny man on the settee leans forward. "My Madge is not well, you know," he says confidentially as though she cannot hear him. "Trouble with her nerves. Had it a long time."

"That's why we're here," I say triumphantly. "To get her better."

"How are you going to do that then?" puts in the woman with the baby.

"First, we'll go out for a short walk, say, to the post box." We had passed the post box just 20 metres along the road. I turn to

Mrs. Hewittson. "You might have a letter you want to post and we could do it together."

"Sammy takes all my letters. He delivers them and takes whatever I've got. Don't need to post anything, thanks all the same."

"Anyway, it's an assessment, a sort of test, to see how far you can go. You don't have to go far," I add hastily. "Just as far as you feel you can go."

"I can't do that, doctor. Sorry, I can't do that at all."

"Oh." This blanket refusal takes me back. "Well," I press on gamely, "what about going out of the front door and down the path to the gate? It's only a couple of yards. I'm sure you could do that with our help."

"I would do it, sir. But it's the fits, you see. Can't risk it. I have these terrible fits."

"She does," interjects the man in the grey suit who I take to be her husband. "She has these fits. She's a martyr to them."

I sense I am losing the battle. What are these "fits"? Could they be epileptic fits? If they are, what do Graham and I do if she has one? I have never seen an epileptic fit. All I know is what everyone else knows from the films, how you have to grab the tongue, but then what? I curse myself. I should have read Mrs. Hewittson's case file before we came. Before I have time to say anything, the front door opens and in breezes another youngish woman with a two-year old in tow.

"Madge, darlin'," she starts, then stops having spotted us. "Sorry, love, didn't know you had visitors."

"They're from the hospital. Psychiatrists," says Madge.

"Psychologists."

"Sorry, didn't mean to offend and all that."

"No offence."

"Thing is," says the new arrival, "I was hoping you'd look after Darren while I go to the Social."

"No problem, love. You leave him here with me." Mrs. Hewittson turns to me. "Very sorry about the walk. But you see I've got my hands full. Another time, doctor."

"Yes. Right," I say decisively. "What about Friday morning? At 11?"

"That would be ticky-tack. I'll be more meself then, I expect."

Unfortunately, that's exactly what worries me.

Friday morning comes and Graham and I make our way back to the Dog Kennel Hill estate, to Arlington House, No. 7. I have found Mrs. Hewittson's case file. A bulging, tattered, beige-coloured, wallet with letters, documents, case notes, and other bits of paper loosely packed into it. I have waded through it all. There is no mention of epileptic fits. Just panic attacks, which I suspect is what Mrs. Hewittson meant. As we approach the door, we see pinned on it a scrap of white paper, fluttering in the wind. I fold it down so we can read what is on it.

Too the Doctors. Very sorry, had too go to the dentists for me tootheyk really bad it is. Mrs. Hewittson.

We try to peer in through the windows but the curtains are closed. There is not a sound from inside. But I knock a couple of times anyway.

"It seems," Graham says, "that a visit to the dentist is preferable to a visit from us."

"Maybe it was an emergency."

"Yes, of course that might be it." He gives a half smile.

I take the paper off the door and, beneath Mrs. Hewittson's scribbled message, I write:

Sorry about your toothache. Hope you get it fixed. We'll come again on Monday at 11.

I am not about to give up so easily.

On a bright, sunny Monday morning Graham and I are again standing outside No. 7 Arlington House. This time there is no scribbled note on the door. We knock but there is no response. The curtains are not completely drawn on one of the windows. Peering in, I see that the front room is empty and the TV is off. There is no sign of occupation. I step back and look at Graham. He shrugs. Just then a young girl, a similar age to the ones we had seen playing around the Wendy house, comes skipping down the street towards us. She skips right up to us and proceeds to skip round us as though we are part of some game she is playing.

"Are you," she says as she skips, "the doctors?"

"I suppose so. Yes, I mean."

"To see Mrs. H?" *Skip, skip.*

"Mrs. Hewittson, that's right."

Skip. "She left a message." *Skip, skip.*

"And?"

Skip, skip. "She's gone to the Isle of Wight." *Skip.* "To visit her brother-in-law." *Skip, skip.* "For the whole week." At that she skips off the way she came.

As we trudge back to the car, Graham says: "You could say we had a great success. After all, we got her out of the house."

"Drove her out," I say with a grin.

"And in one session."

"We should write a paper. 'One session treatment for agoraphobia: a breakthrough in behaviour therapy.'"

We did not write a paper, of course. Nor did we return to bother Mrs. Hewittson again. It had taken me a while to get the message but I did get it in the end.

Anyone who practises as a psychotherapist for any length of time will soon learn that people are unpredictable. What may work with one person does not necessarily work with another. Behaviour therapy however was based on the opposite belief that once something works, it will work full stop. It was assumed that behaviour change followed widely accepted scientific principles, the so-called "laws of learning". So if one agoraphobic is successfully treated by exposure, then, all things being equal, others will follow suit. Much is hidden in that phrase, "all things being equal". When are they ever? Mrs. Hewittson was a case in point. It might be argued that this determined lady was simply not motivated to overcome her agoraphobia. Without a doubt. It was her daughter who suggested therapy, not her. Here was another lesson that I failed to learn at the time: never take a referral from a relative or friend without checking that the patient wants the treatment too. Years later when I started my own private practice, I would often get a phone call from a distraught parent asking if I might help her adult son or daughter who had shut herself in her room, or was failing to study, or had an eating, drinking or drugs problem. While I understood the parent's anxiety, I would only accept the referral if the son or daughter made contact themselves and then only after a careful assessment of their willingness to do some psychological work. Sometimes people opt for psychotherapy to prove that they *can't* be helped. A husband comes for anger management mainly because he has been persuaded to do so by his wife. He does not truly believe he has a problem but if he shows willing and the therapy does not work, he can claim he has done his bit.

But in my evangelical behaviour therapist guise I paid such matters little heed. After all, I was getting good results. My colleagues were too. Research studies showed that behaviour therapy worked. Okay, there was the occasional Mrs. Hewittson but she was offset by people like Gary and Jackie. Then along came Gillian.

**

A couple of years into my work on the psychogeriatrics ward, the opportunity came to move to an adult psychiatric ward at the Bethlem Royal Hospital in Kent. This ward catered for what might be called the *special* patients, that is, the sons and daughters of doctors and professors who had gone off the rails (the sons and daughters, I mean, though the doctors and professors might have too for all I knew). A young girl, Gillian, had been admitted to the ward, barely 19. She had a similar obsessional disorder to Gary. She feared contamination and washed her hands repeatedly. This was a chance to repeat our first success and make her better. It was not so much general dirt Gillian obsessed about. She believed something more peculiar: that places became contaminated by invisible specks spread by animals. Cats were the worst. Her family had a cat and Gillian had eventually confined herself to her bedroom in order to escape the cat's presence. *Modelling and response prevention,* I immediately thought. Get Gillian to confront cats, the source of her anxiety, while preventing her from doing anything to reduce her anxiety.

Gillian had a single room in the ward that she carefully preserved as contamination-free. She was a quiet, shy girl, not given much to talking, seemingly deeply unhappy though not showing classic signs of depression. I was given the green light to try my new therapy. The problem was how could I contaminate her room so that I could get the therapy going? I needed ... well ... a cat. If I found an amenable cat as I had found Flossie the dog for Jackie, then I could combine elements of both therapies. A double whammy! I had some friends who owned a longhaired Siamese, Sherry. In a moment of inspiration I thought I could borrow Sherry for the day, take her to Bethlem, introduce her to Gillian, let her wander all over Gillian's room and, hey presto, contamination! Now to say Gillian was not too keen on this idea is putting it mildly. But I wore her down.

I was the boss, the expert, the professional. The fact that I had barely three years of experience as a therapist and could count the cases of behaviour therapy I had done up to then on the fingers of two hands did not deter me. Gillian caved in. My friends, amused and intrigued, lent me Sherry. Therapy began.

The best laid plans of cats and men. I have to say Sherry was a reluctant therapist. I do not think psychotherapy was exactly her vocation. She did not like the cat box. She hated the car journey across London. She was aloof to the point of disdain with me. She took an instant dislike to the Bethlem especially as I did not dare let her out into the wonderful grounds and kept her in a pokey room with a neurotic and unhappy patient who did not want her there in the first place. But I persisted. Gillian's room was thoroughly contaminated by Sherry's invisible specks. Gillian was told not to wash or clean anything. The stage was set for recovery.

It did not happen. Firstly, Gillian rationalized the contamination. It was bad but not as bad as at home. Then Sherry was not the right sort of cat.

"But she has invisible specks?" I asked.

"Oh yes."

"And you haven't gone down with some awful disease because of Sherry's invisible specks, have you?"

"That doesn't mean that won't happen later," Gillian said primly. *And then you'll all be sorry* hung in the air between us unsaid. "Anyway, it's a stupid therapy, a stupid cat and ..." She stopped in mid-sentence but I could fill in the blank. After three traumatic sessions Gillian withdrew her cooperation. My attempt at behaviour therapy had failed.

Gillian's volte-face made me grumpy. I had wanted another great success like Gary's. I had not managed it. Not only that, my friends were rather frosty with me. Apparently, ever since her trips to the Bethlem, Sherry had turned into an anxious, whining, irritable beast who wanted nothing to do with them. My treatment had not only failed to cure Gillian. I had actually made Sherry neurotic!

It did not occur to me at the time that a 19-year-old girl might be unhappy at home and had found a way to make her unhappiness a very powerful tool in the family dynamics. I had not yet seen any bulimics or anorexics at that point in my fledgling career.

When I did, I rapidly learned how a psychological problem could have a power of its own that makes it very difficult for the owner to give it up. So I suspect it was with Gillian. The problem had been identified as hers, thereby focussing all the family's attention on her. As the family therapists would say, she *carried* the problem for the family. By focussing on her contamination fears, we—the psychiatrists, psychologists, the whole lot of us—colluded with the family to see Gillian as the problem, not the family itself. Gillian would not very easily give up that role however restrictive it became unless the underlying issues were addressed too. Moreover, there was some significant secondary gain from playing this part: she had power.

Later, when I had seen a few more OCD patients, I realized how much investment they had in their obsessionality. It takes a lot of energy to be a fully-fledged obsessional. For a start you always have to be on your guard. Contamination could be just round the corner. And then there are the rituals. Actions have to be performed in exactly the right order—wash the left hand first, soap each finger in turn starting at the little finger, rinse under the tap, then the right hand, fingers again, rinse. Repeat five times always in the right order. And if you get it wrong or someone or something interrupts, then you have to start all over again. This fills the space, mental and physical. You have all this vital stuff to do. And then others get drawn in, parents, spouse, friends, all anxious to help. This is where the power lies: it gives someone like Gillian a means of controlling her family whereas before she probably felt neglected or unimportant.

Sometimes actively seeking a solution can become a problem in itself. Curing Gillian's obsessions, the solution I was seeking, failed to work. Yet people—family, friends, teachers, the GP, the specialists—persist in seeking that very solution despite the failure. The problem gets further and further entrenched. As treatment after treatment fails, despair sets in and the patient is seen as "intractable" or "resistant". She becomes angry, then helpless, and then depressed. Her self-esteem plummets. She has started on the road to becoming a career psychiatric patient with a bulging case file and increasing isolation from mainstream society. I do not know if that happened to Gillian. I hope not. But I know I did not help her and I might well have made her worse. Behaviour therapy was proving not to be as simple as it first seemed.

> *How many psychologists does it take to change a light bulb?*
> *One. But the light bulb has to want to change.*

Psychologists tell this joke against themselves. Jokes can function as a defence against accepting an unpalatable truth. What if it turned out that behaviour therapy, far from being the great new hope of psychotherapy, turned out to be another flawed enterprise? But then, against that, there was all the new scientific research that endorsed its effectiveness. Surely, I thought, the research cannot be wrong. I was keen to add my own contribution. I could do my own research trial and show that behaviour therapy really worked.

CHAPTER FIVE

Fail again. Fail better

In the early 1970s the randomized controlled trial (RCT) had just become the gold standard of psychotherapy outcome research. Patients were randomly allocated, usually to one of three groups, the treatment of choice, an alternative or placebo therapy, and a no treatment control. Pre- and post-measures were taken. A straightforward statistical comparison would show if the new treatment was better than both the alternative and the no treatment condition. A follow-up assessment—six months and/or a year later—would show if the changes lasted. To me it seemed simple. Already there were several published studies of behaviour therapy using the RCT model and in all of them behaviour therapy was proved the winner. I would join the select band.

One decision I had to make was what patient group to focus on. While research was already underway on specific phobics, agoraphobics and obsessionals, I noticed there was one group of patients no one had yet done a proper outcome study on: social phobics. There were just a few case reports in the behaviour therapy literature. Mainly, they showed that Wolpe's *systematic desensitization* or a version of it seemed to work. But no substantial research trial had yet been done. In the psychiatric literature social phobics were defined as people who felt excessively anxious in the company of others. Someone who blushed easily perhaps, who felt tongue-tied and shy, avoiding the company of others. In personality assessments they would score high on the dimensions of introversion and neuroticism. Many psychology theorists—my boss H.J. Eysenck was a leading figure in this regard—thought this was a basic temperamental difference with a strong genetic basis. Behavioural theory on the other hand pointed to a learned component just as in any other phobia. People could become conditioned by anxious experiences in social events, it was argued. Certainly when I began seeing social phobics, they recounted tales of humiliating and embarrassing experiences that had been burned into their memory. Being picked on at school because of a slight stammer and then mercilessly bullied. Asked to read in class and being laughed at for blushing. Trying to sign a cheque in a shop and trembling so much they couldn't do it. Of course these incidents did not prove that the learning theory explanation was necessarily right. People could start with a temperamental sensitivity that made them more vulnerable to experiencing anxiety in social situations. An interaction between temperament and learning seemed the most sensible explanation.

But, as I soon discovered, the diagnosis of social phobia covered a multitude of often quite disparate people and problems. Some social phobics reported pervasive and crippling anxiety. They would try to avoid people at all costs and led very restricted and lonely lives. In contrast, some had a specific phobia like a fear of blushing or trembling or writing in front of others but were otherwise socially confident. It was not a well-defined diagnostic category. Social phobics merged into agoraphobics: for example, both felt anxious in crowded places although social phobics tended to worry less about panicking than about people talking to them. Some were depressed. Others were given a concordant diagnosis such as personality disorder. A few were psychotic. Later, when the research was well underway, I realized how social problems cut across all psychiatric diagnoses, so much so that my patient group proved to be highly variable in the extent and nature of their social anxieties. This was to have a huge impact on the research in a way I completely failed to anticipate.

Those who had used Wolpe's technique of systematic desensitization treated the patient like any other phobic. They constructed a hierarchy, reduced their anxiety, encouraged gradual socialization first in imagination and then in reality, and, hey presto, the patient would get better. It all seemed so simple. But what if many of these people were anxious because they did not know how to handle a social situation? Going to a party where you know no one for example. Suppose you are shy, unsure of yourself, full of doubts. Then what happens? You stand on your own sipping your drink, hoping someone will talk to you. But if they do, you stammer or dry up or say something stupid. You fail to impress. In fact, you do so badly, you leave after half an hour. That confirms your worst fears—you are a hopeless case. This all rang rather too true for me. To this day I remember the poor girl at one party who had to endure my long silences as I desperately racked my brain for something to say.

So, I thought, what if these patients also lacked social skills? I knew about social skills from the lectures that the social psychologist Michael Argyle had given in Oxford.[1] Argyle maintained that social behaviour, even at its most complex, could be broken down into a set of verbal and non-verbal skills. Holding a conversation with someone. Listening. Taking someone out on a date. Giving a lecture. All involved verbal skills of course but also non-verbal ones such as making eye-contact, maintaining appropriate social distance, reinforcing others through emotional expressions, using gestures, *body language* as it is now called. Argyle drew a parallel with perceptual and motor skills, arguing that the same principles were involved. Moreover, he claimed it was possible to train people in social skills just as someone could be taught to drive a car, hit a golf ball, or operate a machine.

---

[1] For a man who studied social skills, Michael Argyle was well known for his odd social behaviour. He had a large, braying laugh and he loved playing practical jokes on people, especially fellow academics. I watched him once listening to a colleague explain in loving detail a brilliant overhead kick Pele made in the 1970 World Cup. Michael waited until the colleague reached the climax of his story and in the pause that followed, he innocently asked: "And what was that game? Golf?" The colleague stormed out of the room. Michael was a great lecturer. I still remember his opening remarks on the topic of the authoritarian personality. "We social psychologists like to study the authoritarian personality because to do so tells us about social behaviour, we also learn about the interaction between personality and social attitudes, and ..." (pause) "... because we can't stand the buggers." It brought the house down. Perhaps Michael should have been a light comedian. He seemed to think he was.

Social skills training! Like the kid in the cartoon, the phrase seemed to spring vividly into my head in great flashing neon lights. This is what I would do. This would be the new and successful behavioural treatment. I would be a pioneer. Patients could be taught basic social skills like how to hold a simple conversation or to tell a story about themselves or to listen to other people or to tell a joke. Wolpe and others had done something like this using a technique they called *assertiveness training*. This involved the therapist and patient role-playing conversations in therapy to increase their self-esteem and assertiveness. Taking something faulty back to a shop or learning to say no to a request or talking appropriately and interestingly about oneself. But this was relatively crude and not grounded in a skills-training model.

Feedback is the *sine qua non* of learning new skills. People need to see what works and what does not. I found some socially anxious patients and began to experiment, trying a social skills training approach first using an audiotape recorder and, later, a video camera and recorder. I had no training in this approach. I just thought about how people did simple social tasks like holding a conversation. I read what the psychological literature had revealed about eye contact, social distance etc. I put together a simple, didactic programme and got started. Once I had an interaction in front of me, an audiotaped, role-played conversation for example, it was easy to pick up on social errors and suggest improvements, or so I thought. And at first I found that this seemed to work pretty well. The feedback generated by the recordings helped people not only to see where they went wrong, but enabled me to model a different and what I took to be a more successful approach. Initial success made me confident that this method would really work. This was dramatically brought home to me by Colin.

I had moved wards yet again and was now the psychologist on the psychiatric ward in the Maudsley where the consultant was Jim Birley, an enlightened and socially committed psychiatrist, who was keen on psychological approaches. He knew of my interest in social skills training and he suggested I might try this new therapy on a man I will call Colin. Colin was in his thirties, married with two young children. He had been admitted following a serious overdose that had almost killed him. Some months before his admission Colin and his family had emigrated, looking for work. But he had been unsuccessful, either failing to get jobs or getting fired from them soon after he was taken on. In the end he and his family were booted back to England. This had sent him into a depressive spiral and led to the overdose.

On the ward Colin's mood was very labile. He could switch rapidly between intense depression and extreme anger. In one bout of anger he had punched the psychiatric registrar in the face and then had broken down in tears. Colin always insisted that all he wanted was a job, a chance to earn money and look after his family. The trouble was he could not get one because of his aggressive, challenging attitude. Jim Birley wondered if I might try using social skills training to teach Colin to be less aggressive so that he could get and hold down a job. Sure, I said, I'll give it a try.

In a side room off the ward Ed, the video technician, and I set up the video equipment. A bulky black camera perched on top of a tripod is directed at one of the two chairs in the room. I test out the angle by sitting in the patient's chair and my picture emerges shakily on the small black and white TV monitor we have placed on a table. Brought in on its own trolley because it is so heavy is the chrome, Ampex tape recorder from the back of which heavy-duty leads run to the camera, the monitor, and the socket board Ed has brought since there is only one electrical outlet in the room. Ed and I make a test recording of me saying "Baa, baa, black sheep" and then Ed leaves because it is after 5.30 and his day has ended. I am left on my own to operate the equipment. It is not difficult. All I have to do is press the "Play" and "Record" buttons simultaneously on the Ampex and the recording is underway. No scope for camera angles, close-ups or fancy lighting effects.

Colin has a thin, foxy face with lanky, black hair that falls across his forehead. He is wearing a cheap suit that has seen better days. His shoes—black brogues—are badly scuffed. I wonder if this is what he wears when he applies for jobs. At my direction he sits in the chair opposite the camera. I can clearly see the physical tension in his body, in the rigid way he holds himself, the right foot jigging up and down on the floor, and the strained paleness in his face. I am uneasily aware of his outbursts of sudden aggression. I remember how he attacked and punched the registrar. I wonder if what I am doing is exactly wise. Too late to back out now.

I have already told Colin what we are going to do. I start the video and run through it again so that his consent is taped. We are to role-play an interview for a job and afterwards view it on video.

"Is that okay?" "Yeah," he says. As the tape rolls and I sit in my chair opposite Colin, I realize that I know nothing about the unskilled labour market. I worked as a golf caddy once but got the job just by turning up. I was interviewed for a place at Oxford but that is absolutely no help here. I will have to wing it, asking a few basic questions and see how Colin responds.

"Okay, Colin, thanks for coming," I say with probably unnecessary politeness. "We've a vacancy as, um, a builder's labourer. So I want to start by asking a few questions about yourself first. Are you single? Married?"

"Why do you want to know?" Colin shoots back venomously.

Startled, I mumble something about it being company policy.

"It's got nothing to do with you," says Colin glaring at me. "That's personal, that is."

"'Okay," I say, switching tack quickly, "let's see, where was your last job?"

"Sydney, Australia. Building site. Labourer.

"'How long were you there?"

"Three days."

"*Three days?*"

"Yeah. Fucking useless Aussie git was the foreman. He gave me the push."

"And how long were you in Australia?"

Colin glares at me again. His foot starts beating time faster on the floor.

"Woz that gotta do with anything? I'm here now, ain't I?"

"Okay," I say again wondering if there was any way I could get onto safer ground. "Before, in England, I see you worked for British Leyland. How long for?"

"Six years."

Oh good, I think. "And why did you leave?"

"I hit a bloke. Ended up in hospital. They said it was my fault, but he started it. He was a smarmy git. Got what he deserved."

I change the subject again. "You're back in England now. I see you haven't worked for six months …"

"So what? Not a crime, is it?" Colin stares at me balefully.

"No, no, of course it's not a crime. I just wanted to know …"

"That's the trouble with you lot. You always want to know. You poke your nose into things that are personal, nothing to do with you.

I was in hospital, understand? A bloody loony bin. Useless dump with stupid doctors and social workers and other useless prats." I think I come into the last category. Colin is ranting now, leaning forward in the chair, spits of saliva coming out of his mouth, his hair falling over his face, his fists tightly clenched, his right foot dancing an Irish jig on the floor.

"Let's stop now," I say quickly. "Just sit back, Colin. Remember, this is just a role-play." To my relief, he does just that. I stop the tape and rewind while Colin says nothing, staring into space. The next step is to show him the recording. How will he react? I am aware of the quiet of the side room and that it is the end of the day and there is no one about.

As the black and white recording plays I watch Colin watching it. He stares intently at the TV screen. His expression is hard for me to fathom. The recording comes to an end. Silence.

"What do you think?" I eventually say with studied nonchalance.

Colin sits forward in the chair. He looks me straight in the face. "If I met that guy in the street," he says, referring to himself, "I'd punch him."

I laugh. I can't help myself. Fortunately, Colin laughs too.

"I didn't realize what a stupid arsehole I was. I wouldn't give meself a job." He shakes his head. "Never clocked it 'til I saw meself on the telly."

We spend the remainder of the session talking about job interviews and how to deal with personal questions and how not to be aggressive. We do a retake and this time Colin is more relaxed and answers all my questions without sounding off. He is clearly pleased when we view the result.

I did not see Colin again. Some time later Jim Birley told me that he had got a job and had been discharged. Whether this was due to the video feedback is impossible to say. But there was no doubt that Colin's seeing himself on the monitor had an immediate and pronounced effect. This reinforced my view that social skills training could be a pretty powerful therapy indeed.

I decided on the study. I would compare social skills training (SST) with an established treatment, Wolpe's systematic desensitization (SD), and a no treatment control group (NTC). I would do pre- and post-test assessments and a follow-up at six months. If SST was as good or better than SD and both better than the control, I would have done what I had set out to do, prove that this new approach really worked. The first thing I needed to do was to find the subjects for my research. Easy, one would think. I was part of a large psychiatric complex that took in three major hospitals, the Maudsley Hospital and St Francis Hospital in Camberwell and the Bethlem Royal Hospital in Kent. I drafted a letter explaining my research plans and sent it round to the psychiatrists, GPs, and any other professionals who might be able to refer patients to me. This was before research ethics committees, before every proposed study is subject to rigorous scrutiny for any possible ethical problems, the bugbear of anyone seeking to do research these days. I simply wrote down what I intended to do, showed it to my supervisor and sent it off. I was blithely confident that I would behave ethically, ensuring the patients understood the study and that they consented to it in writing or on tape, allowing them to leave at any time, making arrangements for those who were not suitable to be helped to be seen elsewhere, and having plans in place if by chance any got worse.

The control group was the only ethical issue that gave me pause. Was it right to withhold therapy even if we did not know whether the therapy actually worked? I found a way of dealing with this. Those randomly assigned to the no treatment group would be placed on a waiting list, reassessed at the end of three months and offered whatever therapy was most suitable to their clinical needs. This meant that everyone who was referred and proved suitable for the research would get therapy at some point. If patients were on medication, as many were, I decided they would need to continue taking their drugs under the supervision of their psychiatrist or GP. I was confident that even if the control group showed improvement as a result of medication, the two treatment groups would outstrip them.

I sat back and waited for the referrals to come in. It is a sort of universal law, like Sod's Law, that as soon as you start a research project, the subjects dry up. I got no more than a trickle of patients referred to me. Some were suitable but others were not at all what I expected. They had diagnoses like Schizoid Personality Disorder with long histories of in-patient admissions, self-harm and criminal behaviour. Some had been diagnosed as clinically depressed and showed absolutely no confidence that anything I could do would get them better. Others were strange, lonely, shy people who found even coming to the clinic extremely difficult and spoke in monosyllables or not at all. This was not the population of social phobics that I had seen described in the literature, ones where a phobic anxiety was the defining problem from which all else flowed. They had problems that were more diffuse and more complicated. But I saw everyone who was referred except psychotic patients as I had excluded these at the outset. And because I was desperate for subjects I even extended the definition of my subject sample to include those with broader social problems whom I labelled arrogantly as "social inadequates". Looking back I think I know what happened. Many referrers seized the opportunity of my research study to get rid of their most intractable patients, the ones they had been unable to make any headway with, the ones who frustrated them and made them feel helpless, the career psychiatric patients whom no one wanted. Shirley was a typical example.

Shirley is a small, plump woman with dark curly hair and round, light grey eyes set in a chubby face. She is clearly nervous. She has had a five-year history as a psychiatric outpatient and has been variously diagnosed as depressed, alcohol dependent, and socially anxious. Various attempts have been made to help her in the past without success. She was referred to a stop smoking clinic but failed to attend. She was put on a list for re-housing by the council but so far nothing had happened. She had been tried on different combinations of psychiatric drugs. She had been supported by a psychiatric nurse for the best part of a year until the nurse moved on. It was a pattern of attempted help that always seemed to fail. Had I been more experienced, I would have been wary of starting something new and repeating this pattern. But in my naïve enthusiasm, I see this as a chance for me to help Shirley properly, to make a difference. I am pleased when the random allocation places her in the SST group.

Shirley hesitantly tells me about her life. In truth, there is not a lot to tell. She lives at home with her elderly mother. She has a clerical job in the accounts department of the Post Office. She has no friends and never goes out. She used to have friends, she says, and even one or two boyfriends, but that was at school. Twenty years ago. Nothing recently.

"I'm too fat," she says.

"You're not fat," I say, truthfully, for though on the plump side Shirley is not fat. In fact, she's an attractive, pleasant woman.

"Yes I am," she says adamantly. "I have a double chin, triple chin really, and my eyes are too small. And they're too close together.

"You shouldn't let that put you off meeting people," I say with breathtaking condescension. "People often perceive themselves as fatter than they really are. Scientific studies have shown that." I am citing one study on anorectics that a colleague of mine has just carried out. Shirley looks unimpressed by my reference to the wonders of science.

"How do you feel when you go out to meet new people?"

"I don't meet any new people these days."

"But if you did, how would you feel?"

"Nervous. I've no confidence in myself. Other people make me feel like I'm inferior. Even at work." Shirley then tells me about Alan, a man in her office who is constantly putting her down. Her supervisor, a woman, is no help as she puts on airs and treats Shirley like a servant. She goes on for some time about how difficult her work is and how unappreciated she is. Eventually I get the chance to bring her back on track, my track anyway.

"Do you know what to say when you meet strangers, say, at a party?"

"I'm too nervous. I get tongue-tied. It's why I drink or used to anyway. I'd have two or three glasses of sherry before I went out. It relaxed me. But then I still found myself on my own or stuck with some sad bloke who couldn't talk either. It was embarrassing, humiliating. That's why I gave up going out."

"Suppose," I say, "I offer you the chance to learn some social skills. How to talk to people, how to hold a conversation or ask people questions. We would do this in your therapy. We'd practise it in the clinic and then you'd try it out outside."

Shirley looks doubtful. I press on. "The idea is for you to regain your self-confidence so that you feel okay when you meet people. You will have things to talk about and strategies to use." Shirley looks more interested now. "It gives you back control," I say confidently. "You learn social skills like any other skill, like riding a bike or driving a car. Breaking the task down into the components, practising them, putting them together into the whole, trying it out, getting feedback, improving your skill." I make it sound terribly easy. Eventually Shirley agrees to try this new therapy. As we come to the end of the session, I ask her my usual end-of-session question, how would she like to be different if the therapy were successful?

"I want to be happy," she says, "to have friends, maybe to get married."

"I can't guarantee getting married," I say in a feeble attempt at a joke, "but if all goes well, you should be able to make friends again and you should feel happier. Is there anything else?"

"Yes," she says and her face creases into a puzzled frown. "What do you think about plastic surgery? A facelift maybe? It might give me confidence, mightn't it?" Her eyes search out mine and I can see the desperation in them. With a sinking feeling, I have my first suspicion that helping Shirley might prove rather more difficult than I imagine.

Rather to my surprise, when we got going on SST, Shirley responded really well in the sessions. I concentrated on starting and holding conversations, reasoning that this would give her confidence when meeting new people. I showed her strategies for opening a conversation, discussed eye contact and social distance, stressed the value of getting others to talk by asking questions and advised on judicious self-disclosure. In a small room in outpatients we role-played conversations, recording our attempts on a tape recorder and playing them back. I was pleased with the way Shirley participated. Her conversational skills improved. However, a major stumbling block was that she never carried out any of the homework tasks we set. Each week she always had some reason why she could not do what we had agreed.

"Did you go to the table tennis club?" I would ask.

"No. I wasn't feeling too hot that night. Bad headache."

"Did you try asking Alan about his car?" I ask another time. "You know he likes to talk about it."

"No. It didn't come up."

"What about going into a shop and starting a conversation about the weather?"

Shirley screwed up her face. "I'd just feel silly if I did that."

However much I stressed the value of trial and error, of not giving up, of learning from experience, Shirley did not follow through on anything. She became more depressed as it became obvious that therapy was not making a difference to her social life. I became more desperate trying to select very easy targets but however easy they were, however much we ran through them in role-play, however much Shirley insisted she would definitely try them out, she just did not do them. She began to ask about other treatments, plastic surgery, hypnosis, anything. After 15 fruitless sessions, we brought things to an end. Both of us felt deflated. The treatment had been a complete failure.

Fortunately, not everyone in the trial proved as recalcitrant as Shirley. Some people took to the training, built up their confidence and got somewhat better. But most had the same problem, transferring what we did in therapy to real life. It is obvious really. Like teaching someone swimming by miming the strokes on dry land and then saying, now jump in the water and do it. There is a world of difference between role-playing in the safety of the therapist's office and trying to strike up a conversation at a party.[2]

When I completed the research trial and analysed my results, it was crystal clear that not only had I failed to show that SST had worked, neither of the two active treatment groups had done better than the no treatment control. There was not much improvement anywhere. I had failed. Others were producing positive results for behavioural treatments. I had got no improvement. Of course in scientific terms a negative result should be as important as a positive one. Scientific advances are all about disconfirming hypotheses, the principle of falsification that Karl Popper had elegantly enunciated. But the hard reality was that what researchers want are *positive* findings. And I had not delivered.

---

[2]Many years after my research study there was a television programme called *Would like to meet* in which shy and unself-confident people were taught the social skills needed to meet a member of the opposite sex. Experts totally reconstructed the volunteers, redesigning the way they looked, dressed, and moved, as well as telling them what to say when meeting someone for the first time, how to flirt, even how to tell jokes. They were given assignments that were recorded on camera and fed back to them. It was remarkably successful in contrast to my puny efforts. I could conclude, rather caustically, that anyone willing to submit themselves to this trial by television cannot be that shy. But in truth the methods were more rigorous and, more importantly, took place in a real environment rather than the therapist's office.

Failure is not easy to take. I went into a spiral of depression and self-doubt. My confidence had been severely dented. Had I done something wrong? Was it me? Years later, I could look back on my PhD research and see the serious flaws in the design that would have prevented anyone from getting positive results. Because I had found it difficult to recruit subjects, I ended up with small numbers in each of my groups. The statistics I used needed much larger numbers to show up a significant effect. Moreover, as there was huge variability in the sorts of problems people had, this resulted in too much variance *within* the groups. Small numbers and large within-group variance act against demonstrating a statistically significant effect. It is like pulling against a strong current. You have to work so much harder to get anywhere. I am not claiming that my treatments worked but the research failed to show it. For people like Shirley it is clear that the approach did not work. A more fundamental lesson remained to be learned about psychotherapy outcome research. But that was to come much later on in my career.

Samuel Beckett once wrote: "Ever tried. Ever failed. No matter. Try again. Fail again. Fail better." One learns from mistakes. That is certainly in part what he meant. But also that the very human demand for unqualified success can be counterproductive, the drive towards perfection always leading to disappointment, to a sense of failure. Far better to aim for something less grand, less exacting and more realizable—a better failure. The day I write this there is an interview in *The Guardian* newspaper with the psychoanalyst and writer, Adam Phillips. A comment from one of his books leaps from the page:

"Tyrannical fantasies of our own perfectibility lurk in even our simplest ideals, Darwin and Freud intimate, so that any ideal can become another excuse for punishment. Lives dominated by impossible ideals, complete honesty, absolute knowledge, perfect happiness, eternal love are experienced as continuous failure."

CHAPTER SIX

"Whatever happened to flaming June?"

In 1975 I finally completed my doctorate. The findings on the effectiveness of the two treatments may have been negative but I needed to write up the study paying careful attention to the theoretical and methodological matters that had led me to it in the first place. I had added another research project, one that was not to do with evaluating treatments, but was drawn from the data I had obtained from the pre- and post-treatment videotaped assessments of patients in conversation with a confederate, that is, someone neutral whom I trained for the task. Painstakingly, I analysed these into categories of verbal and non-verbal social behaviour and examined how much they correlated with each other and with my more general measures such as self-ratings of social anxiety and self-confidence. I was keen to see whether some behaviours might be indicative of the sorts of problems my patients had. This proved fascinating though, as the mass of data accumulated and the correlations reached their hundreds, the picture became highly complicated. Fortunately, a friend who happened to be a biometrician suggested a new statistical technique called multiple regression that somehow simplified the many correlations into a few key ones, thereby extracting meaning from the confused and confusing picture. As I waited for my *viva*, my worry was that my external examiner, Michael Argyle, would ask me penetrating questions about it and I would flounder horribly. But Michael cheerfully confessed he had never heard of multiple regression. So I was able to explain it to him with an airy confidence that belied my tenuous grasp of how it worked. I was awarded my doctorate subject to some minor changes. Hooray! But getting my doctorate did not feel like a great achievement. In truth, I felt a bit of a sham. I gave up science in the third form at school and now I had somehow obtained both a master's and doctorate in science. How could that be except by some sort of sleight of hand?[1]

Even though I had not yet published the results of my study in an academic journal, I rapidly became known as an expert on social skills training. I was invited to convene a symposium at the grandly titled First European Conference of Behaviour Therapy, which was held in an anonymous modern hotel near Heathrow airport. I contacted three leading researchers, two from the UK and one from America, and asked them to present their work. As symposium chair I did not have to make a presentation myself and, if anyone asked me about my own research, I would say that the results were still being analysed or some such non-committal remark. A coward's approach but I was not ready to face the shame at not getting the positive findings everyone else seemed to be achieving. The symposium proved memorable though not for the right reasons. The first presenter, a psychiatrist who had begun a project evaluating SST with groups of disturbed psychiatric inpatients, began confidently, outlining an ambitious study. But after five minutes, he stopped in some confusion. I realized he had nothing more to say. The research had not gone beyond the planning stage. Hastily, I thanked him and asked the second speaker to take over. Peter was part of Michael Argyle's team and had been involved in SST

---

[1]Like many of our early self-perceptions, my notion of myself as a non-scientist was formed by a significant emotional experience. At school I was in a class being taught general science by an irascible and bombastic teacher. On a test at the end of the first term, not knowing the answer to one question, I had written "I have no idea" (only I had mistakenly written "I have know idea.") This infuriated the teacher and he berated me for my ignorance and stupidity in front of the whole class. He gave me 50 lines and when I protested he doubled it and doubled it again until I shut up. Whatever interest in science I had had evaporated.

the longest of any of us. I knew he had completed one study and was in the middle of a second. At least he had something tangible to report. Slightly nervous, Peter reached for a glass of water as he got up, knocking it over onto his and everyone else's notes. This completely flummoxed him. Stammering out apologies he tried to mop up the water, which only made matters worse. I shooed him to the podium but he found he could not read his soggy notes. And worse, his carefully prepared overheads were smeared and illegible. Red in the face, Peter apologized repeatedly and stumbled through an incomprehensible talk. After ten excruciating minutes I rescued him from his humiliating predicament. For a symposium on social skills, the speakers were not exactly good role models for the approach! Fifteen minutes gone, 30 to go and just one more speaker. Fortunately, the American psychologist I had invited was bright, likeable and highly efficient. Using a series of well-constructed slides he showed us some impressive results using SST as part of a residential behavioural programme for aggressive adolescents. Brits saved by the Yanks yet again!

Not getting the results you expect in a research trial should not be a problem. It should galvanize the intrepid researcher into asking further questions, trying to explain the unexpected results. It should lead to further studies that would help illuminate the reasons for the negative findings. This is the rational view of scientific research. But rationality is only part of the picture and perhaps not the most important part. What had driven me to my doctorate research had been the desire to make my mark in behaviour therapy. I was part of a movement. My study was supposed to be a step on the gas, propelling behaviour therapy forward to new areas and greater effects. But my study was a sharp touch on the brakes. It was neither what I wanted nor what the pioneers of the movement expected. I was thrown into a confusion of uncertain feelings. Science demanded honesty, made a virtue of it, and I subscribed to this absolutely. There was no way I could pretend that I had not got the results I had. So, gritting my teeth, I published a paper in a major behaviour therapy journal disclosing my negative findings to the world, well, the tiny fragment of the world of academically minded therapists who read journals. I waited for the explosion. Nothing happened. It was as though I had not written the paper at all. The world turned another revolution. Behaviour therapy continued on its headlong course.

My study was a mere pebble in a river that was flowing inexorably onwards. I had greatly overestimated my own importance.

***

At the Maudsley the distinguished child psychiatrist, Dr. Mike Rutter, was near the beginning of his lifelong research into childhood autism. Hearing of my interest in social skills training, he wondered whether SST might be helpful for adult autistics, particularly those who had language and were towards the normal end of the spectrum, who nowadays would be labelled as having Aspergers. I was intrigued and, despite the failure of my doctorate, I agreed to give it a try. Enthusiasm overrode what little common sense I had. I was flattered to be asked and thought, wrongly as it turned out, that I might be able to make my mark by helping this group of singular young men. It was to be another failure but curiously it was to lead on to a better understanding both of social behaviour and of how therapy works. I saw only about half a dozen people but one of these, David, made a lasting impression on me as he did on everyone he met.

Like a good behaviourist I adopted a rigorous scientific approach to the project. I decided I needed a baseline of social skills, a way both of assessing what people's deficits were and of quantifying these in a way that would enable me to demonstrate unequivocally whatever improvements occurred. I devised a conversational test and decided to record it on video just as I had done with Colin. I persuaded Mary, a psychologist colleague at the Institute, later to become my wife, to take the part of the confederate in this simulated conversation. She gamely agreed though she had no idea of the travails she was letting herself in for.

David and I enter the small seminar room where I have arranged the assessment. The video camera is behind a one-way mirror. Mary is waiting in the wings. In the lift on the way up I have made several attempts to engage David in small talk. Disconcertingly, he never once looked me in the eye, answered my questions in monosyllables, jigged around from one foot to another, and hummed a tune under his breath. In appearance he is frankly unkempt. His hair is a wild mass of dark tight-knit curls. He is wearing a thick tweed jacket, a checked shirt, and a bottle-green tie, which is askew, one end considerably longer than the other. He reminds me, I suddenly realize, of a certain type of absent-minded academic.

"What I want to do, David," I say as we are seated, "is to make a video recording of you in conversation with a friend of mine ..."

"Man or woman?" he interjects.

"Er, a woman who ..."

"Good."

I wait for David to say something further but he is staring at a reproduction Monet on the wall of the room and says nothing. I explain what the recording is for and how it will be kept secure and that we will erase it at the end of therapy. All the while David stares around the room. I have no idea whether he has grasped what I have just said. I decide to take the plunge. Before the recording starts, I give David his instructions: he is to initiate a conversation with Mary and keep it going for five minutes. I stress that it's up to him to keep the conversation flowing. David says nothing but nods when I ask if he's understood.

I bring Mary into the room, introduce her to David and skedaddle to the video camera next door. I press the record button just as David launches into the conversation.

"Whatever happened to flaming June!" he cries, hand raised aloft in a cod Shakespearian gesture.

"Well, I don't know," says Mary taken aback by this unexpected remark. There followed a quick-fire exchange that went something like this.

"Where are you from?" David asks.

"I work here."

"Which floor?"

"The fourth, I think."

"Number?"

"Pardon?"

"What number is your office?"

"Oh. 414."

"Did you take a bus here?"

"No. I came by car."

"Manual?"

"Sorry?"

"Manual or automatic?"

"Oh. Manual."

"Do you like jazz?"

"Yes. I like Miles …"

"I don't. My mother hates it. What time is it?"

"Quarter past two."

"Have you had lunch?"

"Yes. Have you?"

"I had a salad with English mature cheddar cheese, but not grated, and no onions!"

And so it went on. David chopping and changing topic, firing off questions barely listening to the answers, all the while fidgeting in his seat and never once making eye contact with Mary. She told me afterwards it was like being blown all over the place by a skittish and unpredictable wind. When Mary has left, I sit with David and together we watch the recording. For the first time he is completely still, staring with fascination at himself on the monitor. I am wondering which of the many social skills deficits he will pick out. I worry that he will be upset at seeing how odd his performance is. When we get to the end, I say rather nervously, "David, can you tell me anything about yourself that you want to change?"

David pauses a second and then says confidently: "I definitely need a haircut."

Theories about the genesis of autism have been debated ever since Kanner first described the condition in the 1940s. From emotionally cold mothers to a developmental disorder in language acquisition. From a specific genetic fault to the side-effect of the MMI injection. In the last decade a consensus has emerged among psychologists that autistic people show a failure of empathy. They lack what has been called a "theory of mind". People like David do not seem to grasp how their behaviour is registered by others, or if they do, they show no emotional understanding of the other person, no empathy in other words. This fitted David perfectly. He had no idea how odd or off-putting his questions to Mary were. There was no sense of his grasping that she might be put off or see him as odd. Despite this unpromising start, I took David on for SST and for many long sessions tried to get him to pay attention to other people, to take their interests and concerns into account, to adapt his behaviour accordingly. It was a fruitless task. This was brought home to me when, in exasperation at the end of another hopeless session, I told David he had to make a real effort with people and try to find out about what mattered to them. He had to practise conversations like practising the piano, which he excelled at. Five minutes after he left, I got a call from one of my colleagues. "'John," she said, "I think I have one of your patients here." She had met David in the lift on his way down to the exit. Without warning he addressed her with the following remark, "Dr. Marzillier says I have to practise talking to other people. Are you Jewish?" This epitomized the extent of the problem. Interestingly, my colleague was Jewish. This suggests David was not totally deficient in social perception. However, he had absolutely no sense that this was an inappropriate question to ask a complete stranger.

Unlike my doctoral research, my failure to help David, and indeed the other young autistic men Dr. Rutter sent me, did not depress me. Instead, it got me thinking. I was too focussed on *behaviour*. More important than what David or others said or did is how they *perceived* themselves and other people. In plunging into the behavioural aspects of SST, I had neglected an important component, namely, that skilled social behaviour depends upon the capacity to perceive how others are behaving and adjust your behaviour accordingly. In any skilled task there has to be constant feedback and calibration of performance. In social life this is done through subtle evaluations of social cues, registering other people's response to yours, interpreting their emotional expressions, knowing when to hand over the conversation and so on. If you have an impaired or absent sense of what goes on in other people's minds, you are severely handicapped socially whatever behaviours you try out. Perception was the key. But perception was not behaviour. To focus on how people perceive themselves and others is to enter into their minds, something behaviour therapy had steadfastly resisted on the ground that it was unscientific.

In the first decade of the 21st century no psychologist questions what has come to be known as the cognitive revolution. Cognitive psychology—the study of perception, memory, attention, thinking— lies at the heart of academic psychology. Theories about mental processes are an integral part of the science of psychology just as theories about quanta or quarks are in physics. Watsonian behaviourism with its crude attempt to limit psychology to studying only what can be publicly observed deprived psychology of what mattered most, understanding what goes on in people's minds. That is what I had been interested in when I first elected to study the subject. In fact, unbeknown to me, the scientific study of mental processes had been well underway for at least two decades. The experimental approach was just as applicable to studying the cognitive strategies of humans in various problem-solving tasks as it was to the behaviour of pigeons pecking at disks in cages. Inferences about the nature of people's thoughts or mental strategies were tested in increasingly ingenious experiments. Various models of the mind were formed, often drawing upon the advances in computer technology that were beginning to appear. One of the most influential books on cognitive psychology, *The Study of Thinking* by Bruner, Goodnow and Austin, was first published in 1956. I am ashamed to say that it had passed me by or, more accurately, I had passed it. Belatedly, I began reading books and journals on what came to be known as *cognitive psychology* and began a process of liberation from the narrow bounds of the behaviourist's dicta.

I did not give up on SST. I changed focus and concentrated more on how people perceived themselves and others, using video recordings to focus on different perceptions. This was still allied to behaving differently for, in the end, if you wanted to improve your social skills, you had to try out certain strategies and see how successful they were. I collaborated with a colleague and we saw a cohort of socially anxious patients, using single case methodology to track the changes in their social skills with more success. I took on post-graduates and supervised research into SST in a youth club for shy adolescents and for young offenders in local authority care. I put aside the idea of showing that behaviour therapy worked in favour of a more modest goal, seeking evidence that certain strategies worked better than others and for certain groups.

You might say I grew up a bit. I moved out of that narcissistic, adolescent stage where I was convinced I was right, and became more reflective and self-critical. This fantasy of perfectibility was part of behaviour therapy in the 1970s. And it was also part of me. At the same time as my PhD had unravelled, my marriage to G, the French girl I had met in Heidelberg, came to an abrupt end. I saw this as another failure. It was time to move on, to do what people do when things do not work out, escape to exotic places. I ended up in Birmingham.

SECTION II

MICROBES IN THE VAST UNIVERSE

CHAPTER SEVEN

Speaking prose

"I sometimes wonder," says Angie, speaking very carefully as though the exact words were crucial, "if I could get taken over by the Devil. Like in *The Exorcist*." She looks at me and there are tears coursing down her cheeks. I feel moved by her evident distress. "Do you believe in the Devil?" she asks.

"No. But you do. Is that what you're saying?"

"No. I don't know. I don't know what I believe any more."

Angie continues to cry. I do not know what to say. We are in a small side room of a GP surgery in Harborne, Birmingham. I have been invited to work here by one of the doctors as their visiting psychologist and behaviour therapist. It has been four months and I am beginning to build up a caseload of patients. Angie is one. This is our second session.

Angie is 30, married with two very young children. She had worked as a dental receptionist but now stays at home to look after the children. Keith, her husband, works on the North Sea oil rigs. He is away from home for long stretches of time, as he is now. The GP referred Angie to me because she had become depressed a few months after the birth of her second child. He had diagnosed post-natal depression and suggested antidepressants. But Angie had refused medication. He had been seeing her supportively when she told him about the horrific fantasies that had first appeared after the birth of her second child. Angie confessed that she had awful thoughts about killing her children.

In his referral letter, the GP wrote: "I am convinced that this is pure fantasy. She has never harmed her children and seems to love them dearly. I am sure they are not at risk. But Angie is so obsessed with the worry that she might harm them that her whole life is affected. She locks away all the kitchen knives, scissors, even nail scissors, and spends hours in deep distress, ruminating. I am sure she's depressed but there's an element of phobic anxiety in all this and I'm wondering if you could practise a bit of your behavioural magic and help her overcome the phobic anxiety ... ."

Magic. The Devil. Violent attacks on children. What is this about? In our first session Angie had told me about her fears and how she hid knives away in case she might harm her children. Now she wants to know why she has these thoughts. Is she going mad? Her GP apart she has not told anyone about them, not even Keith because she is ashamed of having them. What sort of person thinks such things? I have young children myself and I could empathize with Angie's anxiety. I have had thoughts about the horror of waking one morning and finding one of my children dead in her cot. I tell her this. I wonder whether our fears are similar in the sense that we both are so attached to our children that we worry about all sorts of dangers however remote. The fantasy may be just an extreme form of worrying, I hypothesize. This reformulation seems to calm Angie. It also makes psychological sense, something I am beginning to realize was crucial if I am going to find the best way of treating the problem.

I decide that, instead of rushing in with a behavioural treatment, whatever that might be, I will construct a *formulation*, answering such questions as, why is Angie prone to these anxieties now, are there any obvious triggers, are there any other anxieties around, are there any pressures on her, what is Angie like as a person, what was her childhood like, and what is her attitude to violence generally? If I do all this I hope that it will lead to a therapeutic strategy though exactly what that might be is far from clear.

"Tell me when these thoughts began, Angie. Was there a particular time, one that stands out that you remember?"

She looks at me for a moment. A weary sigh. She doesn't want to talk about it.

"Sometimes," I go on gently, "it can help just to talk. You don't talk about it very much, do you?"

She shakes her head vigorously. "I don't tell anyone."

"So when did they first happen?"

"It was after Jessie was born. My youngest. I was fine after Tom. Jess was a long labour. Over 24 hours. I was exhausted. When I got back home, I had Tom to look after as well. Keith had to go off on a job. He didn't want to but we needed the money badly. His mum came to help."

I sensed from Angie's tone that her mother-in-law coming to stay had been a mixed blessing.

"Was she a help?"

"She's such a perfectionist. She doesn't like me. Well, no one's good enough for her Keith. To be honest, it made matters worse."

"So, a long labour, you're tired, exhausted. Keith's away and you have his mum as well ..."

"And Jess had this awful skin problem. Terrible eczema. She couldn't sleep because of it. Keith's mum said it was our house, that it was dirty. But it wasn't. I took her to the doctor's and he referred her to the specialists. That took a while. Eventually they found out it was an allergy to cow's milk. When I switched to soya, it cleared up."

"That all sounds terribly stressful, Angie. You've been through the mill."

"But these thoughts about the kids. It's awful to think that."

"You've never acted on them, have you?"

"No. I wouldn't, definitely not ... ." She looks horrified at the suggestion.

"Thinking something is not the same as doing it." I search around for something concrete, an example. "Take the IRA bombings. You can imagine what it must be like to go and do that, plant a bomb somewhere, blow people up, but just because you can imagine it, doesn't mean you'll do it." I am not sure that this is a good example given the violence, but it is too late. "A thought is not the same as a deed."

"But *why* do I think these thoughts? They're such horrible things to imagine. It's such a vivid picture."

I sense something important. "Tell me exactly what the picture in your head is."

Angie shudders. At first she refuses, but I manage to get her to tell me. The image in her head is of plunging a large kitchen knife into Jess's and then Tom's heart. Though I try not to show any reaction, it shocks me.

"Is there anything that might have brought this on? A TV programme? Or something you read?' I strike lucky. Slowly, Angie tells me how she read in the newspaper about a couple who had ritually murdered their child. Shortly after she had read it, she had the first fantasy. Vicarious traumatization. Becoming traumatized second-hand through seeing or reading or hearing about traumatic events. The newspaper account was the trigger. I summarize what Angie has told me.

"So at a time when you were under a lot of stress, the long labour, Jess's illness, Keith away, Keith's mum, two young kids to look after, probably not much sleep, at a time when you were really *vulnerable*, you read this horrible account and that puts the thought in your head: 'Suppose I did that?' And once it was there it was hard to get rid of, however much you wanted to, even though you had absolutely no wish to hurt your kids, quite the opposite, you wanted to protect them. But this thought gnawed its way into your mind and frightened you. Is that right?"

Angie nods. "I hate violence. Always have. Even as a kid I couldn't watch violent stuff on the films. They terrified me."

Another piece of the jigsaw. Angie, for whatever reason, grew up as being particularly sensitive to violence. Perhaps it is her temperament. Perhaps something about her upbringing. Or a combination. Her sensitivity is being expressed now in these violent fantasies. The films are replaying in her head and she believes she cannot stop them.

I am aware of another factor. The sociologists George Brown and Tirril Harris discovered five significant risk factors in young depressed women living in Camberwell, London. Two of them are the absence of good social support and having children under five. Both apply to Angie. This makes sense. Not only is there the strain of looking after two young kids, but it can lead to feelings of isolation from other adults. The only person Angie might confide in is Keith, but she feels she cannot because of what the thoughts are about.

She keeps the thoughts to herself and tries not to think about them. When they come into her head anyway, she tries to stop herself thinking them. A form of avoidance. And as behaviour therapy has shown, avoidance prevents the anxiety from going away.

I have my formulation. Angie's fantasies were triggered by reading a newspaper account of parents who ritually murdered their child. Always sensitive to violence, she began to wonder if she might do the same. A specific horrific image came into her head and, however much she tried to dispel it, it returned. She begins to think she is mad or even possessed by the Devil or some sort of supernatural force. She hides knives and other sharp objects. She feels unable to tell anyone, even Keith, and so is at the mercy of her own thoughts and her worries about having them. Add to this a general vulnerability in her circumstances as a fairly isolated mother of young children, and we have a possible explanation for why Angie developed the fantasies and why they persist.

I discuss the formulation with Angie. I outline what I think we might go on to do in therapy. We will first get a record of the fantasies. I draw up a monitoring record on an A4 sheet putting headings so that Angie can note down each day when a fantasy occurs, how long it lasts, what she is doing when it starts and how upset it makes her, using the familiar 100-point scale. This is my good behavioural/scientific side coming out. The record will be a quantitative baseline against which to evaluate progress. I also hope it will show Angie that she has some control over her fantasies. Research on self-monitoring has shown that it often leads to a reduction in the experience being monitored: putting things down on paper triggers the desired change. If that happens, it should reverse her belief that her thoughts are out of her control.

What next? Again I apply what I had learned from behaviour therapy. Not thinking about the fantasies, understandable as that is, is a form of avoidance. Let's counteract that. I suggest that Angie go through the fantasies with me in detail in the sessions. It should take away their sting by seeing them as what they are, just fantasies, not her wickedness, not ideas planted by a malevolent supernatural force but her anxious sensitivity. After considerable persuasion Angie agrees to do this.

"But what do I do when I have the fantasy at home?" she asks, reasonably enough.

I am thinking on my feet. This is new territory. "How about," I say cautiously, "facing up to the fantasy rather than stopping thinking about it?"

"What do you mean?"

"Explore the fantasy, telling yourself, 'This is a fantasy, an extreme form of worry, it's not real.' Describe exactly what you are thinking to yourself. Maybe even write it down ..."

"I couldn't do that," she says, urgently.

"Okay, not writing it down. Not at the moment anyway. But don't avoid thinking about it. If you do, it just comes back. But if you face up to it like this, then you take away its power."

"And the fantasies will go away?"

I hear the eagerness in her voice. I don't know whether they will or not. I have not done this before. I should not raise her hopes too much.

"Yes. They'll go away," I say confidently.

It took only a few sessions for Angie to feel better. The self-monitoring records showed that her fantasies declined in frequency and they were far less intense and distressing when they occurred. She no longer talked about supernatural forces. Keith returned and I suggested she might talk to him, perhaps bring him into therapy. But Angie refused. It was her choice and, although I thought it might help them, I did not press it. Some six weeks later I was able to discharge Angie. I had worked my "behavioural magic".

***

At this time I was employed as a lecturer in the Department of Psychology at the University of Birmingham, helping to run the training course in clinical psychology. I had no formal NHS commitment but spent a day a week as a therapist in the Harborne GP practice. Birmingham in the 1970s was not the most inspiring of places. Many of the old Victorian buildings in the city centre had been destroyed and in their place a soulless cluster of concrete edifices erected that were already showing signs of decrepitude. A ring road ran right through the city centre in a series of swooping tunnels and curves that was supposed to be closed once a year to become a racing circuit though I do not think that ever happened. The best thing about that ring road, the locals said with characteristically mordant humour, is that you're out of Brum before you're in it. Taxi drivers would ask bemused visitors if they knew that Birmingham had more canals than Venice. True perhaps, but Venice it was not. Yet I grew to like the place. I stayed seven enjoyable years in Birmingham, during which time I divorced, remarried, had two daughters, moved house, played football and lived the life of a carefree academic when Research Assessment Exercises, top-up fees, performance targets, and government interference were still a few years away.

I remained a behaviour therapist and even reached the eminence, if that is the right word, of becoming chair of the national organization, the British Association for Behavioural Psychotherapy (BABP). But I was increasingly unhappy with the simplistic strictures of the behavioural approach. In particular, I could not see how as therapists we could focus exclusively on behaviour, the patient's or the therapist's. What about thoughts? Treating these as "hypothetical constructs" and consigning them to secondary status behind behaviour struck me as missing the point. What people like Angie thought determined how they felt. Angie found knives and other sharp objects frightening *because of what she thought she might do*. Her belief led directly to her anxiety. By helping her confront her belief, defusing its toxicity, I had reduced her anxiety without doing anything behavioural at all. I did not expose Angie to sharp objects in order to let her phobic anxiety decline as I later heard a colleague describe in a similar case. All I had done was listen and talk, making some practical suggestions, counteracting Angie's more extreme beliefs with alternatives. I had done this intuitively, sensing how best to help. Across the Atlantic in Philadelphia a psychoanalyst, Aaron T. Beck, was doing something similar, delving into his patients' thoughts and formulating a new brand of psychotherapy, cognitive therapy, that was very soon to sweep all before it. Was that what I had done in helping Angie? When later I trained in cognitive therapy, I was reminded of M. Jourdain, Moliere's *bourgeois gentilhomme*. This gentleman, on being told that the language he was speaking was called *prose*, announced: "Mon Dieu! For more than 40 years I have been speaking prose without knowing it."

CHAPTER EIGHT

"I think I'm wasting your time"

The essence of cognitive therapy is summarized in a much quoted remark of the Greek philosopher, Epictetus, "People are not disturbed by things, but by the view they take of them."[1] If, for example, someone experienced a severe and unexpected pain and thought it signalled a major illness, he would be likely to be anxious. If he dismissed it as a minor muscle twinge, he would not. The perception determines the feeling, not just the experience on its own. In 1976, Beck's book, *Cognitive Therapy and the Emotional Disorders*, was published, launching cognitive therapy as the successor to behaviour therapy. Beck's psychoanalytic training had alerted him to the need to attend to what goes on in the patient's mind. However, psychoanalysis, still very much under

---

[1] Epictetus was a Stoic. He liked aphorisms such as "First learn the meaning of what you say and then speak", "If you wish to be a writer, write", or "He is a drunkard who takes more than three glasses though he be not drunk", the last of which might be incorporated into the Department of Health's guidelines on sensible drinking. Nothing hindered his good spirits, not even death. "I must die. Must I then die lamenting? Does any man then hinder me from going with smiles and cheerfulness and contentment?" Or as Eric Idle sang in *The Life of Brian*, "Always look on the bright side of life. Da dum, da dum."

the influence of Freud's ideas about the unconscious, focussed on interpreting behaviours as signs of deeper disturbances with their origins in the patient's past. The method was a slow, painstaking analysis of potential meaning using the analyst-patient relationship as the cauldron in which that meaning eventually emerged. Beck became aware that there was another aspect of thinking that had been largely ignored. He noticed that patients often experienced a continuous train of thought that ran parallel to the thoughts they expressed in therapy. One patient, angry at Beck, reported feeling guilt at his anger, which made sense as, psychoanalytically, anger is thought to lead to guilt. But he experienced another train of thought which he described as continual self-critical thoughts, a disturbing commentary in his head about his shortcomings that he had not reported until now. Working with other patients Beck discovered that they too were experiencing similar streams of thought, usually negative and critical of the self. Moreover, when these thoughts were brought out in the open, they bore a direct relationship with the feelings that brought the person to therapy in the first place. A woman's anxiety turned out to be provoked by her doubts about her ability to express herself in therapy and a belief that she appeared foolish. A man's depression was deepened by his sense of being a failure as a patient, believing that his therapist saw what an inadequate person he was. Beck labelled these as negative automatic thoughts (or NATs). He decided that instead of delving into the past, it was more valuable to bring these immediate thoughts out into the open and to work with them therapeutically. The thoughts were always extreme and often irrational yet had a powerful grip on the patient's thinking. Beck began to experiment with ways of changing the thoughts so that they became more realistic, less extreme and, most importantly, ceased to have such powerful emotional effects. Cognitive therapy was born.

I read Beck's book from cover to cover, aware that here was a way of getting to what most mattered, what was in the patient's mind. In contrast to psychoanalysis, there was no arcane theory about unconscious dynamics or early experiences or transformed sexuality or the Oedipus complex. There was no need to interpret the patient's thoughts as being about something else, the aspect of psychoanalysis that at that time bothered me most. As with behaviour therapy, what the patient said was taken at face value, the difference being this was not so much about behaviour but about the patient's thoughts. And the methods of treatment were direct and straightforward as in behaviour therapy. Monitor what the patient was thinking, list the thoughts, write them down on a record sheet, point out their extreme and irrational form, challenge them and seek alternative, more realistic, more positive, and ultimately more liberating ways of thinking. Cognitive therapy married the best features of behaviour therapy with what I had always felt was vital to therapy, attending to what went on in the mind.

Just as I had done with Angie I began trying out these new ways of seeking to uncover and change the patient's thoughts. I had been invited to work at the GP practice as a behaviour therapist. But the GPs, unlike many of my psychiatrist colleagues at the Maudsley, were unconcerned about exactly what I did. They were eager to have a psychologist to help them and trusted me to do my job. At that time it was rare for a therapist to work in a GP practice, unlike now where almost half the practices in the UK employ a counsellor, psychologist, or similar. Epidemiological statistics showed that 90% of mental health problems were managed within primary care, only a small minority getting through to specialist psychiatric services. There were many anxious and depressed people around for whom there was either no treatment or at best some form of medication. For psychologically minded GPs the idea of helping people as and when they presented, without having the delays and the difficulties of referral to specialists, was welcome. Working in a general practice meant that I could see people at the moment of crisis rather than many weeks or months down the line. It gave me the opportunity to make the most impact, to intervene at a time when the person was most responsive, and perhaps even prevent major problems arising.

"I've just seen a woman, Naomi, who should be a good candidate for behaviour therapy," says one of the GPs as we meet in the corridor. "She works for Social Services. She had a panic attack when driving an elderly woman to a care home. I think she's in danger of becoming a full-blown agoraphobic. I think you could help her."

When Naomi's appointment comes up, I find there is nothing much of note in the patient's medical file. She is 36, unmarried. Her parents are still alive and live locally. She has no history of psychological or psychiatric problems. When we meet, I immediately take to Naomi. She is wearing a dark suit and white blouse. Her black hair is tied in a bun from which strands have got loose and fall either side of her face. Her hazel eyes search me out with a disarming directness. She seems at ease but I detect an inner tension as though she is just about holding herself together.

"I think I'm wasting your time," she says. "There's really nothing much wrong. I got into a bit of a panic. That's all."

"Why don't you tell me about it?"

Naomi tells me that as part of her job she ferries elderly people around. She has done this for years and usually enjoys it. This time was different. She started to feel hot and light-headed. She thought she might be coming down with a bug.

"Did you have a bug?"

"No. Nothing." She frowns, hesitates and then goes on. "Traffic was backed up along the Harborne Road, which was a pain. I tried to shrug the feelings off, but they seemed to get worse. I thought I might pass out and who then would look after Mrs. Timms?"

"Did you say anything to Mrs. Timms?"

"No." Again the frown appears. "I really should have done. Suppose I had passed out or something. She would have been left on her own." She makes a wry face, self-deprecating. "Not very professional, was it?"

"But very human. We can't always act professionally."

She looks at me surprised as though I had said something revolutionary. Naomi carries on with the story, which ended with her delivering her elderly client successfully to the home. But the next day she felt terrible, a raging headache, and she called in sick.

"I feel bad about that too," she says. "I'm never sick. But I just couldn't face going to work." It emerges that she took two days off. Then, after the weekend, she returned to work, only to break down in tears. Her supervisor sent her home. She had been off work ever since. It is now three weeks since the incident in the car.

"What have you been doing during this time?"

Tears appear in her eyes. "Nothing! That's the stupid thing. I can't go out. I feel …" She stops, searching for the word, "… vulnerable."

"Do you worry that the feelings might recur?"

"Yes! I tried to go on a bus but I couldn't do it. The bus came and like a lemon, I just stood there. I couldn't get on. The driver wasn't too pleased. 'Make up your mind, dear. Not got all day.' I felt humiliated. It was so ..."

"Unprofessional?"

She smiles. "Yes. Though what's professional about taking a bus escapes me."

I am beginning to see a pattern. But I need to know more. So I ask Naomi some questions about herself, her family, her life in general. A picture gradually begins to emerge like a photograph appearing in developing fluid. Naomi has an older brother, Crispin, who has disappeared, fallen beneath the family radar. He had been very bright when young, a gifted child, but he dropped out after school. He had travelled around the world and then got involved in some hippy-type commune. Crispin never gets in touch with them. The family had not spoken to him for over 15 years. The last they had heard he was living on an island in the Aegean. Her younger sister, in contrast, had taken a more conventional route. She was happily married to a London solicitor with a family of four. I ask if Naomi sees much of her sister.

"She's very busy," says Naomi. "The kids. Lots of charity work. Mummy's always complaining that they don't see her often enough."

"How often?"

"Three or four times a year."

London is no distance from Birmingham. It does not seem like a lot.

"And you? How often do you see your parents?"

"Oh, I'm on hand, so most days."

Something in Naomi's face leads me to stay quiet.

"Daddy's been very ill," she says. "Mummy copes but it's hard on her." She looks at me and again there are tears in her eyes. "Cancer. Secondaries in the liver."

"A very tough time for everyone."

"Yes," she sighs. "But then he's over 80 and these things happen."

"But it's always a shock when it's your family, your father."

She nods mutely.

I change tack. "What about work? How's that going?"

Naomi seems to pull herself up. "Okay," she says brightly. "Lots of changes in Social Services in the last few years."

"My God, yes." Naomi tells me how the recent reorganization has affected the work. Not for the better. They have fewer staff and have to spend more time on paperwork and meetings. She is rushed off her feet.

"So quite stressful," I say.

She smiles at me. "It's 'stress,' is it? That's what's wrong. I can't cope with stress." There's a playful tone to her remarks though I sense it masks an underlying worry.

"Maybe. But let's find out a bit more about the panic attack if that's what it was. Tell me what went through your mind at the time."

"At first I thought I was becoming ill. It *felt* like a bug or flu. Then as it got worse, I thought, 'God, what I am going to do?' I should have told Louise—she's my colleague—that I wasn't well. I'm an idiot."

"So you were feeling unwell before you set out?"

"Yes, but I didn't say. That's what I should have done. It was ..."

"Unprofessional?"

"Yes! I'm not like that. I am very well organized. I do things by the book."

"And later, when you got back home, what went through your mind then?"

"Oh, savage thoughts," she says vaguely.

"Such as?"

She sighs. "Like I'm useless."

"And?"

Naomi seems to have to gear herself up to tell me. "Like I'm going mad. That I'll never get better. That I've made a mess of my life. And I'll become a burden to the family."

"Wow. All this from one small panic attack."

"I know. Stupid, isn't it?"

"Not stupid. The panic attack was perhaps the straw that broke the camel's back. There's been a lot going on in your life in the last year or so. It all came to a head."

She nods and tears now fall unrestrained down her cheeks. As we talk I discover more about Naomi, how two years ago, she was about to get married and her fiancé suddenly broke it off. He had been seeing another woman, she found out subsequently. Since then she has not had a relationship with anyone. I feel her loneliness and now with the changes at work and her father's terminal illness, there is a lot to worry about. I say this to her and suggest we spend a few sessions to see if she can turn things round. I outline an anxiety management programme, essentially the behavioural approach I am familiar with, but including tackling her anxious thoughts. Naomi brightens up at this for, as I am discovering, she is a true professional and the therapy holds out the promise of getting back her sense of herself as a strong and successful person.

Naomi came to see me eight times over six months. I introduced her to an anxiety management programme and she took to it with enthusiasm, learning the skills of relaxation and controlled breathing as a way of bringing her anxiety under control. This gave her confidence and her worries about panicking receded. We talked about the losses in her life, the fiancé who had let her down, the imminent death of her father, and about her loneliness. Having read Beck's book I was particularly interested in the negative thoughts that Naomi had told me about. She was intensely self-critical and we focussed on how easily these thoughts came into her head and how they made her feel. We listed them one by one. I pointed out how irrational and extreme they were. I also pointed out that she was a conscientious, good person who looked after her parents in contrast to her brother and sister. It was hard for Naomi to acknowledge her own goodness and the negative thoughts never totally went away. But they became less powerful and she felt better. Naomi recovered quickly. She returned to work. I had helped her get over her panic and anxiety. But what exactly made a difference? Was it the combined cognitive and behavioural treatment? Was it something more amorphous like the support I gave her or the fact that we got on well together? Was it that she had someone to confide in about her loneliness? Might she have recovered anyway? It was impossible to answer these questions in a single case. All I knew was that I found this way of working congenial. More than that, it felt right. At last I had found a therapy that combined the strengths of the behavioural approach with a level of sophistication about the workings of the mind. I decided I would train as a cognitive therapist. When my time in Birmingham came to an end and I found myself in Oxford, I was given the opportunity to do exactly that.

CHAPTER NINE

Going cognitive

I left Birmingham to become the Oxford Regional Tutor in Clinical Psychology, a much grander sounding post than it actually was. My job was to re-start clinical psychology training in the Oxford region after the university's MSc course had ground to a halt for typically academic reasons (squabbling over which group of neuropsychologists should be invited to lecture the students). Although I was back in the NHS I had no formal clinical commitment. I established myself as a therapist in a GP practice in a small market town in Oxfordshire, working in the same way as I had in Birmingham, seeing the patients the GPs referred me. Here I adopted the more cognitive approach I had tried out on patients like Angie and Naomi. In Philadelphia, Beck and his colleagues had set up a Cognitive Therapy Center, which served both as a centre for research and a base for training others in the new approach. Several UK psychologists went over to learn at the master's feet. As it happened, two of them, John Teasdale and Melanie Fennell, were in Oxford, working in the university department of psychiatry. I knew them both well. John was a colleague from my Maudsley days and Melanie had been a student of mine at Birmingham. One day John stopped me in the corridor and told me he was starting a cognitive therapy training course in Oxford. Would I like to be in the first group of trainees? I did not have to think twice. This was exactly what I was looking for, a chance to formalize what I was already putting into practice, to become a proper cognitive therapist.

***

Six of us are squeezed into a small office in the university department of psychiatry. John and Melanie, the two tutors, and four would-be cognitive therapists, Stan and Ruth from the Maudsley course in London, and myself and Ivana from Oxford. The idea is that once we are trained as cognitive therapists, we can go on to teach our own trainees, thereby disseminating cognitive therapy through the clinical psychology profession. A cascade approach. Like pyramid selling. Or being part of a cult where the leader tells the followers to go out and bring in new members. I have a momentary twinge of unease. I have never liked being strongly identified with a group, put off by the cast-iron ideological certainties and the emotive force of mob passion. I had joined the Labour Party when I was 16 but had never been to a single meeting and let my membership lapse after a year. I was still a member of BABP, the behaviour therapy organization I had helped to found, but my doubts about behaviour therapy had driven me more to the periphery. Yet here I was signing up to a new ideology. What happens if I do not become converted? If I do not think that cognitive therapy is the answer to everything? But I put these doubts to one side. After all, I have seen how valuable it is to ask patients what they are thinking. Cognitive therapy is simply a formalized way of doing this. How can it be anything but a good thing?

John and Melanie tell us that we are to work with depressives. In my therapeutic work I had come across many depressed people but had not been sure about how best to treat them. Behavioural methods did not seem particularly useful. Some ideas were quite bizarre. One recommended not reinforcing depressive talk so the therapist would respond only when the patient said something positive. Negative comments would be ignored. This was based on the notion that if you did not show any depressive behaviour (e.g., talking in a depressed way), then you could not be depressed, an idea so daft that it seems like satire. Another suggested that severely depressed people, who are almost always very passive, had to be provoked into some form of behaviour, which could then be reinforced. It was suggested that they were given a meaningless task like sandpapering a block of wood and then told they were doing it the wrong way. After they reversed the process, they were told that was now wrong. This would go on until the depressed person protested or perhaps threw the block of wood at the therapist. Behaviour at last! It did not seem to occur to the inventors of this technique that it might just reinforce the depressed person's sense of the meaningless of his existence.

"Depressives can be tricky," Melanie says. "Don't expect that your client will go along with everything you suggest. They'll find all sorts of ways to wriggle out of doing cognitive therapy. 'The dog ate my homework,' that sort of thing. 'Sorry, couldn't fill in the activity schedule because I lost my pen.' Or, 'I didn't think there was any point in trying to challenge my negative thoughts since they're obviously true!'"

"We call it the 'YES-BUT' phenomenon," says John. "It's part of the depression, a negativity that seeks to undermine anything positive, including the therapy itself."

"Particularly the therapy," interjects Melanie.

John glances at her. "Maybe," he says. "Not for everyone though. It's not always an uphill struggle."

I sense that John does not want us to be put off, to think that cognitive therapy is going to be terribly hard work. But I am also thinking about something else, the difference in their personalities. John is a highly intelligent academic with a quiet, gentle manner that masks a steely determination. Melanie is a breezy extrovert with a strong sense of humour and a playfulness that I remember liking when she was my student. I am wondering how these differences might affect their work with depressed people, a thought that I was to return to later.

"A necessary condition of cognitive therapy," says John, "is that you establish a good positive relationship with your clients, a collaborative one where you work together to counteract depressed mood and thinking. The feelings of hopelessness so characteristic of depressives can extend to the therapy too. *No one can help me. I am a hopeless case. What's the point of therapy? Nothing's worked in the past. Why should it work now?* These thoughts have to be tackled first and the best way to do this is to spend time specifically on developing a sound therapeutic relationship."

I am impressed. Little was said about the therapeutic relationship in behaviour therapy. It was assumed that people wanted to get better and would go along with what treatment the therapist suggested. When people did not, as with Gillian, Mrs. Hewittson, and several others I saw, they were written off as not motivated and the therapy brought to an end. Cognitive therapy recognized something that I was to understand better in years to come. Change is not always wholeheartedly welcomed even if you desperately want to get better. And a significant change always entails a significant loss.

The first supervision session ended. The four of us trainees dispersed with the mission to find some depressed people to try out this new therapy on. I asked the GPs where I was based to look out for depressives, which they were very happy to do. They referred two people to me, Frances and Brian. My experience treating them was to revolutionize my whole approach to therapy.

Frances is a tall, striking woman, smartly dressed, who shakes my hand firmly when we meet. She is in her thirties, single, owns her own flat and works as an administrator in a firm of local solicitors. She has a history of episodes of depression that stretches back to her early twenties and is in the middle of one now, according to her GP. She has been signed off work for a month. The first thing she tells me is that she has tried everything to get rid of her "horrible depression." Acupuncture, the Alexander technique, homeopathy, spiritual healing, all sorts of diets, exercise, meditation, yoga, several different antidepressants, psychotherapy—the list goes on.

"And nothing worked?"

"Oh yes, sometimes. But only for a while and then the depression comes bouncing back."

"I suppose you must be wondering if this new approach will be anything different."

She gives me a surprised look. "That's exactly right."

I tell Frances what cognitive therapy is about. I stress the collaborative element to it, the way we will work together to identify and counteract negative thoughts. I explain the cognitive model, how feelings like depression are coloured by the way we think. I give a textbook example. "Suppose you see a friend over the other side of the street. You are about to walk over to have a chat when she walks on, ignoring you. How would you feel?"

"Pretty upset actually. Something quite like that happened a few weeks ago. I was in Waitrose and this woman I know, Julie, completely cut me. I was already feeling low but that made it much worse."

"So what did you think at the time? Do you remember?"

"I thought she clearly doesn't want to talk to me. She probably finds me boring."

"And naturally that made you upset."

"Of course."

"Suppose you thought something different like 'Julie mustn't have seen me.' How would you feel then?"

"But I didn't."

"I know. But bear with me, suppose you had."

"Then I wouldn't have minded."

"Exactly. How you appraise the situation affects how you feel. If your first thought is a negative one—'Julie doesn't want to talk to me because I'm boring'—then you are going to feel bad. But if you thought something different like ..."

"But I didn't," says Frances again, emphatically.

"I know but it doesn't mean you *couldn't* have thought something different. Suppose you had the thought 'I wonder if she's seen me' and even gone up to her and said hello. Suppose she gives a start and says, 'God, I didn't see you there, Frances. I was in a world of my own', and you two have a nice chat, you'd feel a lot better, wouldn't you?"

"Yes, yes," says Frances impatiently. "I follow. But the point is I didn't think or do that."

"That is exactly the point," I say eagerly. "Cognitive therapy is about changing your thinking so that you can directly influence what you do and how you feel. Because of your history of depression I suspect you have a tendency to interpret events negatively. Many depressed people do. Then you act accordingly, which can provoke the very reaction that you fear will happen. You avoided Julie because now you think she finds you boring ..."

"I did exactly that. You're right."

I grab a piece of paper and sketch a vicious cycle of negative thinking, depressed feeling, withdrawal, further depression, more negative thinking etc. A grid of boxes and arrows that I have got from Beck's book. Frances looks on, clearly interested.

"Depression and negative thinking are closely interrelated. It is negative thinking that maintains depression but often people don't even know they are doing it. The thinking is automatic and so familiar you take it for granted. The notion that you should examine your way of thinking, test it out and change it is not even thought about, let alone tried. Yet if you do this, and do it systematically and with help, it is quite possible to challenge the thoughts and stop yourself getting depressed."

End of speech. Frances sits back. I look at her as she reflects on what I have said, wondering if I have convinced her of the value of cognitive therapy.

"I understand the logic," she says eventually. "I admit it makes sense."

"Perhaps you're thinking, 'It may be logical but I have tried things before and they didn't work.'"

A wry smile. "You are a bit of a mind reader, aren't you?"

"It's an understandable thought given all the therapies you've tried. But is there anything else you're thinking? Something even more negative perhaps?" I know that Beck has argued that more powerful negative thoughts often underlie the ones nearer the surface.

"Only that I'll never get better."

"That certainly is a negative thought. But is it true?"

Frances gives me a searching look. "I was going to say yes but I'm beginning to follow. I can't know I'll never get better. It's a negative thought, one that I have a lot."

"And if you believe it, it will certainly make you depressed."

Frances and I look at each other. I am aware of a sense of closeness, a moment of understanding. I feel ridiculously pleased. If this is cognitive therapy, then it works a treat.

"So let's try it out. Why don't we get started and meet for six sessions and review your progress. If nothing changes, then you haven't lost much. But I have a hunch that cognitive therapy will help you, Frances."

"No negative thoughts on your part at least," she says.

Beck's cognitive therapy involves paperwork. Lots of it. There's a depression inventory, a series of multiple-choice questions that the patient fills in before each session. For example, she must tick one box out of "I do not feel sad", "I feel sad much of the time", "I am sad all the time" or "I am so sad or unhappy that I can't stand it". There are 21 of these items, all aspects of depression, each item's scores ranging from 0 to 3, resulting in a maximum of 63. On the first administration Frances scored 34, which is at the bottom end of the "severe" category. Then there is a weekly diary or activity schedule, which consists of noting down what she did every waking hour and rating the activity out of 10 for Pleasure and 10 for Mastery. The idea is simple enough. It is a chance to get a snapshot of what Frances does and see what gives her pleasure, if anything, and what she does that requires effort. Later, there are thought records and a complicated form for challenging negative thoughts.

I explain the weekly activity schedule to Frances and suggest she fills it in.

"But I'm not doing much," she protests. "Certainly nothing interesting."

"Don't worry. That's not the point. Put down whatever you do. Cleaning your teeth, making lunch, going for a walk, watching TV, washing up. Fill it in as you go along if you can."

"What's the point of it?"

I explain that it will act as a baseline, that we will examine it next time and plan activities for each week. "It may seem simple but one strategy is to increase pleasurable activities and ones that require a bit of effort. That way you take back control of your life and start to climb out of the depression."

"Homework. A bit like being back at school."

"I suppose in some ways cognitive therapy is a sort of re-education."

I realize I have not asked Frances anything about herself. I discover she comes from an ordinary, middle-class family. No dark secrets, she says. No skeletons in the closet. She had gone to a private school where she had been known as a bit of a swot. Not that she studied hard, she told me, just that she was good at it. She got four A levels, all grade As. She studied history at London University and graduated with a First. She had been accepted to do a master's in social anthropology at LSE but at the last minute dropped out.

"Why?"

"I thought it would be too much for me. And that was the time I first felt depressed."

Frances, unsure of whether she should do the master's, had consulted her parents. They had thought she should get a job to get some money and security. She took a fast-track secretarial course and began work as a secretary for a firm of solicitors. It seemed a step down for someone of her undoubted academic ability.

"It was pretty dull stuff," she says. "But I'm a good organizer and very soon I was promoted to an admin post. That's how my glittering career as an administrator began."

Frances has had boyfriends but none serious. And no one at the moment. She has a few women friends, some of whom she occasionally goes to concerts with though she has felt too low to do that in the past couple of months. She has a cat. She used to ride horses but has not done so for years. As she tells her story I sense that, beneath the veneer of competence and efficiency, there is something missing. But I cannot put my finger on what it is. I ask about her episodes of depression. She says they occur every few years for no reason she can fathom. She starts to feel low, sleeps poorly, gets very tired, and it comes to her that her life is a waste of time. She stops going to work and stays in bed. She has some suicidal thoughts but has never acted on them.

"It's as though there's a barrier between me and the world. I just can't get engaged in anything. Sylvia Plath wrote about a bell jar descending, muffling the world. It feels exactly like that."

"And then somehow you come out of it?"

"So far. But it's hell when it's happening."

"And now, how do you feel at this moment?"

Frances is silent. "I don't know," she says eventually. "I like the idea of the therapy. I can see it might work. But ..."

"... it might just be another false dawn. Sure. But let's give it a go. Keep the weekly diary and in a notebook jot down whatever is going through your head when you feel really depressed. All your thoughts, however bizarre or extreme they may be. We'll look at them next time."

After Frances leaves, I make some notes to take to supervision. The session has gone extremely well, more or less according to the book. Frances seems an ideal candidate, depressed but not excessively. Intelligent, verbal, organized, and interested in the approach. Yet at the back of my mind there is a nagging doubt. Had I missed something? But unable to make any sense of my nagging doubt, I dismiss it. The proof of the pudding is in the eating, I tell myself. I shall soon find out if cognitive therapy really works.

CHAPTER TEN

Microbes in the vast universe

I have a confession to make. The cognitive therapy supervision is the first formal training I received in any form of psychotherapy. My training in behaviour therapy consisted of observing Jack Rachman and a few other pioneers, reading books, and attending workshops. Mostly I made it up as I went along. Almost all the early behaviour therapists did this for there were no training courses then. Nowadays every new therapy has to have a formal training programme. Often these are lengthy and almost always costly. In 2007 a professional training in cognitive therapy can last between one and two years (one day per week) and can cost as much as £6,000 per annum. Even very simple techniques become formalized into a therapeutic school that is zealously guarded by the acolytes. Training with John and Melanie is informal, so much so that it hardly feels like training at all. We follow the recommendations in Beck's books, adapting the methods to the patient's needs. My fellow trainees are all experienced therapists, committed to becoming cognitive therapists, eager to learn. Our tutors have only just learned the approach themselves. The feeling generated is that we are all in this together, working it out as we go along.

In supervision I present Frances as my first case. I have got her to record her negative thoughts on the thought record sheet. Drawing on her administrative skills she has assiduously typed them out and when we come to challenge them, she does the same for the thought challenges. Her challenges are good. They produce the desired result, a reduction in how much she believes her original negative thought. We collaborate to reformulate a more reasonable thought and her mood improves. This is how it should work. She is a model cognitive therapy patient. One technique we try appears to be particularly effective. This is capturing a negative thought and then listing the "pros" and "cons", i.e. what evidence supports the thought and what is against it. Frances comes up with the thought, *I'll never get better*, which she rates as 90% for believability. In the "pros" column, she types the following:

I get depressed every few years whatever I do.

I have tried lots of therapies and none had a lasting effect.

I think that I have a depressive personality—for me the cup is always half empty.

My depression is my fault—I should try harder but I never do.

In the "cons" column she lists:

I have got better in the past and remained well for a number of years.

Just because nothing has lasted in the past doesn't mean it won't in the future.

Cognitive therapy makes sense and research has shown that people do get better.

I am a resourceful person—if I apply my mind to it, I should be able to succeed.

Then comes the key test. I ask her to re-rate her original thought, *I'll never get better*. She rates it at 60%, still high, but a definite improvement. I point out to Frances how her original thought is an example of absolutist thinking, one of the cognitive errors that Beck says depressed people make.[1] Can she change it to make it less absolute? She comes up with this modification.

---

[1] The other errors Beck identified are *arbitrary inference* (drawing a conclusion in the absence of evidence), *selective abstraction* (focussing on a detail while ignoring other salient features), *over-generalization* (making a general rule out of one or more isolated incidents), *magnification/minimization* (erroneously over- or under-estimating the importance of an event) and *personalization* (relating everything to oneself). While

I tend to think I'll never get better because I'm depressed. But I have got better in the past and I am in therapy now. When I am less depressed I don't tend to think I shan't get better because I have!

It is a convoluted thought. I simplify it.

I can't know that I'll never get better and I recognize that this absolutist negative thought is a product of my mood state rather than a realistic appraisal of what will happen.

Frances agrees. I ask her how she is feeling now. "Quite optimistic actually," she says brightly. The cognitive therapy seems to be working.

Cognitive therapy provides a structured framework for challenging thoughts. This is what the record sheets and the formal procedures do. Wherever possible things are written down. Painstakingly, negative thoughts are identified, noted down, deconstructed, challenged, tested in reality, and reformulated into more realistic and optimist thoughts. It bears some relationship to the *Power of Positive Thinking*, the self-improvement method developed by Norman Vincent Peale in the 1950s in which negative thoughts are banished by force of will. Cognitive therapists are not keen on Peale though. His methods, which included self-hypnosis and harnessing God's power to improve your mind, are a hotch-potch of odd techniques. He believed in unconscious conditioning via the repetition of phrases and suggestion. Cognitive therapy is a rational and conscious process. It does not use rhetoric or suggestion but entails hard work that the patient has to do under the guidance of the therapist. And, as I discover, it is indeed hard work. There is much to do in a cognitive therapy session—monitoring the homework tasks, selecting a problem to be worked on, identifying and challenging thoughts (which can take most of the session), setting up behavioural experiments to test out beliefs, examining and filling in record sheets, agreeing the homework tasks, getting feedback on the session from the patient, and filling in the Beck Depression Inventory. We are told to set an agenda at the beginning of the session so that we can allocate the

---

Beck believed that these errors were characteristic of depression, most of us will make them at one time or other. But when we become depressed, we are more likely to show them and less likely to realize we are.

time appropriately. Even so it is not easy to squeeze everything into a session. I struggle to keep to the structure. I find I have to interrupt my patients and bring them back to the task in hand. I feel vaguely uncomfortable doing this but do so anyway since that is what the therapy requires. And in Frances's case it seems to be working. She has become adept at the written process, at challenging her negative thoughts and finding new ones. Her mood has definitely improved.

***

One week Frances failed to attend a session, something she had never done before. We were well into the therapy. We had moved on from changing negative thoughts to identifying the underlying beliefs, what Beck called *schemas*.[2] These are the major drivers of depression, ideas that are often formed in childhood and become reactivated in current crises. They can be encapsulated in key phrases or prescriptions like *To be happy I have to be accepted by everyone all the time, I must succeed in whatever I do, I have a fatal flaw in my personality, I am fundamentally a bad person.* According to Beck, to produce lasting change it was essential to get to these core beliefs and deal with them.

In the session before Frances failed to attend, she had complained that her work as an administrator was boring. I asked why she did not try to get a more demanding and interesting job, something that drew more on her academic ability perhaps. She said vaguely that there was no point. Puzzled, I pursued this and we came to an example of a powerful underlying belief. *Life is meaningless*, she claimed. *In the end we all die.*

"How do you know life is meaningless?" I ask.
    "I just do."

---

[2]Beck uses the word *schema* to describe a stable cognitive pattern, a way of looking at the world that has been established over many years, rather than a mental picture or plan, the common meaning of the word. It is an abstraction such as the way people may describe themselves or others, "I'm an optimist by nature" or "He does not suffer fools gladly", the latter a polite way of saying he is an irritable bastard. While we can be aware of these descriptions, Beck's idea of a *schema* goes further, suggesting that fundamental beliefs are unconscious at least until brought out into the open in cognitive therapy.

"Come on. You know that won't do. Let's do some cognitive work on this. List 'pros' and 'cons,' for example."

Frances says nothing. I try to read her face but I cannot. It is expressionless.

"Don't you want to challenge this belief?"

"I can't see the point."

"To get better. To deal with your depression."

"*Deal* with it," she says sarcastically. "You don't *deal* with the meaningless of our existence."

I am startled by Frances's tone. It is the first time I have heard her talk in this angry way. I backtrack. "Okay. I'm sorry. A poor choice of words. But I do think we should examine this belief, don't you? It seems central to your depression."

Frances stares at me. For the first time in the therapy I feel unsure. More than that. I have a sense of unease.

"Maybe," she says at last. "But not today. Can we leave it to next time?"

"Okay."

Later, I wonder if I should have agreed so readily. Was this avoidance on my part? Up to now the therapy had been going smoothly. Frances was the model patient. This was our first glitch. I had told myself that it would be better not to push this. We could work on it in the next session. The only problem is that Frances failed to turn up for the next session.

I ring Frances. I do not normally do this when patients fail to show up. I wait a couple of days and if they do not contact me, I drop them a line. But Frances is a special case, my first cognitive therapy patient, and I am worried about her. The phone rings on and on. I am about to hang up when at last she answers, a slow "Yes, who is it?" as though I have just woken her up.

"Frances, it's John. I was wondering if you were okay."

"What time is it?"

"Just after two. Have you been asleep?"

A long pause. "Sorry. Just very tired."

"You didn't make the session this morning. I wanted to know if you're alright and if we should reschedule."

Another long pause.

"Are you feeling depressed?"

"You could say that."

"Is that why you didn't come to the session?"

"What's the point? I'm not going to get better."

"That's your depression talking, Frances. You've had a downturn in mood. All the more important for you to see me at this time. We can work on it together and help you get out of it."

"I don't know."

"I do." I am being the decisive, no-nonsense therapist though it is the last thing I feel at this moment. My shoulder muscles ache with tension. My heart is beating fast. At the back of my mind is the thought that Frances will kill herself. "How about later on today, at 6? Or tomorrow morning?"

"No. I need a bit of space. I'll come to next week's session. Don't worry, John. I'm not going to do anything stupid. I haven't the courage to do that anyway."

I try to persuade Frances to see me earlier but she is adamant. She promises to come next week. I wring a further promise from her that she will contact me immediately if she feels suicidal.

What has happened? The therapy was going along really well. Is it just a blip, a random change in mood? Has something happened to Frances to trigger the increase in her depression? Was it related to our discussion of her core belief that life is meaningless? I ponder these matters but come to no conclusion.

When Frances comes to our next session, I immediately notice a change in her manner. There is a slowness to her movements, a hesitancy that I have never seen before. She does not look directly at me and when I study her face, all I can see is blankness. I ask her how she is. She takes a while to respond. She says she feels lousy, tired, depressed, no energy, completely zonked. All signs of depression.

"I'm sorry you're feeling so bad but I'm glad you came," I say. "It's a chance to do some work and improve your mood."

She looks at me and sighs. "The good doctor's going to make me better. Hooray."

"Well, I'm going to try. Tell me right now and in all honesty what you think of coming here."

"A waste of time."

"Why?"

She shrugs. "Nothing works and anyway what's the point. I get better for a bit and then I get worse. I'm just useless."

"Several very negative thoughts in that statement, I'd say. Do you remember how we dealt with, I mean, worked on your negative thought, *I'll never get better*? We listed the 'pros' and 'cons' and came to a more realistic thought. I have it here."

I search through my notes and read it out to her:

I can't know that I'll never get better and I recognize that this absolutist negative thought is a product of my mood state rather than a realistic appraisal of what will happen.

"Do you believe that now?"

"It's irrelevant what I believe," she says in a lethargic tone. "Life's meaningless anyway. We are microbes in the vast universe. Specks of cosmic dust. What does it matter? What does anything matter?"

"Something mattered enough for you to come here today. You're depressed, Frances. Something brought you right down in the last week. I don't know what. But I am absolutely convinced that your view that life is meaningless is caused by your depression."

"It's not," she says emphatically. "Life is meaningless. It's not a product of depression. It's true. And anyway I've *always* believed it so it can't be a response to a change in mood."

For the moment I am stumped. I am also feeling pissed off with Frances, with her certainty and resistance to my attempts to help her.

"Always?"

"Always."

"So you sprung from your mother's womb with the thought, *Hey, why am I here? Life is meaningless. Let me back in?*" I have spoken without thinking. I have let my feelings show. I have broken a cardinal rule: do not mock your patient. I am a crap therapist. But a small smile appears on Frances's face.

"Okay," she says. "Not always. But from a long way back."

"And when was that?"

"When I went to school. My secondary school."

"Tell me about it."

She gives a huge sigh. "I got a scholarship to this posh, private school. All my friends went to the local state school. Not me though. From the beginning I hated it. Hated the teachers, hated the stuck-up kids, hated the long journey to get there."

"Did you tell your parents?"

"I told my mum. But she just said it was a great opportunity and all that crap. No point in talking to my dad. He was dead set on my bettering myself."

"So you stayed at the school."

"Yes."

"And where does the belief that life is meaningless come in?"

"Oh that. Yeah, well, one day in assembly when the headmistress was droning on with some bible sermon I just had the thought that God didn't exist and that human beings were tiny specks in the vast universe and that life was meaningless."

"How did you feel?"

Frances turns to me with a puzzled look. "That's the odd thing. It was strangely comforting. I thought if life is meaningless, I needn't worry about things anymore because it didn't matter whatever I did."

"So you weren't depressed?"

"No. Which is why I told you that the belief preceded the depression. And it's true, isn't it? Life *is* meaningless."

Frances waits for me to answer but I do not know what to say. I am not sure if life is or is not meaningless. Drawing on my philosophy degree I could deconstruct the question. What do we mean by meaningless etc? My philosophy tutor, Jonathan Cohen, had written a book called *The Diversity of Meaning* in which he analysed all the different ways we give meaning to things. But instinctively I know this will not be helpful here.

"I don't know if life is meaningless or not. Maybe it depends on how you look at it. But I know that you are depressed, Frances, and that's not a great state to be in and that my job is to help you get better ..."

"But what's the point? I'll only get worse again."

"You don't know that. We have only just started cognitive therapy. This is the first blip. If we give up now, it'll just reinforce the belief that you'll never get better. But if we keep going, at least we'll test it out. At least you'll give yourself a chance to get really better. What do you say?"

A crucial moment. Frances says nothing. She is staring out of the window of my office at the buildings opposite. We sit in silence. I am desperately thinking what to do, trying to remember what Beck says in his book. I know I am supposed to challenge this core negative belief but I do not know how. There is a supervision session in two days. I can raise it there but what do I do now? Then it comes to me: when people become severely depressed, go back to basics.

"Frances," I say with an authority I do not remotely feel. "I'm going to give you an Activity Schedule to fill in. In fact, let's start it now, together, going back over yesterday and today. I know you think this is a waste of time as life is meaningless, but *I* don't. You need to take back control over your mood and this is the way to do it." I get out a schedule and cajole a reluctant Frances into filling it in, rating each activity for Pleasure and Mastery. Most ratings are 0; a few are 1s and 2s. However, listening to *The Archers* on the radio gets a 5 for Pleasure. I seize on this and suggest that she makes sure she listens each day. I also tell her that, however she feels in the morning, she must get up when she wakes up, have a shower, clean her teeth etc and have a decent breakfast. She should do things, simple things like having a walk or feeding the cat. The aim is for her to get through the week but doing so by taking charge of her life again.

"Can you do that," I ask?

Frances takes the Activity Schedule, carefully folds it and puts it in her bag. "Okay," she says quietly.

After Frances has left, I sit lost in thought. Why had Frances become more depressed? Was this perhaps a reaction to the therapy? How could I challenge negative beliefs like life is meaningless? Was it a question of rationality or something else? I have my first inkling that cognitive therapy's positivism might not be as straightforward as it first appeared.

CHAPTER ELEVEN

"The heart has reasons that reason cannot know"

"In my view life *is* meaningless." Stan throws this comment diffidently, almost languidly, into the discussion. The supervision group has been grappling with my difficulty in getting beyond Frances's core belief. We have not got much further than it is part of her depression, a debilitating hopelessness that needs to be challenged immediately if the therapy is going to work. Stan, normally on the periphery of the group, has said nothing until this bald comment.

"But isn't the belief that life is meaningless a sort of meaning in itself?" says Ruth. She is a perceptive and sensitive therapist who was later to co-edit a book on "wounded healers", therapists who themselves had been psychiatrically ill.

"Perhaps," says John, our tutor. "But the point is not whether or not the belief is true but that it encapsulates the central core of Frances's depression. She's held this belief for a long time. When she's well, it lies dormant and doesn't have the impact it has now. Why has it become active now?"

"I wish I knew the answer," I say. "The therapy was going really well. Frances grasped the method of challenging thoughts and up to that session, her mood was good. She scored only 18 on the Beck Depression Inventory. That has gone up to 43, the highest it's been."

"Perhaps it's a mood swing," says Ivana. "It could be a biological change related to something else. The menstrual cycle?"

"I'm afraid I didn't ask about that."

"Whatever the cause," John goes on, "you need to work hard on the belief until it shifts."

"But how?" I ask. "You said that it didn't matter whether the belief is true or false yet Beck's approach is to look at the evidence for and against, the 'pros' and 'cons'. There's no unequivocal factual evidence for or against the belief that life is meaningless."

"But you can do the 'pros' and 'cons' differently," Melanie interjects. "You ask the question, 'How helpful is it for me to hold this belief?' Evidence for, evidence against. More to do with function than fact. For Frances the consequence of the belief is to tip her into depression. It doesn't help her."

My other cognitive therapy patient, Brian, was also proving difficult to help. He was not as depressed as Frances but there is a depressive, Eeyore-ish quality to his view of the world. Nothing ever seems to go right for Brian. We had got to one core belief quite quickly, namely that other people looked down on him. For this reason he led a predominantly solitary life and had no close, intimate relationships. I decided to challenge this belief and was looking for some way of doing that when Brian told me that he had not received the renewal of his tennis club membership. Tennis was his main hobby. Lugubriously he proclaimed that the others at the club did not like him and did not want him as a member. That was the reason his membership had not been renewed. I was a member of a tennis club and knew that unless someone stole the silver, pranced around in the nude or batted the opposition senseless with his racket, their membership would be automatically renewed. I asked Brian if there might be other reasons why he had not received the membership form. Typically, he could not think of any.

"Could the form have been lost in the post?" I asked.

"Possible, I s'pose," he said grudgingly.

"Or some delay in getting them out. You could check it out. Ring the club and ask."

Brian did not want to do this at first. When he gave in to my pressure, he was told there had been a delay at the printers but now the renewal forms had come through. He would receive one the next day, which he duly did. In cognitive therapy terms this was a result. A core belief is disconfirmed by clear evidence to the contrary. I asked Brian how he now rated his belief that others at the club saw him as inferior. After all, he was not rejected as he had believed.

"No," he said. "But they still see me as not as good as them. I just know it."

The core belief had not been shifted one jot by the disconfirming evidence.

When I see Frances again, her mood is much the same. She has however filled in the Activity Schedule though it is not typed up this time. We go through it together. She has listened to *The Archers* regularly and apart from one morning, she has got up in good time. A few activities are rated as much as 5 or 6 for Pleasure. I point out to her that, although depressed, she has done what we agreed and that some activities improve her mood. She should build on those, gradually increasing them. Frances is not exactly enthusiastic.

"It's pathetic that I can't do basic, simple things. And anyway I think it's a waste of your time my coming here. I think I should stop.

My first cognitive therapy is going to be a massive failure. No way will I let this happen. Frantically I cajole Frances into going on for a bit longer.

"Let's work on that core belief that life is meaningless."

Frances sighs.

"Now I want us to forget about whether it's true or not, and concentrate on whether it helps you to believe it. In other words, list the 'pros' and 'cons' of simply holding this belief."

When we do this, Frances comes up with just two statements as 'pros,' *It's what I have always believed and therefore true to myself* and *It's strangely comforting.* As 'cons,' and admittedly with a lot of prompting from me, she lists *It stops me doing things, It's a depressing thought* and *It reinforces my negative view of the world.* I ask Frances if she can reformulate the belief. With considerable help from me, she comes up with *Life may well be meaningless but holding on to that belief makes me feel depressed and so it's better not to dwell on it.* She rates this reformulation as 60% true, not a massive endorsement but positive at least.

Can a belief be both *strangely comforting* and *depressing*? It is an odd conjunction. I am puzzled by it. I mention this to Frances and she says something revealing.

"It's comforting because then I don't have to worry about doing things, like improving myself, for what's the point?"

"But depressing," I say, "because you are stuck with yourself and you are not happy, are you?"

Tears spring into her eyes. She shakes her head and begins to sob. At last I get a glimmer of what might be going on.

"When you first had that belief, at school during the headmistress's boring sermon, you were stuck in a place you didn't want to be. A posh, private school. Your friends were all at the state school. But there was nothing you could do about it. Your parents wanted you to be there, to improve yourself. I think the belief that life is meaningless acted as a sort of protection, a way of coping with your unhappiness. If life was meaningless, your unhappiness didn't really matter. You had to just get on with things. And you did."

Frances is still sobbing but I sense she is listening to me.

"And now this belief comes back with a vengeance just when you're improving with the therapy. Maybe something similar is going on now. If you continue to get better, then where does that leave you? You're bright and working in a job that doesn't stretch you or give you that much fulfilment, does it? But to change jobs is a bit like changing schools. Somehow it's not allowed though this time not by your parents but by yourself."

I have to admit that I doubt very much if I said this as clearly as I have written it here. But I recall that moment when I realized that Frances's belief and indeed her depression was a defence against change. And for the first time I felt I understood her. And for the first time too she had shown me her vulnerability as opposed to her competent, capable side.

I would like to tell you that Frances rallied and that cognitive therapy pulled her out of her misery, that she went on to examine her life and change it for the better, moving to a more interesting job, being more positive about herself, socializing more and conquering her recurrent depression using cognitive behavioural techniques.

Nothing as dramatic as that happened. Frances did get better. She came out of the depressive depths she had sunk into. But by our last session she was not much different from the competent, controlled super-administrator I had first taken on. She said she found the cognitive techniques helpful and felt she understood herself better. But her core beliefs did not change. For all I know to this day Frances believes that life is meaningless.

***

Out of the blue I was asked to write a long article on Beck's cognitive therapy for a prestigious academic journal. A year or so previously I had published a speculative paper on the different ways behaviour therapy might become more cognitive. An American academic, Phil Kendall, had read it. He thought I could do a similar forensic evaluation of cognitive therapy. It was too good an opportunity to miss. I eagerly accepted. I plunged myself into reading everything Beck and his acolytes had written. I wrote to Beck, asking for unpublished material including accounts of the therapy in operation. He very generously sent me a wodge of unpublished papers and a selection of tape recordings. The latter were invaluable. Listening to the tapes I heard how adept Beck was as a therapist, combining a ruthless pursuit of negative thoughts with warmth and clinical sensitivity. When I eventually met him in person, he proved, like other pioneers of new therapies, to be an exceptional man. Charming, charismatic, intelligent yet approachable, determined to the point of stubbornness, he swept all before him, patients and psychologists alike.

It was not difficult to write the first part of the article showing how Beck had developed and shaped the therapy from his clinical experience. Modifying depressive mood using the cognitive therapy armamentarium (mood inventories, activity schedules, thought records and challenges, behavioural experiments) was something I understood and increasingly valued. But when it came to changing core beliefs my nagging doubts clanged even more loudly in my mind. A core depressive belief such as *To be happy, I must be accepted by all people at all times* is challenged by finding evidence that contradicts it, such as times when your happiness is not dependent on the evaluation of others or the fact you are quite unbothered by *some* people's indifference. Therefore, it is not rational to hold this extreme belief. There is evidence against it. But I had seen in Brian's case how evidence against a dearly held belief can be discounted. Surely, I thought, Beck and his colleagues were being a bit too literal. When we formulate a core belief, it is often expressed in absolute terms. *I am a complete failure*, one might say in moments of crisis. The fact that you have passed O level Spanish and therefore cannot be a *complete* failure is not the important thing. You *feel* a complete failure. This is not about rationality but feelings, and feelings are not in their nature subject to rational argument. Have you ever tried to reason dispassionately with your nearest and dearest when they are really pissed off with you? How effective was that? Blaise Pascal put it very well: "The heart has reasons that reason cannot know." Core beliefs may be irrational in their literal form but what matters is the intense, elemental feelings they encapsulate and this explains why they are so resistant to change.

In 1983 the psychologist, Dorothy Rowe, published a book on depression that was awarded the MIND Book of the Year. The book was addressed directly to depressed people, one of the earliest in a genre of self-help books that have since flooded into bookshops in their tens of thousands. I read the book and was impressed by Rowe's perceptive understanding of depression, not least because of her own experience of it, which she readily talked about in the book. In Rowe's view depression was a metaphor that people used in different ways. To psychiatrists, in its severe form it was an illness requiring treatment, usually antidepressant medication. To cognitive therapists, depression was a disorder of thinking. In both cases the thrust was that there was something wrong requiring adjustment. Instead of drugs, cognitive therapists used thought challenges and behavioural experiments. Drawing on the work of the cognitive scientist, George Kelly, Rowe thought of depression differently. She saw it as a *personal construction*, the unique way each individual understands the world around them. What was needed to help people escape from the deadening passivity of depression was above all an understanding of how they saw themselves and the world. Only through personal understanding could any real change come about. Rather than impose meaning on depression as psychiatrists and cognitive therapists did, it was essential to uncover what depression meant to the individual. After that, it was a matter of establishing trust, generating a sense of safety, and encouraging exploration of meanings other than depression. I was intrigued. I read that Rowe was giving an invited talk at the Tavistock Clinic in London, the very place that I had gone for the two-day selection process 15 years ago at the beginning of my career. I decided to return to the clinic and hear what Rowe had to say.

I walk from Belsize Park tube along wide thoroughfares lined with large, leafy trees that in the first press of autumn are slowly beginning their perennial transformation. On either side are tall, imposing Victorian and Edwardian mansions in dark red brick exuding wealth and prestige. Nowadays most are converted into flats. Many have become the domain of private psychoanalysts who trained at the Tavistock and set up on their own. Discreet brass plates by the front doors attest to the intense relationships going on inside. This could have been my life, I muse, but the thought has little impact. I had been too young and impatient to apply myself to the lengthy rigours of psychoanalysis. Even now I am wary of this privileged and hermitical therapy. Despite misgivings I still hold to the belief that scientific evaluation, the open and democratic process of deciding what actually works, must be applied to all psychotherapies. Psychoanalysis, I believe, has never proved itself in that arena.

I turn the corner and ahead of me is the Tavistock Clinic. An ugly, glass and concrete five-storey building, no doubt the state of the art in the 1960s, it is more worthy of Prince Charles's "monstrous carbuncle" epithet than the extension to the National Gallery ever was. Inside, the lecture theatre is packed. A buzz of noise greets me as I arrive. I know no one and find a seat near the back. Dorothy Rowe is introduced by a suave, dark-suited male analyst in a way that suggests that it is daring of the Tavistock to invite this flagrant rebel into their midst. In truth Rowe is an unlikely looking rebel. A small, middle-aged woman with a nice smile and an Australian accent, she charms the potentially hostile audience with her fluency and gift for communication. She does not pretend to be familiar with psychoanalysis. She has no truck with conventional psychological theories or the latest therapies. She is, she says artlessly, a George Kelly disciple, a man who was ahead of his time, the true founder of cognitive therapy. Slowly and in ordinary language she articulates the personal construct position, what later came to be known as social constructionism. All of this is familiar to me. I had given numerous lectures on Kelly and his theories. I wonder if I have wasted my time. Then Rowe starts to talk about depression. She talks about the many depressed people she had seen when working in the Whiteley Wood Clinic in Sheffield and what she had learned from them. She is extremely good at telling their stories and I am immediately engrossed as she tells of her battles with very depressed and often suicidal people. And "battles" is the right metaphor, for what Rowe is saying is something that makes everything clear to me. I understand now why Frances and Brian resisted my attempts to change their core beliefs. This is because these beliefs define their very identity. Though they may hate the crippling depression that descends upon them, and though they desperately seek help, there is another part of the self that nurtures that very depression. Rowe calls it the "vanity" of the depressive, that part of them that secretly supports their maladaptive, extreme negativity, the sense of their own badness. Depressives build their own prison, she says, and so when therapists or others try to knock down the walls, they fiercely resist. Only the individuals themselves can knock down the walls and that will only happen once they feel safe enough to do so. Therapy is about creating that sense of safety.

I leave the talk in a daze. I walk up and down the leafy avenues oblivious to my surroundings letting Dorothy Rowe's comments reverberate in my head. Thoughts whirr round and round in my mind as I try to make sense of them. At some deep level I believe Rowe is right. I am not persuaded of this by rational argument; it comes to me as a revelation all the more powerful for being unexpected. And surely that is the way core beliefs actually change? Through emotional experience not through reason or experiment. That is what was wrong with cognitive therapy. Certain types of beliefs, ones that are central to our very identity, are tenaciously held on to while others, less central, less emotionally important, are amenable to change by argument and demonstration. I think of Thomas Kuhn's book on scientific revolutions, his analysis of how paradigm shifts occur in science. He describes a battle of minds with protagonists lining up on either side and doing everything to attack the other side. A psychological process, he says, not a rational one. This is also what happens when significant personal beliefs are threatened even if those beliefs are in the end responsible for misery and unhappiness. A full frontal attack on core beliefs, the method that was integral to cognitive therapy, would not work. It needed something else, something more subtle, something directed at the emotional component of the beliefs, of why they were so important and why change was resisted. I do not know what that might be but the idea of finding out excites me. I descend the steps at Belsize Park station and push my way through the busy throng of commuters, still immersed in my thoughts. Might there be a way of incorporating these new ideas into cognitive therapy? Could one combine its pragmatic rationalism with the more personal and emotional way of working that Rowe was advocating? Or was I deluding myself? Was I, like Voltaire's *Candide*, vainly seeking the best of all possible worlds only in the end to be perennially disappointed?

CHAPTER TWELVE

The power of negative thinking

The inspiration provided by Dorothy Rowe's talk led me to her other writings, in particular her book, *The Construction of Life and Death*, a theoretical analysis of the beliefs human beings hold about the world. Fundamental beliefs such as those about the meaning of life and death are, according to Rowe, *metaphysical* not rational. A belief in God for example is a statement of faith; no amount of evidence will shake it. This was brought home to me vividly a few years ago when I was on a visit to Egypt with my family. We were shown around the Valley of the Kings by an urbane and cultured guide, Rifaat, who had previously worked in Egypt's Office of Antiquities. The indefatigable Rifaat was immensely knowledgeable about Egyptian culture. An intelligent and excellent teacher, he even taught us the basics of hieroglyphics. When we were there, a tsunami devastated Thailand and other Asian countries. More than 200,000 people died. Innocent people going about their daily business. How, I thought, is this compatible with a just god? I asked Rifaat what he thought. Why had this happened? Was it God's will? Yes, he said simply. They must have done something to deserve to be punished. His belief in God was not shaken by natural disasters or evidence of other awful events that had no apparent purpose. It was central, a given, an axiom from which everything else flowed. As believers are wont to say, God works in mysterious ways. We mere humans cannot always fathom His purpose.

I do not share Rifaat's faith in God. In my view the notion of a god or gods is a human construction designed to give meaning to the mysteries of life and to justify certain courses of human behaviour. I remember when this first came to me at the age of five. I realized suddenly that the biblical claim that God created man in his own image was an inversion of the truth. Man created God in his own image, which was why God was always portrayed in a human way and indeed why he was always portrayed as male. My conviction that this is true is just as robust as someone else's faith in a supernatural deity. If, for example, a modern Jesus appeared in the world, turning water into wine and performing other miracles, I would see him as a David Blaine figure, a magician or trickster. I would remain convinced that what he did could be explained scientifically and even if scientists failed to show immediately how the miracles worked, I would simply believe that eventually the trick or method would be exposed. After all, science can work in mysterious ways. We humans cannot always fathom exactly how.

Rowe contrasted metaphysical and rational beliefs. This is how she summed up the difference:

The main difference between metaphysical and rational beliefs seems to be in their capacity of proof and the ease with which they are given up. Rational beliefs are capable of proof, and when disproved can be relinquished. Metaphysical beliefs do not lend themselves to proof, not in this world at least, and once held are not easily relinquished.

There is a world of difference between the claim that a certain fertilizer results in better plant growth and the belief that one should love one's neighbour as oneself. The former is a factual statement that can be tested by empirical evidence. We can find out if it is true and, if it is not, then it makes no rational sense to hold on to it. The latter is a moral statement that is not capable of being changed by looking for evidence or by rational argument. Discovering, for example, that people who do love their neighbours as themselves lead happier lives is not the point. The belief describes what one *should* believe; it epitomizes certain values. As I wrote my article, the major flaw in Beck's cognitive therapy became clear to me. The therapy did not take into account the different forms of belief but assumed that all beliefs could be changed by argument and reason. The more fundamental beliefs that depressed people can hold, what Beck terms *schemas*, seemed to have the quality of moral beliefs. My patient, Brian, had accepted that his belief that he had been singled out not to receive renewal of his tennis club membership had been disconfirmed. To maintain it in the face of clear evidence to the contrary would have been quite irrational. But his belief that people at the club looked down on him was not changed one bit. This belief expressed a fundamental certainty that Brian held to, that he was inferior to others, a moral judgment he made on himself. Similarly, Frances's belief that life was meaningless enabled her to come to terms with the low level of unhappiness she felt and get on with her life. Occasionally, however, her unhappiness was too great and the protection the belief gave to her wavered, which was when she plunged into depression.

What is the implication of this distinction for cognitive therapy? Quite simply, that challenging core beliefs on the basis of their irrationality is misguided. To put it bluntly, it will not work. Because people are strongly attached to their core beliefs, they will not be persuaded by rational argument. Nor will the bludgeoning approach that some therapists adopt work any better. Albert Ellis, the founder of rational emotive therapy, was notoriously aggressive in challenging what he saw as patients' irrational beliefs, sometimes resorting to sarcasm and even verbal abuse. Apart from this being a quite anti-therapeutic strategy, an attack on core beliefs will just strengthen the hold that they have. Think of political or religious differences. How successful are full frontal attacks in changing the views of core believers?

None of my concerns had any impact on the general enthusiasm for cognitive therapy. Whatever the shortcomings of Beck's ideas about the way beliefs change, there were many attractions to this new approach. Most behaviour therapists felt liberated from the straitjacket of simplistic practices and outmoded ideas. Cognitive therapy allowed them to do what most had already been doing, attending to what their patients were thinking. The systematic methods that Beck and his colleagues advocated, the use of self-monitoring records, structured thought challenges and behavioural experiments, appealed to the scientific practitioner that most psychologists wanted to be. This was not airy-fairy speculation. You did not make it up as you went along or postulate unconscious conflicts that no one could see. You followed simple yet powerful procedures. You identified negative thoughts, challenged them, and your patient got better. Even psychoanalysts cast their eyes with interest on this brash newcomer, drawn by her bright new clothes, youthful good looks, and effervescent manner. There were attempts to integrate cognitive and psychoanalytical ideas, the most successful being Tony Ryle's cognitive-analytic therapy, of which more later.

As with the development of behaviour therapy in the 1970s, research studies came thick and fast supporting the effectiveness of cognitive therapy for all sorts of problems, not just depression. Generalized anxiety disorder, social anxiety, obsessive-compulsive disorder, panic disorder, agoraphobia, eating disorders, addictions and, even later on, psychotic delusions, all succumbed to the new method. Twenty years on cognitive therapy is a successful and highly esteemed psychotherapy. In 2007 the Labour peer, Lord Layard, called for 10,000 cognitive therapists to be trained in the UK, asserting that the future of human happiness lay in their hands. But in the late 1980s I was beset by doubts. On the one hand, I could see that Beck's cognitive therapy provided a much-needed structure for tackling the anxious and depressive thoughts of many patients. It also worked, at least to a degree. Key thoughts were identified and recorded. Their relationship to mood plotted. Thought challenges such as listing the "pros" and "cons" loosened the hold that entrenched thoughts had. Irrespective of the question of rationality, the methods opened up the possibility of choice. There are alternative ways of thinking, the cognitive therapist says, and here are some. What happens if you choose to think differently? How do you feel? What can you do? Let's try it out. The pragmatism of cognitive therapy is its great strength. You may be feeling depressed now, but with certain adjustments to your thinking, you could feel a whole lot better.

Had Beck been content to describe his therapy as a synthesis of techniques for changing mood via thoughts, I would have had no qualms. But Beck, aware that at the heart of depression lie core beliefs or schemas, asserted that the therapy must tackle these to be truly successful. If Rowe was right, then cognitive therapy was not the way to do this. My own experience with Frances and Brian indicated that such beliefs do not readily change. I needed to re-examine my whole approach to therapy. Before I could do this, Beck arrived in Oxford on a short sabbatical. I had the opportunity to meet the man himself. Pictures of Beck on the dust jackets of his books showed him to be a dapper, silver-haired, distinguished-looking man who sported a tweed jacket and bow tie. And indeed this is exactly how he was. But just as people say about TV and film stars when they see them in the flesh, Beck seemed smaller than my impression of him from the photo. When I was introduced to him, he shook my hand warmly and then, registering my name, gave me a second glance.

"You wrote that excellent chapter in the Advances series," he said. "I really enjoyed reading it."

Thrilled, I stammered my thanks to him for sending so much material.

"Not at all. And you know," Beck said, leaning confidentially over to me, "those criticisms you made of cognitive therapy, I thought they were very interesting."

I had argued the case that Beck and his colleagues had misleadingly focussed on the rationality of core beliefs whereas these beliefs were more to do with basic values. I had liberally quoted from Beck's and his colleagues' books and journals to show this.

"Do you know something even more interesting," Beck went on in his confidential tone, "not one of the extracts that you quoted in your article was actually written by me." Smiling, he turned away to talk to someone else. Inwardly, I smiled too. Here was a good example of exactly what I had been arguing, how core beliefs persist in the face of the evidence. Beck's powerful investment in cognitive therapy meant that all criticism was deflected in this case on to his colleagues. The fact that the extracts came from books or articles on which he was usually the senior author seemed to escape him. Nor was he going to respond to my argument with counter-arguments of his own.

***

Successful cognitive therapy occurs when negative thinking is replaced by positive, more realistic and rational thoughts. But experimental studies did not support the assumption that those who are not depressed are more realistic in their thinking. While it is generally true that depressed people selectively attend to more negative information than non-depressed people, i.e., they have a negative thinking bias, those who are not depressed are not bias-free. They tend to be more attuned to an overly positive view of the world, a "rose-tinted spectacles" effect. It occurred to me that depression is not about accurate or rational thinking but more about the extent to which strong feelings colour perception. When feelings run high, or when we have an intense personal investment in something, rationality goes by the board. You do not have to be a psychologist to observe this phenomenon. You can see it every day wherever people engage in debate—in pubs, in Parliament, on the television, in academic seminars, and in family life. When Beck was in Oxford, people hung on his every word. He ran seminars and workshops. He gave video demonstrations of cognitive therapy in action, sometimes using role-plays and sometimes with actual patients. I saw some of his demonstrations, which were very impressive. Beck was adept at getting through to people, articulating their thoughts, translating them into cognitive therapy language, illustrating alternative ways of thinking, encouraging them to take action, and reinforcing their progress. I thought how good it must be to be treated by such a powerful yet empathic person, someone who exuded confidence and optimism, who came with an impressive track record, who was utterly convinced that cognitive therapy was going to be helpful. One of my colleagues told me, with a mixture of amusement and awe, that Beck had said in one session when discussing the progress of a patient, "Well, if it works, it must be cognitive therapy". Perhaps—and I can imagine this—Beck said it with a twinkle in his eye. Yet it illustrates how much strong belief can override rationality.

I had embarked on training as a cognitive therapist in the hope and expectation that this new approach would not only work but would feel right. I was uncomfortably aware that, for me at least, it did neither. I was also aware that others did not share my reservations. My colleagues in Oxford embraced cognitive therapy. Many went on to become leading figures in the cognitive therapy movement, initiating major research projects, running teaching workshops, setting up cognitive therapy training courses and, in Oxford, establishing an independent, self-funding Cognitive Therapy Centre within the Oxfordshire Mental Health Service NHS Trust. The tide was in full flood. The British Association for Behavioural Psychotherapy (BABP), the organization that I had helped to found in the 1970s, renamed itself the British Association for Behavioural and Cognitive Psychotherapy (BABCP), reflecting the inevitable reality: we were all cognitive therapists now. All except me, or so it seemed. Perhaps I was wrong, my reservations unnecessarily pernickety. Did the question of rationality matter? After all, there were many good things about cognitive therapy. Could I not embrace the general ethos, go with the flow, and play a major part in this new movement as I had done before with behaviour therapy? And then an uncomfortable memory surfaced. Back in 1969, as part of my training as a clinical psychologist, I had written a dissertation on behaviour therapy. I examined the claim that behaviour therapy was based on scientific knowledge. I had expected to describe a secure foundation in psychological science, how learning theories closely underpinned the new therapies, how methods like Wolpe's systematic desensitization were clearly derived from animal experimentation and that outcome studies provided a bedrock of support for their effectiveness. I found nothing of the sort. If I applied the meagrest form of critical analysis, it was clear that the link between the science of psychology and the practice of behaviour therapy was at best tenuous and most likely non-existent. I struggled to finish the dissertation on a positive note, talking about "the difficulty of the task" and "work in progress". And then I forgot about it. I wanted to be a behaviour therapist. I saw this as the way forward. I did not want anything as inconvenient as the truth to get in the way of my desire.

I would not repeat my error. Fifteen years ago I was a different person. In the 1970s I knew almost nothing. Now at least I knew something. My adolescent narcissism had been tempered, to a degree at least, by experience. I had learned something from my patients, from my failures and my successes. I felt secure. I did not need to establish a name for myself. I was good at my job, enjoying teaching and running a training course. And I was curious. What was the nature of depression? What were core beliefs or schemas? If they were essentially irrational, how did they arise? Most importantly, what could make them change?

***

There was one other occasion during Beck's sabbatical that he and I spent some time together. We had an exchange that almost dramatically changed the course of cognitive therapy for good. Nothing to do with a discussion, rational or otherwise, about changing core beliefs. Something much more important. Tennis.

On a hot, sunny summer's day Beck and I meet up at the tennis court in the grounds of Wolfson College, in north Oxford, where he is staying. He is a keen tennis player and I have volunteered to give him a match. Beck is not in his usual sunny mood. He tells me he hasn't slept well. Although the college is a nice enough place, the room is small and the bed is uncomfortable. The food is poor too. He grumbles on in this way, clearly put out that he has not been better looked after in his time at Oxford. There is nothing I can do about it and anyway I am not overly sympathetic. Wolfson College is beautifully situated with lovely lawns that stretch down to the banks of the Cherwell river. Many people would be very happy to spend a couple of months there on sabbatical. We knock up and take measure of each other. Beck's forehand and backhand show that he has had good coaching, something I have noticed that many American tennis players have. He is an accomplished player but he is in his sixties and I am in my forties. I wonder if we should just hit a few strokes, get some rhythm going.

"Okay," says Beck. "That'll do. Let's start."

"You want to play a game?"

"Sure. Don't you?"

"Yes. No. Er, absolutely."

We toss for serve. Beck wins. His serve is medium paced but heavily spun. It takes me a while to get the hang of it. He wins the first game. As we change ends, the thought crosses my mind that I could lose deliberately. It would help restore Beck's mood and put myself in his good books. Who knows, I might want to get a job in Philadelphia one day. I dismiss the thought. The only time I have deliberately lost any sporting encounter is against my children and then only very rarely. I once played table tennis left-handed against my younger daughter, Sarah, but, as she would keenly remind me, I still won.

Gradually, my relative youth turns the contest in my favour. I do not play a power game. I tend to play a variety of what I think of as subtle shots—spin, lobs, backhands down the line, cross-court forehand drives, disguised drop shots. I move Beck to and fro across the court. He chases every ball. The sun beats down. We are both sweating profusely, but he far more than me. I am becoming concerned. At the end of the first set, which I win 6–2, I suggest we might stop. Beck refuses. He wants his revenge, he says grimly. We play on. The same pattern occurs as he runs, scuttles and scrabbles for every ball. Then suddenly, after one lengthy rally, he stops dead in his tracks. He is red in the face. His breathing is fast and shallow. He drops his racquet. He grasps his chest. I rush round the net, my mind filled with the image of the distinguished Professor of Psychiatry and Founder of Cognitive Therapy collapsing with a fatal heart attack on the tennis court. I am about to gain the unenviable reputation as the man who killed Professor A.T. Beck. Fortunately, it turns out to be no more than hyperventilation brought on by the heat and the exertion. Gradually, his breathing returns to normal.

"Right," Beck says, picking up his racquet. "Let's continue."

"No way," I say decisively. "Enough's enough. We've had a great game but we should stop."

"You wanna stop?"

"Sure. I'm whacked. It's enough for me."

With more than a little reluctance Beck agrees to call it a day.

"Good match." I say cheerily. "Call it a draw?"

"You won the first set 6–2 and are 3–0 up in the second. How rational is it to call that a draw, John?"

"You might have come back at me, worn me down."

Beck pats me on the shoulder. "You won, John. But maybe next time I'll beat you."

Fortunately, we never played again.

SECTION III

GETTING PERSONAL

CHAPTER THIRTEEN

Crossing the Rubicon

Some years ago one of my daughters gave me a book called *Shrink Rap* featuring jokey cartoons about psychologists and psychotherapists. A recurring cartoon was of a defenceless patient lying on a couch being listened to (or not) by a small, bearded, middle-aged man who, if there was dialogue, is shown speaking with a heavy Viennese accent. This popular image of psychotherapy is one of the many legacies that Freud has left us. Even today, some 70 years after Freud's death, most people see psychotherapy as Freudian psychoanalysis, the patient lying on a couch, the therapist a silent, inscrutable, European-looking, older man who seems excessively interested in his patient's early sex life.

Simple, stereotyped, negative, and highly distorted views can be remarkably persistent even among those who should know better. In the late 1980s the vast majority of academic psychologists, with a few rare exceptions, regarded psychoanalysis as at best an old-fashioned, outmoded therapy and at worst a form of deception. Their view was no different from that of the cartoonists: the sadly deluded patient lies on a couch, day in, day out, year after year, while the hidden analyst makes portentous, ridiculous interpretations about entirely hypothetical and unverifiable psychic processes. No benefit could come from this approach, it was believed. This view was bolstered by various critiques of psychoanalytical psychotherapy claiming to show it was no better than placebo. But for academic psychologists their major objection was theoretical. Freud's ideas about the workings of the mind were, in the dispassionate language of modern science, arrant nonsense. His "hydraulic model", for example, in which unconscious sexual drives build up until they somehow overflowed into the psyche, causing neurotic symptoms, was pseudo-scientific, 19th century thinking at its worst. The division of the mind into the holy trinity of *id, ego* and *superego* could not be sustained given what we knew of the workings of the brain. The idea that there were stages of development, *oral, anal, pre-genital* and *genital,* and that adults can get neurotically fixated at a certain stage, did not fit with modern research into child development. The various psychic processes that Freud had elaborated—*repression, resistance, denial, displacement, projection, introjection*—were regarded as little better than mumbo jumbo. In other words, academic psychologists saw psychoanalysis as fundamentally unscientific. Its theoretical concepts did not meet the Popperian criterion of falsifiability, namely that scientific hypotheses should be capable of being disproved by evidence. Hypothetical mental processes that acted unconsciously on the person are difficult, many thought impossible, to put to experimental test. Take psychological defences. Freud had suggested that when a significant intrapsychic conflict is exposed, say, in a therapy session, the patient will unconsciously defend against acknowledging it because it is too frightening to do so. They may staunchly deny that they have any such feeling (anger, lust, jealousy, love, whatever it might be). This defence is known, appropriately enough, as *denial.* The analyst however knows better. But how then, the academic psychologist asked, can one test out the truth of the analyst's assertion? If the analyst's hypothesis is true about the unconscious feeling, the patient denies it. If it is false, it is also denied. Heads the analyst wins; tails the patient loses. The concept of denial, as with many other psychoanalytic concepts that are unconscious, is incapable of being scientifically disconfirmed for this reason.[1]

---

[1] It is possible to think of ways in which denial in the psychoanalytic sense can be distinguished from ordinary denial. Verbal and non-verbal clues could be seen as an indication of an unconscious process behind the denial. This is encapsulated in the expression lifted from *Hamlet*, "Methinks the lady doth protest too much," suggesting that excessive, disproportionate denial is a clue to something else going on behind the scenes. But to do this scientifically is no easy matter and few psychoanalysts have attempted it.

To a large extent I had gone along with this critical judgment. Like my colleagues I did not know anything at all about modern psychoanalysis. I was suspicious of a form of therapy that seemed to stretch out for years and the goal of which was something nebulous called *insight*. But my experience as a therapist had taught me that there are more things in heaven and earth than are dreamed of in scientific psychology. The simplistic rigour of behaviour therapy was unsustainable given the complexity of human behaviour. Cognitive therapy's attempts to incorporate cognitions into the mix raised more questions than it answered. Above all, I was increasingly aware of how important personal and interpersonal variables were in therapy. How different would it be if you were a patient of the serious and gently determined John Teasdale compared to the extroverted and playfully humorous Melanie Fennell? Or, to jump back a century, if you were the patient of the urbane and cultured Freud compared to the stiff, intellectual pastor's son, Jung? I knew that psychoanalysis placed the therapeutic relationship at the heart of the way the therapy worked although I had only a hazy idea as to what that meant. I decided to find out.

I kept pretty quiet about my interest in psychoanalysis. I did not want my colleagues to know. It felt as though I was doing something slightly perverted, like looking at pornography or admiring Margaret Thatcher. After my years as a hard-nosed behaviour therapist, times in which I had poured scorn on psychodynamic ideas and techniques, this felt like a betrayal. On the other hand, I was intensely curious. What was psychoanalysis really like? Would there be something that gelled with my personal therapeutic style? Or would I be repelled by the arcane ideas and old-fashioned practices? My first foray into reading psychoanalysis was not a great success. The classic British introductory text, the one all budding psychoanalysts are enjoined to read, is called *The Patient and the Analyst* by Sandler, Dare and Holder. I took the book out of the Warneford medical library and began my voyage of discovery. I found it hard going. The abstruse language of psychoanalysis felt like an impenetrable wall. The authors of the text took great pains to explain what they meant in Freudian and post-Freudian terms, but there was no attempt to bring them down to earth, to ordinary experience. It was all highly esoteric. I felt like an initiate into a new religion who has to make the plunge and immerse himself into a completely new language and way of thinking. Did I *really* want to do this? My second problem was more prosaic. *The Patient and the Analyst* is a dull and boring book. There is no sparkle to the writing. There is little in the way of case material to stimulate or entertain. The effect was to make my eyes glaze over. My mind would wander and I would have to steel myself to carry on reading the grey, anonymous text and the dry descriptions of these unfamiliar and arcane processes.

Despite these difficulties, Sandler, Dare and Holder brought me face to face with something that I realized was vital to successful therapy, the therapist-patient relationship. Psychoanalysis places great stock on this relationship; it is the crucible in which all meaningful change takes place. There are two aspects of the relationship that psychoanalysts see as particularly important, the *treatment alliance* and *transference*.

The *treatment alliance* had been defined some 20 years before by two analysts, Greenspoon and Wexler, as *the non-neurotic, rational, reasonable rapport which the patient has with his anaiyst and which enables him to work purposefully in the analytic situation*. In other words, it is the normal basis for seeking help: the patient wants to get better and comes to trust the therapist that he or she will make him better. All therapies require a treatment alliance as is obvious from times when it is clearly absent.[2] I certainly did not establish a treatment alliance with Mrs. Hewittson, the chronic agoraphobic lady on the Dog Kennel Hill estate. Nor with Gillian, the obsessional with her fear of contamination by invisible specks from cats. I was familiar with this idea of course, expressing it usually as the patient's motivation to get better. But then Sandler et al wrote *the treatment alliance should not be equated with the patient's wish to get better*. Why not? Because the motivation to get better may carry unrealistic or magical expectations about therapy. Wanting to get better is not enough. It must be remembered that psychoanalysis is not about immediate symptomatic improvement, but about uncovering deeper, unconscious conflicts that apparently provoke the symptoms. To benefit from it, patients must have a willingness to go beneath their surface desires

---

[2] Without any deliberate irony Sandler, Dare and Holder wrote, "A treatment alliance would not be required in the emergency treatment of the unconscious patient." This was the only humour in the whole book and it was, like the hypothetical patient, unconscious! I wondered what sort of people the legal sounding trio, Sandler, Dare and Holder, were. I did not imagine they would be terrific dinner party guests.

and explore these conflicts however painful this might be. Sandler et al listed the characteristics patients need to benefit from psychoanalysis. They need to be able to introspect, to see themselves somewhat objectively as you would see another person, to tolerate and work with painful feelings, to accept frustration, to trust the analyst even though he or she does not tell them very much, and to agree to a treatment that is long-term and leads to an uncertain outcome. Some list! My initial reaction was to question this. Is this not saying the patient has to buy into the way of working analytically right at the outset and is that not a sort of indoctrination? On the other hand, I could see it made sense. A patient who does not accept the premises of this form of therapy will never be able to work with it. That could be said of other therapies too. In cognitive therapy a patient who refuses to accept that his or her feelings are a product of distorted thinking is not going to get very far. Analysts work hard to establish a good treatment alliance. Regularity of contact for example—the same hour, the same place, week in, week out—is part of the alliance. This is *your* hour, is what the analytically-minded therapist will emphasize, and I am here for you in this hour. Moreover, if the patient begins to fret about the therapy or gets anxious about how deep the therapy will go, the analyst comes back to the alliance, bringing the problem out into the open and working on it in therapy.

Fostering a good treatment alliance seemed to me what any good therapist should do. The other analytical idea, *transference*, was not so straightforward. Like most therapists I understood transference to mean the patient relating to the analyst as if he or she were a figure from the patient's past, most often a parent. And like many of my colleagues, I was wary of the term. The risk was that, from a position of superior knowledge, the analyst interprets the behaviour of the patient as *transference* when perhaps it was nothing of the sort. If the patient is angered by what he or she sees is a crass remark by the analyst, how convenient for the analyst to see the anger as being transferred unconsciously from an earlier relationship. Might not the analyst simply have been crass? Reading Sandler, Dare and Holder made me realize that *transference* was not a simple concept. Like many of Freud's ideas its original definition as the unconscious repetition of earlier desires and feelings had been elaborated and changed over the years. Analysts differed in both how they defined the term and the importance they attached to it. At the extreme were those who believed *all* aspects of the therapist-patient relationship were to be regarded as *transference*, which, as Sandler et al pointed out, makes it useless as an explanation. Some regarded it as referring exclusively to transferring early experiences in the first year of life though others used it in a more general way. Some saw transference as quite specific to the analytic situation. Others believed it occurred, often unrecognized, in other therapies and indeed in relationships outside therapy. Some saw it as always unconscious and others as also at times conscious. Then there were different forms of transference, positive or negative, maternal or paternal etc. It was fascinating but to a novice like myself, rather confusing. If psychoanalysts differed among themselves about the nature of transference, then how was I to work out how useful the idea was?

I could not grasp psychoanalysis entirely by reading books. I thought it might be helpful to talk to some practising psychoanalysts. The Warneford Hospital employed two medical psychotherapists, that is, consultant psychiatrists who had trained in psychoanalytical psychotherapy and whose job it was to give a lead in this therapeutic approach to their medical colleagues. One of them was the distinguished Jungian psychoanalyst and writer, Dr. Anthony Storr. I had been introduced to Dr. Storr when I first arrived at the Warneford. I had heard him speak at seminars and case conferences. He came over as a likeable, affable, and surprisingly unassuming person. What he said usually made good clinical sense whatever therapeutic perspective you came from. I had also heard how approachable he was, how he liked to help those junior to him. I decided that I would take the plunge and make an appointment to see him.

I am walking down the corridor towards Dr. Storr's office in what is known as the Psychotherapy Department, a small suite of offices in a part of the Warneford Hospital. I am in a state of nervous trepidation as though I were back at school and had been summoned to see the headmaster. I could be about to embark on a significant change in direction, to leave behind the security of the cognitive and behavioural methods that I had become proficient in and enter a foreign country where they spoke a different language and where I would be a stranger, a novice again. Fifteen years ago I had turned down the offer of a place at the Tavistock Clinic. Here I was turning to the therapy that I had long dismissed as irrelevant and out-of-date. What on earth was I doing?

Dr. Storr comes out from behind a large, old-fashioned desk as I enter his office. He welcomes me with a friendly smile and a handshake. He has a round face with a ruddy complexion, all curves and irregularities. Under his benign gaze my nervousness instantly vanishes. I glance briefly around the room. It is like any other consulting room, the large desk near the window, from which there is a view out onto the green fields that border the south side of the hospital, a coffee table and a couple of low chairs, a standard grey filing cabinet, but then I notice a divan bed running along one wall. I realize with a start this must be the famous couch. I have a fleeting, panicky thought that Dr. Storr will ask me to lie on it and say whatever comes into my mind. But he gestures to a hard chair to the side of the desk and invites me to sit down.

"What can I do for you?" he begins rather like a sympathetic GP starting off a consultation.

"Thank you for seeing me, Dr. Storr," I begin hesitantly.

"Please call me Anthony. It's John, isn't it?"

"Yes. I'm interested ... in finding out ... something about ... psychoanalytic therapies. Maybe even trying them out." I sound like an embarrassed 15-year-old trying to talk about sex. "I've read Sandler, Dare and Holder."

"Not probably the best book to start with. A bit dry. I'd recommend a biography of Freud. Ernest Jones is probably the best as it's contemporary. Or there's a recent one by Ronald Clark that's not bad. Also try reading some of Freud's case histories. You can find them in Blackwell's. Penguin have published them as part of their Penguin Freud Library."

"Thanks. What about other psychoanalysts? Jung, for example."

"Of course you could, and indeed should read, Jung. In fact, I have just put together a selection of his writings. But I wouldn't recommend it just yet. Begin with Freud. After all, that's where it all started."

There's a pause. I am not sure what to say.

"You worked in Eysenck's department at the Maudsley, didn't you? What did you make of him? He's an odd sort of fellow, I find. Very bright but appears not to understand much about psychotherapy. And very hostile to psychoanalysis."

I tell Anthony, as I am getting used to calling him, about Hans Eysenck. Stories. Vignettes from my time at the Institute of Psychiatry. Like the very critical stance he took against the psychodynamic psychotherapies. How Eysenck, despite never having seen a patient himself, became the leading authority on behaviour therapy, how he embraced controversy, relishing the publicity. And, above all, how he hated Freud.[3] Anthony listens attentively, only occasionally interrupting when he wants to know something more. He is extremely good at this and I relax more and more. As we come to an end, I ask him about getting started and whether he might supervise me if I tried out the psychodynamic approach on a patient. He readily agrees. Later, I realized that many psychoanalysts would not have agreed, at least not until I had embarked on a training course or an infant-observation course that is a prerequisite for anyone contemplating training in psychoanalysis. After all, who was I to dabble in psychoanalysis when others had spent years in training? But Anthony has no such qualms.

"If I may be presumptuous," he says, "and recommend my own book, *The Art of Psychotherapy*, to help you get going. You'll find copies in the Warneford library but it's in paperback and not expensive. I wrote it for junior doctors and trainee psychiatrists, anyone interested in knowing what to do rather than the theory. How to set up the room. How to start the session. That sort of thing. You probably know most of it already but it will act as a guide when you take on a patient."

Our session has ended. I leave feeling a sense of quiet excitement, a keenness to get down to this new way of working, to discover

---

[3] Throughout his professional life Hans Eysenck was a controversial figure. His 1952 critique of psychotherapy caused a huge stir since he claimed that the results from research trials showed it was no better than the passage of time. Arguments raged to and fro about how he had interpreted the data with accusations that he had distorted some of the findings for his own purpose. In the early 1970s he embraced the highly sensitive view that black (Afro-Caribbean) Americans had significantly lower IQs than whites and argued that a large part of this difference was genetic, for which he was physically attacked by students at a meeting at the London School of Economics. The eminent psychologist, Jerry Bruner, wrote a piece in the TLS about Eysenck, saying how there were two Eysencks, the gifted academic psychologist and the cavalier showman. Bruner thought we needed to see more of the former and less of the latter. One day I had the temerity to ask Eysenck what he'd thought of the article. "Utter nonsense," he said gruffly. But I thought Bruner was absolutely right.

how it works and of course if it works. My hesitation has entirely gone. I know that I will take the plunge and study psychodynamic psychotherapy. What has brought this about? It is not a dispassionate, rational appraisal of psychoanalysis. I do not have enough knowledge to do that. My qualms about cognitive therapy certainly play a part. Struggling with trying to change deeply seated beliefs has brought me to question the rational, scientific approach that underpins both behaviour therapy and cognitive therapy. I am drawn towards something else, the personal relationship and the part it may play in therapy. And it is something personal about Anthony Storr that has brought this about. His warmth perhaps. His curiosity. The way he simply accepted my interest in psychoanalysis without qualm or question. His willingness to help. Had I then been attuned to the sort of introspection that psychoanalysis encourages, I might have detected something else. Might I be experiencing an idealized transference in my very positive response to Dr. Storr? Neither my father, who was emotionally distant and often uncomprehending of what I was doing, nor my mother, who was highly critical and sceptical about everything and everyone, had responded to me in such a straightforward and accepting way. Those 20 minutes I had with Anthony Storr changed my life. I resolved to train in psychoanalytic approaches to therapy. I would start by taking on a patient under Anthony's supervision and then, if that worked out, consider embarking on a proper training course. I had crossed the Rubicon.

CHAPTER FOURTEEN

Dipping my toe in the water

How could I set about being a psychodynamic psycho-therapist when I knew so little and had had no training? Had I a right to do this? And if I did try it out, how do I explain this to whichever patient I selected as my guinea pig? Do I tell him or her I am trying out a new approach? That I am under supervision? That I was a complete novice? That there was no guarantee of success or even what success would look like? Would any sensible patient not run a mile? On a training course these ethical matters would be worked out in advance. All novices in any new therapy had to confront them after all. I had told my two cognitive therapy patients, Frances and Brian, that the therapy I was trying out was new to me and that I was under supervision. That had not presented any problems. Yet I was not in the same situation. I was not *training* as a psychodynamic psychotherapist but trying out some of the methods. Anthony Storr was acting more as a mentor than a supervisor. He would see me from time to time and I would talk about what I was doing and present whatever problems might have arisen. He carried no responsibility for what I did, which is very different from a supervisor on a training course who can be held to account if things go wrong. The obvious solution would be to apply for a proper training in psychodynamic psychotherapy, get on an accredited course and spend however long it would take to become a psychodynamic psychotherapist. I did not want to do this. At least, not yet.

I had worked for 20 years as a psychologist and therapist. I had always been confident in my abilities, perhaps too confident in my early years when I was a fervent behaviour therapist. Whatever errors I had made, I had not lost an inner confidence as a psychotherapist. I did not think about this very much, if at all, which was perhaps just as well for conscious reflection could well have undermined my composure. When faced with people who were distressed and beset by difficult problems, I did not hesitate. I was immediately drawn into their world and excited by the possibility of helping them. Somewhere deep inside me I knew I was good at this activity and trusted myself to carry it off. This inner confidence enabled me to make the leap and take on a patient and work in a very different way from the way I normally worked.

Inner confidence is a two-edged sword. Some therapists can come to believe that whatever they do will be successful. They do not look for any disconfirming evidence. This is especially true of charismatic leaders of therapy schools who have powerful vested interests in believing that their approach is right. One of the strengths of my early scientific training was to be wary of certainty, something I took into my experiment with psychodynamic psychotherapy.

***

An opportunity arose quite soon after I had had my conversation with Anthony Storr. A man whom I shall call Jeremy contacted me in some distress. Over a year before I had taken him on for treatment of public speaking anxiety. He was an academic in his mid-forties. Public speaking was a way of life for him, not just giving lectures to his students but presentations at academic conferences, participating in various university committees and in his recent role as vice-president of an international association in his field of work. Outwardly, he was a highly successful academic but his inner world was in turmoil. A few months before I first saw him he had stumbled over his words when introducing a guest speaker at a conference. He felt himself blushing and his recollection was that, as he put it, he *made a complete pig's ear* of the introduction. He spent the whole time the guest speaker was talking ruminating about his stupidity and feeling that the audience had seen how badly he had done and were laughing at him. From then on he began to dread public appearances, often cancelling at the last minute or refusing invitations to speak. Even his lectures to the undergraduates, something he had previously enjoyed, became highly charged affairs as he worried that he might stumble over his words or blush or come to a complete standstill. He became acutely self-conscious and his anxiety was such that his hands trembled and he sweated profusely, which only added to his misery.

At the time Jeremy had seemed to me an excellent candidate for CBT. There was a definite anxiety response at the outset, which had become magnified and had generalized thereafter. He showed clear physical signs, sweating, blushing, a tremor. He had developed a set of irrational and exaggerated self-critical thoughts that added to his anxiety and sustained his negative view of himself. He had begun avoiding situations in case he became anxious again. Jeremy had been nervous about lecturing when he had first started his academic career 20 years before. His family doctor prescribed Propanolol, a peripheral anxiety antagonist, familiar to professional sportsmen such as snooker players who take it to steady their nerves. That had got him through the anxiety and very soon he no longer needed it. He had never taken it again. The only other anxiety he reported was a mild claustrophobia that meant that he avoided lifts or travelling on the tube. Otherwise, he seemed to have had a trouble-free life. He was married with three young children. His wife, a teacher, was American. They had met in the States where he had completed his doctorate and worked for ten years before returning to England. His current job was in a tenured university post. Other facts that emerged when I had first seen him were that both his parents were dead, his mother having died from a stroke six years ago, his father from cancer in the past year. He had not been particularly close to them but they had always been supportive of him. He had been the first person in the family to reach university. His parents, whom he described as ordinary, straightforward people, had been very proud of him. He had a younger brother who was a hippy-type, working hand-to-mouth as a jazz musician and living a rather chaotic life. Jeremy had had to bail him out on more than one occasion.

I had seen Jeremy for 12 sessions in which he completed a course of anxiety management for his public speaking. I had taught him a method of physical and mental relaxation that he was able to apply successfully to his main fear. We also identified key negative thoughts such as *People think me ridiculous because I blush and stumble over my words when speaking in public* and *I am a fraud and others can see that* and *I am weak and useless because I can't get over this silly problem.* Using cognitive therapy methods Jeremy was able to challenge these thoughts and change them into more reasonable and realistic ones. By the end of therapy his confidence had been restored and he was managing to talk in public with only minimal nervousness. I remembered him as being very grateful for my help. I had put him down as a clear success. But here he was just a year later apparently as anxious and upset as he had been before. Perhaps this would be an opportunity to take a different perspective and try out a psychodynamic approach?

How to begin? In his book, *The Art of Psychotherapy*, Anthony Storr declared that the psychodynamic psychotherapist should *get the patient to talk as freely as possible, whilst he himself stays in the background.* This is best done by means of the technique of free association that Freud pioneered. It is the main route to the problems and conflicts that are presumed to lie beneath the surface of the patient's consciousness. To work psychodynamically I would need to do this. I would have to listen for the resonances, for the signs or clues that suggest a hypothetical underlying conflict and, through judicious interpretation, bring this to the surface. I would have to forgo a desire to offer practical help. It was daunting to think of doing this. I had never done it before, at least not consciously, and apart from Anthony Storr's supervision, I had no means of checking whether I would be doing it correctly. But first I had to make sure Jeremy was willing to work in this way.

"I've gone right back," says Jeremy mournfully. "I've made a right mess of things. I'm really sorry."

He is sitting opposite me in the consulting room I am using. He looks a picture of misery, his long, angular body bent double in the chair, his head held in his hands. I have never seen him so distressed.

"Why don't you tell me what happened?"

He looks up at me. "I know exactly what happened and why," he says emphatically. "That's the stupid part. In August I was due to take over the presidency of the association. It's their fortieth anniversary this year so a big jamboree was planned. As president I would kick off proceedings and give a keynote talk. I thought to myself, *I'll be okay. I'll be nervous but I know how to manage my anxiety now.* But as the weeks went by and the conference was coming nearer, I panicked."

He stops talking for a moment and looks up at me. There are tears in his eyes.

"I did a really stupid thing, probably the most stupid thing I've done in my whole life. I told the association I had been diagnosed with a serious illness, hinted that it was cancer, and that I had to take time off. I suspended my presidency and said I wouldn't go to the conference. After that, I just went downhill. I couldn't work. I snapped at Jean and the kids. I shut myself in my study and spent hours staring out of the window, doing sweet f. a. The doc signed me off work with depression. Gave me some Prozac. I have the tablets here." He fishes into his pocket and takes out a bottle of pills, which he hands over to me. The bottle is unopened.

"You didn't take them?"

"I don't want to take pills, John. I don't want to be dependent on medication for the rest of my life. I should be able to sort this out myself. Jesus, I've made such a mess of things. Really fucked up this time."

As I listen to Jeremy several thoughts go through my mind. Was he really depressed as the GP thought? Had I missed that last time? Or was it that the presidency of the association was a step too far for him? Should I have foreseen that? Had we stopped the CBT too soon? But he had been so much better and confident that he could manage on his own. He had been keen to stop. Jeremy however was not blaming me or criticizing the therapy. He was castigating himself. He had always been self-critical. I had seen this as part of his anxiety, but perhaps it was deeper than that. Strangely, whereas before I had simply accepted his self-criticism as just the way he coped, however maladaptively, now it pisses me off. I feel like saying to him, *Pull yourself together, man* or something equally non-therapeutic.

For the rest of the session we talk about what had happened and what could be done. I check out how depressed he is and discover a moderate degree of unhappiness and hopelessness, a sense that he is a failure though he knows rationally that is not the case, and pessimism about the future. He is in his mid-forties and this could be described as a mid-life crisis, though that label does not do justice to the intensity of his feelings. I bring things to a close and we talk about what could be done.

"I'm thinking," I say slowly, "that we could reinstitute the anxiety management programme, working to get your anxiety back under control and help you back on your feet." I pause but Jeremy does not jump at the suggestion. "Or we could do something different. We could spend some time exploring what might be going on beneath the surface so to speak. This crisis, if that's the right word for it, could be a signal that something is wrong. Something more than public speaking anxiety." I am watching Jeremy and see that I have his full attention. "What I'm thinking of is that you and I spend some sessions in an open-ended way with you talking about yourself, your family, your early life, to see if, together, we can sort out what has been going on."

I am aware that this is all rather vague. In Storr's book, *The Art of Psychotherapy*, the therapist signals the psychodynamic way of working by saying something like *Last time I asked you a number of questions about your problems and background. From now on I want you to take the lead rather than my asking more questions. After all, you are the only person who knows what is going on in your mind. What do you feel that you need to talk about?* I am trying to say something similar.

"I'd like to do that," says Jeremy decisively. "I think that might be helpful. I'm not saying the anxiety management wasn't helpful," he goes on hastily. "It definitely was. But I know what to do, the relaxation, challenging thoughts and all that. I just couldn't do it."

We end by agreeing that we take six sessions working in this way after which we will review and decide whether to go on or do something else. Jeremy stands up. The misery and distress seems to have fallen from his shoulders. His eyes are gleaming.

"Thank you, John, so much," he says shaking my hand. "I really value what you are doing for me."

Before the next session I make another appointment to see Anthony Storr. I go through Jeremy's case, describing the CBT we had done, the relapse and the reasons for it, and his eagerness to get down to a different way of working. I am more nervous than

I expect to be. I feel under scrutiny. I have the disquieting thought that I might be exposed as a dumb therapist. However, Anthony listens attentively to me without comment.

"Well, that's as far as I've got," I say rather lamely.

"Interesting case. I have seen several people like Jeremy. They can be quite difficult."

Difficult is not the word I would use to describe Jeremy. Quite the reverse. "He didn't seem difficult to me," I say hesitantly. "He was keen enough and he grasped the CBT techniques. He was assiduous in putting them into practice too."

"I understand. But then when things go wrong again, he collapses. He's come back to you for more help, which you then offer and he accepts."

Shouldn't I have offered to help him?

"It's about the process, John," says Anthony in a kindly manner, recognizing my uncertainty. "Put aside the idea of therapy as a medical or psychological treatment and think about what was going on between the two of you. How did you feel when Jeremy came back?"

"Puzzled and then disappointed. He'd done so well."

"Did you feel angry at all?"

"Yes. Once, when he went on and on about how it was all his fault and that he was a stupid fool. I just thought it was rather pathetic of him, which was not very therapeutic, I'm afraid."

"What do you think the anger was about?"

The question surprises me. I was angry because … what? Not that he had relapsed and come back for more help. I was, if anything, gratified by his trust in me. I wanted to understand what had happened and help him further if I could.

"Was being angry the sort of feeling you would normally have in this context?" Anthony goes on.

"No. I was surprised by it."

"Then it was very likely a projection. It would fit the picture I've formed of Jeremy. He's someone who likes to be liked by others, to be admired, and his work as a lecturer enables him to achieve this through lectures and presentations, his research, all that sort of thing. The public self, the one he presents to others, is of a likeable, pleasant and successful man. But let us presume for the moment that his public self masks a very different feeling that for the most part he is unconscious of, an angry, frustrated, unhappy child-like self. The anger you felt was *his* anger projected into you. There is a part of Jeremy that is contemptuous of his eagerness to please but, unable to express it or even to recognize it, he projects it into you."

I had read about *projection*. I understood it, in theory. One of the unconscious ways people deal with unacceptable feelings is by projecting them into others. How often has one heard people criticize others without any awareness that what they are criticizing is something they have themselves? *Why are you so argumentative?* says a highly argumentative man to his wife. *What I hate about X is that they are so selfish,* says someone unaware of her own selfishness. But applying this to therapy is a different matter. Could I have been angry because of something about me? Perhaps at some unconscious level I was really angry that Jeremy had collapsed so readily. I say this to Anthony.

"That's also possible. A form of the *countertransference* is what the therapist brings into the session from his or her own life. But for the moment let's stay with Jeremy. What do we know about his early life that might point to the repression of negative feelings?"

I rack my brain. "His parents were always supportive, or so he says. There's his rebellious younger brother. He might have made Jeremy angry."

"That's more likely to be a conscious rivalry although there may also be envy of his brother's ability *not* to do what his parents wanted."

The penny drops. "You mean that Jeremy was pushed into the role of the good child, the one who succeeds, who carries out the wishes of his parents that he better himself, and that he suppresses any negative feelings, any anger, because it's unacceptable in the family."

"That's what I'd be looking to explore with him in therapy. His early relationships with his parents, both mother and father. As well as trying to get at what he feels about you. You tell me he's always saying how grateful he is to you for all your help. Yet he's no better than he was. Perhaps worse. Here in the therapeutic relationship you have a repetition of his being *the good child* and your part is some amalgam of mother and father. By relapsing he's disappointed you but can he say how angry he is with you for not getting him better? That doesn't seem possible. Yet he needs to get in touch with those feelings if he is to move on."

I leave the session with Anthony, my mind in a whirl. I feel a mixture of excitement and uncertainty. At the back of my mind I imagine my CBT colleagues ridiculing these speculations about unconscious processes, how they are unscientific and, they would say, easy to propose but impossible to verify. Yet, another part of me feels there is truth in what Anthony has said. It makes sense. It fits with what I have come to know of Jeremy. The desire to please me and others, the absence of any anger, even the form in which his problem is expressed. Public-speaking anxiety entails presenting oneself to others and his worry is that he will mess up, that is, there will be cracks in the surface and some other part of himself will show through.

CHAPTER FIFTEEN

"I'm so grateful for all your help"

"I don't know what to say." Jeremy looks at me expectantly. It is the start of what I have called "our exploratory work together". Normally I begin the session by asking him how he is. But not this time.

"Just say whatever's on your mind."

A frown appears on Jeremy's face. He puffs his cheeks and sighs. "I just keep thinking about the conference and the lie that I told to get out of it."

He stops, looks at me. I say nothing, holding his gaze. He looks away and stares out of the window.

"You know," he says after a short while, "what comes into my head is the story about George Washington and the cherry tree. How he told his father he could never tell a lie."

I seize on the word "father". My plan, inasmuch as I had formulated a plan other than to get Jeremy to do most of the talking, was to focus on his relationship with his parents. "How do you think *your* father would have reacted if he'd known?"

Jeremy gives me a sharp glance but looks away immediately. "He'd have been disappointed," he says, flatly without emotion.

151

I manage to stop myself from asking how his father's disappointment would make him feel as it seems too direct a question. Instead, I say nothing. There is a long silence that seems to last an eternity.

"I didn't cry when my father died. I didn't feel anything at all. Is that normal?"

I shrug my shoulders, avoiding answering, but realize immediately that my shrug is a sort of answer. I am aware of my body being tense and tell myself to relax. Easier said than done.

"He was in pain. But he never complained. *Stoical* is the word that comes to mind." A pause. "He lived on his own after Mum died. I mean I visited as often as I could but he didn't let on. Didn't say he was in pain though he must have been. By the time the docs got to him, it was too late. I'm told it's treatable, that sort of cancer, if you get to it early enough."

I am aware that Jeremy used cancer as an excuse for not going to the conference. I try to think if I can bring this in somehow, but I cannot think how.

"He wasn't an easy man. I mean, he didn't show his feelings. Maybe it's a generation thing. Stiff upper lip and all that. Charlie could get a laugh out of him through messing around on the sax, playing things like *Knees up Mother Brown*." He liked that. But Charlie never came to see him, not in the last few months anyway."

"That must have been tough."

"Yeah," he says slowly. "Charlie could have done more. But then that's Charlie."

Charlie is beginning to irritate me. I do not know whether that is a projection from Jeremy or my own feelings or both but I decide to mention it.

"I'm feeling a bit annoyed with Charlie. He seems to get away with a lot, don't you think?"

To my surprise, Jeremy smiles. "Always been that way. He'll never change. Good Time Charlie." The phrase, I suspect, is one the whole family used.

"Doesn't it make you angry?" As soon as the words come out of my mouth, I regret them. It is as though I am saying he ought to be angry rather than exploring how he feels whatever that may be.

"Not really," he says mildly.

I am struggling now. Is Jeremy denying his anger unconsciously? Or maybe he has never felt angry with Charlie, consciously or unconsciously. I decide we need to get out of this impasse.

"Tell me a bit about how life was like when you were growing up."

The session continues with Jeremy telling me about his early life in Leeds. His father worked as a rep for a tool-making company and was often away on business. At home he spent most of his spare time woodworking, which was his passion. Jeremy tells me he was a gifted carpenter. Neither of the boys had his talents though it did not seem that their father ever encouraged them. Jeremy says he was close to his mother, a warm-hearted, sociable woman with many friends in the community. They took in lodgers so the small terraced house they lived in was often full of people. However, his mother made sure that Jeremy could do his homework undisturbed. She got his father to build a desk in the boys' bedroom and he would be up there most evenings working. Charlie did not have Jeremy's academic talent or interest, so he was mostly out with his friends.

I ask whether Jeremy envied Charlie his freedom.

"No. He was four years younger than me. He was just our kid really. He wasn't good at school like I was. Didn't pass his 11+. He just wanted to have fun. Still does."

"Was life fun for you?"

Jeremy pauses as though he has to think about this. "It was on the whole. I liked school. I was bright and encouraged by the teachers. I didn't have many friends and there was a bad time when I was bullied."

"Bullied?"

"Too much of a swot, I suppose. That's the only reason I can think of. And being too small. Believe it or not, I was a runt of a kid, small for my age. So I was picked on."

I look at Jeremy's tall, angular body. It is hard to imagine him as a runt. "How long did that go on for?"

"Two years. Then I suddenly shot up in size. And Terry Brannigan, the leader of the gang, was expelled for extorting money. If you gave him sixpence he'd leave you alone. Sometimes. Pretty crude but also pretty effective."

"Did your parents not intervene?"

"I never told them." Jeremy looks uncomfortable.

"Why not?"

"I don't know. My mum was so pleased with me doing so well at the grammar school. I didn't want to let her down."

"And your dad?"

"You couldn't talk to him about that sort of thing. I tried once, told him about Brannigan and his gang. He just changed the subject."

I take a risk. "I'm guessing here but I think you thought it was *your* fault, that you should have been able to stand up for yourself, should have managed the situation."

"Spot on, doc." His fake jocularity just seems to emphasize the pain of the memory. "But it's all done and dusted now. All in the past."

"Is it?"

Jeremy looks directly at me. I hold the look. For a few seconds we stare into each other's eyes until he slowly looks away. A fanciful thought flits through my mind that he has projected his real feelings into me with that look. But that is not what projection means. It is not the transmission of an ether-like substance through the atmosphere, but a way of conceptualizing what happens occasionally in normal communication. My challenging question took him by surprise. He is registering what it means.

"I *did* think that," he says after a while. "That it was my fault somehow. Typical victim mentality, you might say. And, yes, you're right. I tend to blame myself now. I am very self-critical. Jean's always banging on about it. But it's not all negative. You need to be critical of yourself if you're going to get on. And in this case, I'm right. I lied to people. I let them down. I chickened out of the conference when it should have been my finest hour."

A silence. I do not know what to say or whether to say anything at all. An image of Jeremy's dad comes into my mind, a closed-off, slight, thin man for whom work, doing practical things, was a way of life, and emotions something to be avoided. I imagine him in his workshop, planing a piece of wood, looking for perfection in a dovetail joint. His son watches but his father says nothing. Just planes away in silence. I realize that this is *my* fantasy and it probably says more about me than Jeremy. I consciously bring my attention back to what Jeremy has told me. *Typical victim mentality*, he said. I decide to use that phrase to explore what he feels.

"You said *typical victim mentality*. Is that what's happening now when you castigate yourself for not going to the conference? Is that *typical victim mentality*?"

"I suppose it is," he says flatly. "But I also think one has to own up, take responsibility for what we do and don't do. John, I have *fucked up*. No amount of talking will get round that fact, however unpalatable or typical of a victim mentality it may be."

I feel I have missed a trick, that my question has moved us away from what really matters. We are in danger of getting into an intellectual discussion and I know that will not be helpful. It is becoming very clear to me that this form of psychotherapy is not at all easy. Pitfalls and booby traps lurk around every corner. There is another long silence. I can see from his gaze that Jeremy is lost in thought. I wait for a while and then ask:

"Can you tell me what's going through your mind right now?"

A slow smile lights up his face. "I was thinking of the time Jean and I drove from Pittsburgh to San Francisco one glorious summer. It was before we had kids. It was our Kerouac road trip, staying in cheap motels, sometimes sleeping in the open. I'd just got my doctorate and had two months off before I started as an assistant prof. We didn't plan anything. Just decided one evening we'd do it and took off the next day. It was a fantastic time."

"Free. No responsibilities. The open road."

"'Pity is that we can't do that now."

I wait but he does not say anything more. "There's something important in this memory," I say, not at all sure of my ground, but I press on anyway. "It feels like a loss of innocence, like a missed childhood. Housman's *blue remembered hills*, his *land of lost content*. Does that make any sense?"

"Curious you should quote from *A Shropshire Lad*. It was Dad's favourite poem. He could recite bits of it by heart." Suddenly he is crying. Tears flow down his cheeks unheeded. The outburst of feeling has taken him by surprise. "I'm sorry," he says indistinctly. "It's just … " He does not finish the sentence. I pass over the box of tissues that sit on the table between us. He takes one, wipes away the tears, blows his nose, struggling to get his composure back.

"Thinking of your dad," I say quietly.

Jeremy nods. "I wish I'd told him how I felt. You know, talked properly… Even when he was dying … I just … couldn't."

"And he couldn't either."

"No."

Jeremy gradually regains his composure. We talk more about his dad. The yawning gap between father and son. The realization that with his death he could never put it right. The wish that it had all been different. We do not mention Charlie again or the bullying or the conference. When the session ends, Jeremy tells me how grateful he is to me for putting up with him.

"I'm sure this will be really helpful," he says, effusively. "It's given me a lot to think about."

Anthony listens without interruption as I recount what happened in the session.

"You certainly got to some powerful feelings about his father. It sounds like a delayed grief reaction, doesn't it? He said he couldn't cry after his father died. Now he has. But I wonder if something was missing. Do you have any idea now what that might be?"

"'Anger?'" I do not really know but I am guessing from our previous discussion.

"Absolutely. Each time you've spoken about Jeremy, you tell me how grateful he is to you for all your help. What do you think of his expressions of gratitude?"

I had not thought about this at all but I do not admit that. As I think about it now, I realize it feels like it is too much. I say that to Anthony.

"Excessive gratitude is an inverted form of aggression. A person feels he *should* be grateful and, like Jeremy, he lays it on thick. Yet beneath the surface lies anger at being in the dependent position. Only the anger cannot be expressed probably because it's too frightening. I come back to what I said earlier. The treatment hasn't worked. If anything he is worse. Yet he thanks you all the time. Eventually you'll get fed up, or perhaps he will, and then anger will emerge."

I try to take all this in. Is being excessively grateful a form of inverted anger? And is Anthony implying that I should interpret Jeremy's gratitude as unconscious feelings of anger at my having let him down? But before I have time to say anything, Anthony carries on.

"There's something I should have said last time. If you were seeing Jeremy three or four times a week in an open-ended way, then you would have the time and the space to work through these issues, letting them develop naturally. However, you have only six sessions and while you might go on for more, I have a feeling that won't happen. That means you should set a limit on what you can work on in the time available. The delayed grief reaction at his father's death is probably the best thing. You should also draw on your CBT skills to get him to solve this conundrum of the conference. He needs to get back to an adult way of dealing with that. Don't you think his lie about being seriously ill is a very child-like way of reacting? Like a schoolboy might claim to be ill to avoid an exam or escape being bullied. What would you do in CBT terms to deal with this?"

"Work on the negative thoughts. Getting him to challenge their extreme negativity and formulate a more realistic and helpful way of thinking about what happened. And some simple problem-solving. What he should do now about the conference and his presidency. Listing the various options, looking at the pros and cons."

"I think you should do that, don't you?"

I cannot help feeling disappointed. I want to continue in the psychodynamic way of working. It feels like Anthony has had second thoughts. I ask if he thinks I should abandon the psychodynamic approach altogether.

"It's a matter of expediency. What's right therapeutically for your patient in the circumstances. As I see it, the great virtue of cognitive-behavioural therapy is its practicality. I think many psychotherapists could learn a great deal from CBT. Also you began with Jeremy using that approach, which means that your relationship is on a different footing. Had you been starting from scratch, it would be important *not* to offer practical help, thus allowing the possibility of a degree of regression and, with it, some anger."

"It does sound as though you are suggesting I go back to what I know, which is CBT."

"Is there not a possibility of combining the two approaches? In time-limited psychodynamic work, that is really what psychotherapists do. They select a focus for the work and stick to it. It's practical but still psychodynamic."

I feel confused. How do I do this? I feel disappointed with Anthony. He seems more interested in my using CBT than in helping me work psychodynamically. Should I focus on Jeremy's relationship with his father, the delayed grief reaction? Should I interpret his expressions of gratitude as inverted anger? Do I encourage regression or not? What should I do? But I do not say any of this to Anthony. Of course I should have done. But something holds me back. Instead, I thank him for his valuable help, giving no inkling of my disappointment and uncertainty. I had no idea at the time of how my behaviour mirrored that of Jeremy, that my expression of gratitude hid my unconscious anger and that this anger was more to do with my relationship with my father than anything Anthony had said. Only when I had been through psychotherapy myself did I eventually come to understand this.

Despite my disappointment I did what Anthony suggested and at the next session I brought up the issue of the presidency of the international association. We discussed what Jeremy might do about it. Gloomily, he talked about having *burnt his boats* and that he might as well resign. That's one possibility, I suggested, adopting my best cognitive therapy mode, but weren't there other ways of dealing with this? Could he not say that the illness hadn't been as serious as he first thought and that he was now better and could resume the presidency? Jeremy temporized, putting up all sorts of excuses for *not* dealing with this. When I challenged him, we came to anger at last for he admitted he was angry at having been put in this position. He had never wanted the presidency and had only taken it on to please his academic colleagues. Pleasing others, I suggested, was something that he had done a lot, particularly with his parents. Had he not been pleasing them by being the bright and hard-working schoolboy even to the point of not telling them that he'd been bullied? Maybe, I suggested, he was angry with them, his father in particular, for not protecting him more? Here I was consciously, if perhaps a little obviously, making the link between the present and the past that is a characteristic of the psychodynamic approach. Jeremy simply accepted my interpretation as a possibility and, hardly to my surprise, was grateful for the insight. But there was no emotional response, no tears as had happened at the mention of *The Shropshire Lad*. He confessed that he found it hard to criticize his parents. After all they had done what they could to help him within their limitations. An impasse, or so it felt. I did not push the point any further partly because I was not sure how to and partly because I was aware of what Anthony had said. In the short time we had it was better not to get into deep water especially as the pilot was a novice navigating blindly without any charts. But it illustrated how tricky the psychodynamic method was. Why had my interpretation not had an emotional impact? Was it because *I* made it rather than allowing

Jeremy to reach it himself? Or was something being avoided by both of us? Anger perhaps, if Anthony was correct. Jeremy's unconscious anger at me on the one hand, and my unconscious anger with him on the other. The trouble was that if we were both unconscious of anger, how on earth could we get to it?

In the weekly sessions that followed Jeremy reflected on his sense of himself as a failure, someone unable or unwilling to face up to difficult decisions. I reverted to my tried and trusted CBT methods. I challenged him on his self-evaluation, pointing out how he had in fact made a success of both his career and his personal life. Gradually Jeremy's depression lifted and his confidence increased. The one stubborn barrier was his reluctance to take on the presidency. However we approached it, Jeremy could not see anything other than his weakness and guilt in the lie that he had told. But at least he could accept that it was not a serious character flaw and that he could live with it. The shame was still there, I felt, but the sting of it was far less. As Anthony predicted we finished after the sixth session. Jeremy wrote me a letter a few days after we had ended, expressing his deep gratitude to me for all the help I had given him, saying how much he had learnt about himself and how helpful I had been. Did I take that at face value? Was there anger at me somewhere beneath his gratitude? Had I done enough?

My brief flirtation with the psychodynamic approach had not been an unalloyed success. But it told me something important, that if I sat back and let the patient talk, more might be revealed, emotions in particular. I might well have got to Jeremy's tears through cognitive therapy if I had asked him directly to think about his father. I would never know. But that was not the point. When I sat back, creating the space for Jeremy to talk, when I held back my desire to help him directly, our relationship changed. Jeremy could talk more freely, and I could listen not just to what he was saying but what else might be going on. It changed the nature of the therapy. It had been right to return to the practicalities of cognitive therapy for that is how we had started out. But suppose when Jeremy first appeared, I had done what Anthony suggested in his book, *The Art of Psychotherapy*, and asked him to say whatever was on his mind while I listened without offering immediate practical help. Would we have then got to his anger? I could imagine his frustration at my not helping him directly. If I were confident and skilled enough,

I could turn that frustration to good therapeutic use, using it as a key for unlocking feelings of which he was largely or entirely unconscious. And if his excessive gratitude appeared as it well might, we could explore this together.

I was intrigued by this way of working. I wanted to do more of it. However, I needed to get a proper training, not just dabble in it. And then chance intervened as it had before in my life. I learned that the Warneford Hospital's Department of Psychotherapy was to set up a two-year, part-time training in psychodynamic psychotherapy in conjunction with Oxford University's Continuing Education Department. It was specifically designed for experienced NHS and other public service therapists in order to help them incorporate the psychodynamic approach into their practice. Here, right on my doorstep, was an opportunity to do exactly what I wanted, get a formal training in psychodynamic psychotherapy.

CHAPTER SIXTEEN

"I've told you all I know"

First days are always difficult. I tell myself this as I sit amongst a group of strangers. I have been accepted on the Oxford psychodynamic psychotherapy course and I am at the beginning of the training, one of a small group of highly selected students about to embark on a two-year, part-time course. We are seated in the group room in the Warneford Hospital's Psychotherapy Department. So many disturbed psychiatric patients have passed through this room, I fancy I can sense their distress, the feelings that suddenly erupt, the stormings out, the tears, the hopes raised and dashed. But it is really my own anxiety I am feeling. Now that it has come to it and I am about to start on this journey, doubts assail me. Do I really want to be a student again? I head up my own training course after all and have done for years. I am normally on the other side of the fence, cheerfully giving out reference lists and course programmes to my own quaking bunch of novices. It is a strange, dislocated feeling to be seated this side.

There are 12 of us in all, nine women and three men, a not unexpected gender imbalance. We are in a square-shaped, ground-floor room. Two identical windows on the wall to my right give out onto dark green foliage in the grounds beyond. On the wall opposite there appears to be another window but it is in fact a mirror and one-way screen through which group sessions may be observed from a small adjacent room. Dark-red curtains are tactfully drawn across it in case any of us gets paranoid about being watched. The walls are painted a neutral mushroom colour that looks fresh as though it has just been done last week. I wonder if it's been redecorated in our honour. The only personal touch in the room is a large rectangular, woven wall hanging, done in *faux-naïf* style, all blocks and angles. It depicts a group of men and women, South American Indians as far as I can tell, squat and short in stovepipe hats, doing domestic tasks like cooking on an open fire. The colours are muted shades of brown, beige, and terracotta. The most disconcerting feature is that none of the people has a face. Just dark blocks in place of eyes, nose, and mouth. A strange tableau to hang in a group psychotherapy room, with its implication that individuality is unimportant, that we are all in the end faceless people.

Sid Bloch, the course director who nurtured the course into exist-ence, addresses us. He talks eagerly of his plans and aspirations, of his fervent desire to run a first class academic course yet one that is closely attuned to the realities of clinical work, of his wish to ensure that psychodynamic ideas and methods permeate through the eche-lons of the NHS, social services, education, the prison service, the pri-vate sector, indeed anywhere and everywhere that psychotherapy is practised. He talks fast, excitedly, energetically. I am carried along by his voluble enthusiasm at first but then begin to feel more and more detached. Have we students to carry the banner of psychodynamic psychotherapy like riders at the head of the crusade to Jerusalem to convert the infidel to the new religion? This is not why I signed up for the course. I do not want to lose my sense of perspective. The course syllabus is handed out with details of the weekly Wednesday afternoon sessions that run through the three terms of the first year. A mixture of lectures, seminars, casework, and supervision, plus a sensitivity group run by a therapist external to the course. A long reference list of key books is attached. More than any of us will read of course. I flick through it and my enthusiasm returns. The upside of being a student is that other people give you things—references, articles, their knowledge and opinions, the benefit of their clinical experience—all laid on for us privileged few.

In the first few weeks the lecturers took us through the history of psychodynamic psychotherapy from Freud onwards. I suspended my critical judgment, not wanting to meet every idea or every method with questions about the scientific basis or the psychological research that might or might not support it. I was not here as a demolition expert: there were enough of those in the world of psychology already. Peter Gay's monumental biography of Freud had just been published. I read it avidly. No figure in academic psychology could compare with Freud in terms of the influence he had. Single-handedly, and from a position of relative powerlessness as a Jew in late 19th century Vienna, he had transformed psychiatry and gone on to do the same with Western thought. Freud did not discover the unconscious. Henri Ellenberger's socio-historical analysis, *The Discovery of the Unconscious*, made that clear. But his invention of psychoanalysis as both a system of thought and a method of inquiry showed the many unconscious processes that enveloped everyday life from the minutiae of Freudian slips and nightly dreams to the powerful neurotic symptoms that afflicted men and women of the time. I discovered that many of the disparaging criticisms of Freud, made from the vantage point of the late 20th century, were either obvious, wrong, or a travesty of what he had set out to do. One thing was abundantly clear from Gay's biography. Freud was first and foremost a scientist. His burning ambition was to make an impact on the scientific world. Early on in his career he began a wildly ambitious *Project for a Scientific Psychology* in which he tried to synthesize advances in neurology, physiology, and psychology seeking laws of a Newtonian simplicity that, unsurprisingly given the rawness of all three disciplines, eluded him and he abandoned the enterprise. I realized how ironic it was that modern criticisms of psychoanalysis focussed on its unscientific nature given Freud's total commitment to science. Many of his central notions such as the division of the mind into *id, ego* and *superego* were essentially prototypes of hoped-for neurological advances that would confirm their existence. Were Freud alive today, I conjectured, he would be on the side of the hard-nosed scientists, the biologists, the neurophysiologists, the biochemists, the geneticists. I doubted that he would have had looked very kindly on the modern-day psychoanalysts with their speculative inferences and their belief in subjectivity and narrative truth. He would want data and evidence like any other true scientist.

Yet psychoanalysis is what he is remembered for. He committed himself completely to the method of systematically analysing the patient's symptoms, uncovering clues to their unconscious meaning. The case histories—the Wolf Man, The Rat Man, Dora, Little Hans—and his great works like *The Interpretation of Dreams*, are masterly expositions of how to extract the hidden significance of words, gestures, dreams, omissions, relationships, narratives, all gleaned from the person in front of him. Like so many others before me I was fascinated by Freud's erudition and by his Sherlock Holmes-like determination to analyse the significance of every little event or phrase. But like many others too, I could not but see the glaring limitation of this method of inquiry. So much depended on the man and his patient. To construct a scientific edifice from such material was doomed to failure. It could never be replicated, dependent as it was on the two individuals locked in the intricacies of their own subjectivities. Science needed something else altogether, something more objective and generalizable, something more prosaic. Psychology as it happens.

Freud believed in his new method, asserting with characteristic vigour that if one looked hard enough, the truth would be plain to see. "When I set myself the task of bringing to light what human beings keep hidden within them," he wrote in his account of his patient Dora, "I thought the task was a harder one than it really is. He that has eyes to see and ears to hear may convince himself that no mortal can keep a secret. If his lips are silent, he chatters with his fingertips; betrayal oozes out of every pore. And thus the task of making conscious the most hidden recesses of the mind is one which it is quite possible to accomplish." But it was not true and indeed it could not be true. Extracting hidden meanings is a process riddled with all sorts of plausibilities and implausibilities, not to mention the many ways the analyst could provoke the very behaviour he is looking for. The danger could not be more obvious, the analyst seeing what he wants to see in the array of words and silences that fill the analytic session, finding the answers he is already certain are there to be found. As a scientific method, psychoanalysis is fundamentally flawed. Whatever blinkered prejudices my academic colleagues had against Freudian psychoanalysis, they were right about that. It would never be possible to construct a lasting psychological science using psychoanalysis.

Some have argued that psychoanalysis should not be judged in terms of the positivist approaches that drive natural sciences but in terms of the search for meanings via the process of interpretation that is central to the method (hermeneutics). This is a very different idea of science to the one I have always understood. The word *science* is derived from the Latin, to know, and in that literal sense psychoanalysis is about acquiring knowledge. My experience as a psychotherapist made me acutely aware that there are many ways of knowing, including a tacit sense of understanding that comes from two people exploring their subjective worlds. But I do not think this is scientific knowledge for the simple reason that it cannot extend beyond the particular and if science is about anything, it is about arriving at generalities, making public claims that can be shown by empirical evidence to be true or false.

Scientific validation was not what I was interested in. My overriding desire was to see if the Freudian approach, and the many variations that followed it, offered something to me as a clinician and therapist. The best way to do this was through the supervised case work, taking on a patient and doing what I had started with Jeremy, working as a psychodynamic psychotherapist.

***

Sitting opposite me is Matthew, a tall young man, in a scruffy white T-shirt and faded jeans. In his hands he has a Rubik cube. Each side of the cube is subdivided into nine coloured squares, the puzzle being to twist the arrangements to produce sides of all one colour. Matthew is fiddling with the cube, a frown of concentration on his face. He is my first proper psychodynamic psychotherapy patient. This is our first session.

"I wonder if it might be best if you put the Rubik cube down."

I leave the faintest of inflections at the end of my remark to try and soften the suggestion. Matthew drops the cube into a battered shoulder bag that he has draped on the side of the chair.

"There," he says, flashing me a brilliant smile. "I solved it yesterday. I thought I'd see if I could do it again. I must have gone wrong somewhere."

I could pick up on the wider meaning of his last remark but decide that it is a bit too early to do so and, moreover, it is Matthew who should do the running, not me. I have already introduced myself and explained that we are to work together for up to a year, meeting once a week, holidays apart.

"How about you kicking off," I say. "Just say whatever's on your mind."

We are seated face-to-face. There is a couch in the room but Matthew declined it. I was disappointed as the couch seemed so much a part of the psychodynamic approach.

"What do you want me to say?" he says brightly as though he is here to audition for a part in a play.

"The idea is for you to talk and we take it from there. Whatever is on your mind."

This produces a long silence during which Matthew gazes around the room as though seeking something to latch onto.

"Crap painting," he says pointing at a Monet print of a mother and young girl walking through a bright red poppy field. "I hate reproductions."

Is Matthew saying something about himself in this remark, I wonder? That he is not a reproduction, but the real thing, a true original. Whether he is or not I decide not to comment. I think about what I already know about him from the assessment that Dr. Franklin, the Psychotherapy Department's senior registrar, carried out. He comes from a well-off, middle-class family. He is particularly close to his mother. She gives him a generous allowance and has let him stay, rent free, in a flat she owns in Headington. His father, a successful businessman, is largely absent from home. At school Matthew was regarded as very bright but dropped out in the 6th form. There are suggestions of drug taking and gambling. Since school, he has had periods of temporary work, mainly on building sites, though most recently he worked in an office. None of his jobs have lasted long. He is currently unemployed. Matthew's major complaint is of extreme anxiety, often in the form of panic attacks. These have caused him to retreat to his flat, sometimes staying there for days on end, not seeing anyone.

My reverie is interrupted when Matthew says, looking quizzically at me: "You're not like Doctor Frankenstein. He asked me lots of questions, most of which, actually *all* of which, were stupid. In the end I just made things up. It seemed to make him happy."

Jesus! Now I do not know what of Dr. Franklin's assessment is correct, which is, I suspect, exactly what Matthew wanted.

"I wonder why you did that."

"I wonder why myself." A cheeky smile, inviting me to join in the joke. I cannot help smiling back. There is something very disarming about Matthew.

"When I was at school," he says after a while, "I would make things up. Entertain the troops by telling a few fibs, playing the joker. It got to be a habit. I had this great ex-army greatcoat and me and the other lads hung about, doing dares and that. Wicked!"

He sounds about 16. Stuck in an adolescent time warp.

"Only I lost the coat. Then the bastards threw me out."

Why did they throw you out? It's on the tip of my tongue to ask but I stop myself. Above all, I want not to interfere, to let Matthew talk and me listen. So far he has not told me about anything serious. Not about his uncertain sexuality. Not about his intense feelings of panic. Nor about the time when he took an overdose of antidepressants (the tablets were his mother's prescribed by the family GP). Dr. Franklin had noted all these in his assessment but Matthew does not seem to want to talk about any of this. Of course they might all be fabrications (*fibs to entertain the troops*) but somehow I doubt it. Beneath the veneer of jokiness I sense his vulnerability and unhappiness. The difficulty might well be getting him to talk about it.

Matthew talks more about his school even though it is over three years since he left. He was *brilliant* at English and had two poems accepted by the school magazine. But he stopped working in the 6th form because it was all so *puerile*. Then the teachers tried to get him to see a school counsellor who turned out to be a real *wanker*. I am cast in the role of the eager listener to his tales of schoolboy derring-do. He tells a good story and I think I could just let him do that. But where would we have got to and what purpose would it have served other than to pass the time? The dilemma with the passive stance of the psychodynamic psychotherapist is that someone like Matthew could *entertain the troops* all day long. At a pause I venture to stir things up, unsure if I am doing the right thing and wary of how he will react.

"From what I've heard so far everything seems so hunky-dory that I wonder why you are here in psychotherapy at all. It hasn't been all sweetness and light, has it?"

Matthew does not say anything, which causes my heart to beat faster. I run through the statement I have just made and castigate myself for its anodyne quality. Could I not have been more incisive?

"*Hunky-dory*," he says, drawing out the word in a laconic manner. "Now that's not a word in the psychotherapist's lexicon, I would have thought? Or is it?" He looks at me expectantly, all sweetness and light of course. I feel the stiletto sliding subtly into me. I tell myself to stay mum and then wonder at my choice of words. *Mum's the word*. The phrase floats through my mind as though magically Matthew has projected it into me. Is this an unconscious communication? Do the words mean that we will be okay as long as I mother him, admire his precocity and wit, but if I, taking the paternal role, challenge him, he will hit back? All this flits through my mind in seconds, a blur of semi-conscious thought, as Matthew looks me straight in the eye and waits for me to respond. I say nothing, holding his gaze until he looks away. My beating heart gradually slows. In my previous persona as a cognitive-behavioural therapist, I would have been more active. I would have probably said that *hunky-dory* was certainly not a psychotherapeutic term, just a word that seemed appropriate. I would have smiled, wanting to maintain good rapport. I would have asked Matthew whether he minded the word or if he preferred another. Why do I not do this now? Because my primary role is not to be Matthew's friendly helper, not to make him feel at ease. As a psychodynamic psychotherapist I am seeking to create a space in which we can explore deeper feelings. For that to happen I have to dispense with the niceties and tolerate the discomfort just as Matthew has to do too. I am finding this difficult. It is not just that Matthew, with his air of vulnerability and his boyish charm, invites me (and others, I imagine) to look after him. I realize I like looking after people. That is why I am in this job. Only in this instance *looking after people* means something very different. It is not about making them feel better, at least not immediately, but getting through their defences to the heart of their problems. To achieve this I shall have to use a few stilettos of my own.

The session stutters on. Matthew's breezy insouciance dissolves. He retreats into scowling silences. When he speaks, there is anger and more than a hint of despair. He rails against both his parents, his father for his crass insensitivity and his mother because she is *a very silly woman*. I hear nothing of his brothers and sisters. He brightens up only when he talks about his best friend, Tom, who is about to return from college. Tom is going to stay with Matthew and they'll have fun together again. I cannot help thinking that the fun will be rather hollow. A feeling of sadness pervades the room. Matthew's defences are pretty brittle, I realize. I feel daunted at the task of treating him. After all, I am a novice at this form of therapy. Yet I desperately want to help him, not just because I am on a course and anxious to do well, but because I sense his despair. I end by saying a few words about the task ahead.

"These are your sessions, Matthew. We have up to a year to work together."

"But what's the point? It's just talking. What can talking do?"

"It's an opportunity for you to take a look at yourself, to explore how you feel, to examine what has happened to bring you to this point."

"But I've told you all I know."

"I don't think so," I say more assertively than I had intended. "Do you really think you have?"

A pause. "No. There are other things. Stuff I haven't talked about. *Horrible* stuff. But I don't think I'll ever talk about that."

"Let's see. Next week at the same time?"

"Okay," Matthew says. A flutter of hope, faint and tenuous. I sit for a while in silence after Matthew leaves. I feel drained and empty. Then I pull myself together, reach for my pen and start making the detailed notes I shall need for supervision.

CHAPTER SEVENTEEN

Not waving but drowning

Over the following months Matthew attended every session. He was always on time. As before, he refused to lie on the couch, which I put down to his fear of being vulnerable, and sat, or rather lounged, in the chair opposite me. The Rubik cube never returned though I was aware of its symbolic presence. Could we solve the puzzle and bring Matthew's fragmented parts into a solid whole? But at least he talked. Quite often this was in the same jokey, superficial vein as in the first session. He tested me, making jibes at the stuffiness and stupidity of psychotherapy. He made dark references to secrets that he couldn't possibly share. He entertained me with witty stories about friends and family. He portrayed himself as a sort of cross between Oscar Wilde and Jarvis Cocker of the pop group, Pulp. I sat tight, waiting for the moments when I could make an interpretation or draw his attention to his defences or try to bring him to contemplate what I saw as his truer, deeper feelings. It was not easy. Matthew was adept at deflecting my attempts to breach the walls. If he did not care for what I had said, he disparaged it or simply ignored it. I felt frustrated yet I always looked forward to the sessions. I enjoyed his company and relished the battle of wits. I wondered if this was what should happen in psychodynamic psychotherapy. It did not seem to be how other therapists described what they did. That was altogether more serious, measured and reflective. Was I being unconsciously drawn into Matthew's way of relating as though everything were a game? Perhaps, but I wanted to establish a good relationship with him, a therapeutic alliance. After that, I told myself, we would get down to the real work.

"Tom and I are an item."

Matthew told me this proudly, triumphantly, one hot day in August. It was now six months since we had first met. In that time we had established a rhythm to the therapy. Matthew would tell me what he had been doing in the week. Stories that he would embellish, that he would enjoy telling me about. Some true, some fiction, I suspected. *Entertaining the troops* was my shorthand for this part of the session. I was content to listen. Then, we might get into something more personal and just occasionally some intense feelings emerged. Once he talked about the time he had shut himself away in his bedroom. This was as near as he came to utter despair. He hated himself for what he called his *weakness*. I was sure this was sexual but Matthew would not elaborate however hard I encouraged him to do so. Another time he stormed into the room, ferociously angry. He'd applied for a foundation course in art at a local college. He'd been rejected. In a fit of pique he had burned all his drawings, years and years of work. In these moments I felt close to Matthew. I would try to explore his feelings only for him to veer away from my attempt either by falling silent or by attacking psychotherapy (and me) as a monumental waste of time. I found it very frustrating. In supervision I was encouraged to hold my ground. I was told that with someone like Matthew, someone who was stuck in a primitive narcissistic state in which his feelings varied from wild grandiosity to ferocious anger, the therapeutic relationship was the key. In effect, I was to be the "good parent" he never had. That was all very well but seeing him just once a week meant that my parental influence was very limited. I had no sense of progression. Each new session we had to start again from scratch. Was this a weakness of the once-weekly psychodynamic approach or something about Matthew? Could he only disclose personal feelings if he knew that in a matter of minutes his time would be up and he could escape? And I wondered if a more experienced psychodynamic psychotherapist would be able to handle him better, getting through to his true feelings with greater skill than I could muster.

Then along came Tom. Over the summer vacation Tom and Matthew were inseparable. Matthew's mood lifted. He began making plans. He and Tom would set up a furniture restoring business, marrying his creative talents with Tom's business acumen. He would spend the autumn at Tom's university and join the dramatics society in which Tom excelled. He would be the director. He would write a play. He had an idea that he was sure would take the West End by storm. A play in which Oscar Wilde meets Jarvis Cocker, a sort of two-hander in which he would update and indeed improve upon Wilde's witticisms. In the sessions it was always Tom, Tom, Tom. I knew of his attraction to Tom. Matthew had not tried to hide it. But Tom had girlfriends. As far as I knew he was heterosexual. Yet, as Matthew told me with some relish, they had ended up in bed together. For the long summer months Matthew seemed happy as long as he and Tom were together.

***

Early October. I am waiting for Matthew to appear. He is 15 minutes late. Not that long. But Matthew has never failed to turn up for a session. He has never been even so much as a minute late before. I am worried. I think the worst. He has overdosed or thrown himself under a train. It is with relief I hear a knock on the door and Matthew finally appears.

He throws himself into the chair. His face is ashy white. He looks exhausted. Something has happened. I wait for him to talk but he sits staring at the floor. I rehearse what I might say. *It's not like you to be late.* But that sounds perilously like a criticism. *You seem down. Has something happened?* I imagine Matthew's sarcastic response: *Aren't you the perceptive therapist?* A neutral, *Can you say what's on your mind right now?* But that's banal. Perhaps I should say nothing, allowing the silence to close round us like a blanket. Then, unexpectedly, Matthew speaks.

"Tom's got engaged."

"'Engaged?'"

"The Honourable Sophie Charlesworth, daughter of Viscount Raylston. She's a dumb bimbo, but the family's as rich as Croesus."

A long silence.

"I guess you feel he's abandoned you, let you down."

"I didn't really care for him anyway. He slept with his mouth open. He snored for fuck's sake."

Like a disappointed child, Matthew goes on the attack. But at least he is not entertaining me. He is showing something of how he really feels.

"You trusted Tom," I say slowly. "He was going to be your saviour in a way. But like everyone else, your father, your mother, your schoolteachers, he has hurt you. Deep down I suspect you are thinking that there must be something wrong with you, that you are flawed. I think we could explore this here."

It is too long a statement and as I say it, I feel I have made a misjudgment though I am not sure what.

"*Explore* it? Yes, why don't we do that? That would be fun."

The sarcasm is not unexpected but for a moment I am thrown by it. In my head I can hear myself saying, though I do not say it out loud, *Psychotherapy is not meant to be fun,* sounding just like the critical father/teacher/mother Matthew rails against. I think this is countertransference, a form of projection from Matthew, what he unconsciously expects others to say to him and gets them to do, thereby confirming his view of himself as a bad person and them as insensitive and uncaring people. I know this intellectually but I do not know what I should do. I let the silence linger as I think.

"Tom's at fault to some degree," I say eventually. "While he was here, you and he had fun. He knew you took it more seriously than he did, but he played along anyway. You allowed yourself to hope for something more. Maybe you always knew that it wouldn't work out, but kidded yourself that this time it would. That's what really hurts."

"I know all that." Impatiently. "Tom's a wanker. Always was, always will be."

"And you? What are you Matthew?"

"I don't know." He says this quietly.

"Shall I tell you what I think?" I pause, but he does not say anything. "You like to play the role of the entertainer, the brilliant child who amuses others. It's what you're good at, what you do here a lot of the time, what you did at school too. But a part of you hates that, sees it as trivial and shallow. But for some reason you cannot come to terms with your serious self. There's something wrong, or something went wrong. You punish yourself for it."

Another long silence. Have I done the right thing? I have put into words what I think is Matthew's problem. Then I realize with a start that I have done this, not Matthew. I have not let him come to this conclusion himself.

"I have these sexual fantasies. I've never told anyone this. They're sort of perverted." He shudders. "I can't tell you what they are, John. Don't ask me. Just that they're revolting. Once I've done, I feel awful. Guilty."

"It might help to tell me what they are."

He shakes his head vigorously. "I can't."

I press him to tell me but he is adamant.

"I'm grateful for what you're doing," he says. "I know I piss about. There's a part of me that thinks 'What do you know? I know more than you do. I'm the best psychotherapist, I'm the coolest guy.'" He looks up at me and gives me a wry grin. "Hey, maybe I am. Maybe I should retrain as a counsellor. Waddya think, doc?"

"Matthew."

He shrugs. The moment of emotional contact was there but it is suddenly gone. Matthew's resorted to his tried and trusted jibes and jokes. I try to bring him back to the feeling. I point out what he is doing, how he is defending against letting me get close to him. But he is not having any of it. Instead he is off on a riff of how he doesn't need Tom and that he can do it all better on his own and maybe he should end the therapy as it's only all a load of words and *bollocks really*. When he has gone, the disappointment weighs heavily on me. I go through what I said and imagine what I might have said differently. I question whether I am any good at this form of psychotherapy. There is so much uncertainty. But then that is what the process is about. In CBT the certainty came from the model of therapy and the patient guided into accepting it and working within it. Here there are models too but they are vaguer and there are no clear prescriptions as to what to say or do. This makes it so much harder. Yet, deep down, I feel this is the right way. The fact that Matthew defended against it should not put me off. After all, it is somewhat narcissistic of me to expect to master the approach at the first try and I know that Matthew is not the easiest of people to help whatever the therapeutic approach.

Matthew and I continued in much the same vein week in, week out. Sometimes, he sat in brooding silence, resisting my attempts to get him to talk. At other times, when he was in a good mood, he would tell me stories about his wonderful life, embellishing and elaborating on the smallest of encounters, an argument with a car driver when he was cycling around Oxford which he got the best of, almost getting caught on a shoplifting spree in the middle of town, getting drunk on strong lager with some teenagers he ran into in a pub. Tom had returned to university (*good riddance*) but try as I might, I could not get Matthew to address his sense of loss. He was angry with Tom but refused to talk about it (*what was the point?*). When I pointed out that psychotherapy was about exploring what mattered however painful, he would give me a withering look or launch an attack on what he described as a *stupid talking shop*. I felt frustrated, unable to penetrate the defensive wall he had erected. I held on to the fact that Matthew attended the sessions assiduously. He must be getting something out of it though I was far from clear what it was.

I talked about my doubts and difficulties in supervision. I read up on the various psychoanalytic theories of narcissism. Matthew undoubtedly showed the mixture of grandiosity and contempt that psychoanalysts described as the key feature of narcissism. Underneath all the surface bombast lay a deep sense of hurt. One theory suggested that narcissism persists because of failures in early parenting. A characteristic pattern, one Freud had identified, was of an unresolved Oedipal conflict in which castration anxiety in relation to the father had never been resolved. Sexual desire for the mother was transmuted into a conflicted internalized world in which primitive omnipotence alternated with ferocious attacks on the self. Sexual perversion was often present. Matthew hinted about problems in relation to his father and I knew he had a highly ambivalent attitude to his mother. He had many times alluded to sexual perversion. But I knew so little and the psychoanalytical theory seemed highly speculative. I was not sure I believed in the Oedipus complex. Did young boys really suffer from castration anxiety? Did they fancy their mothers in the way Freud described? It all seemed rather archaic, the ideas redolent of a way of looking at child development that had not kept up with modern psychology.

Yet one aspect of psychoanalytical theory struck a chord. This was to do with identity. People like Matthew, people with a strong streak of narcissism, failed to form a strong sense of their own separate identity. They related to others as extensions of themselves; *selfobjects* was the technical term, the conjoined words summarizing the failure to separate self from others or *objects* as others are known in the jargon of psychoanalysis. I knew Matthew's self-esteem was highly fragile and constantly undermined by the way people behaved towards him (and he to them). The theory suggested that his fundamental fear was of the disintegration of his sense of self, arising out of a feeling of inner emptiness. "The strongest guard is placed at the gateway to nothing ... because the condition of emptiness is too shameful to be acknowledged." Dick Diver, the psychiatrist protagonist in Scott Fitzgerald's novel, *Tender is the Night,* says this, talking about actors but alluding also to himself. At some unconscious level Matthew felt empty and ashamed. He compensated for this by his illusions of narcissistic grandiosity. He was the best psychotherapist. He was the unrecognized genius. He was the witty storyteller, the great entertainer. His destructive rages were exactly like primitive, childish reactions, as when he burned all his paintings or attacked Tom for snoring. My problem was not so much to do with understanding, but what on earth could I do? Whenever I tried to reach out to Matthew, he moved away, often by attacking me or disparaging psychotherapy, or simply refusing to talk. I realized I had to withstand these attacks and gradually build up a strong relationship, a sort of optimal re-parenting in which attachment and firmness were finely balanced. Easier said than done. Nine months had passed. I still had no clear idea of the *horrible things* Matthew had alluded to at the beginning. I was pretty sure they were sexual and possibly involved his father though that was speculation since Matthew would never discuss it. In supervision I was encouraged to do two things as we moved into the last three months of therapy. Get Matthew to talk more about his early childhood and work explicitly on his relationship with me. The idea was to link his past with the present and help Matthew find an alternative way of relating to people via his relationship to me. It was with more than a little trepidation I set out to do this.

"Tell me about your father."

Uncharacteristically I have opened the session rather than waiting for Matthew to begin.

"Why?"

"Because."

"*Because?* Is that supposed to be a clever psychotherapeutic remark?"

I say nothing.

"Okay. I'll tell you. My dear beloved father hates me. He's always wanting me to love him. He says he forgives me. *Forgives me!* I should forgive him, I can tell you."

"What did he do to you?"

Matthew looks directly at me. I hold his gaze. I can see he is weighing up how much to tell me. We have been here before several times and every time he has ducked the issue.

"Don't tell me," I say as though it is a game. "Maybe you want me to guess and then when I do, you can tell me I'm wrong."

"My dear, we are sensitive today."

"It's just that I think you should tell me. You have been coming to see me for nine months and you have wanted to tell me but never could. I think it's because you are ashamed of what happened. But you can get through that, surely."

I have never talked to Matthew quite like this. I have no idea if it is the right approach psychodynamically, but I am not allowing myself to think too much. Something impels me to say it. It could well be countertransference. A projection from Matthew perhaps or my frustration at the way he always turns everything into a joke or an attack.

A brief moment of silence. "Actually," he says, "he's always asking me to forgive him, not the other way round. He felt me up. When I was a kid. He said he couldn't help himself. But they all say that, don't they?"

"How old were you?"

"Six. Seven. Can't remember exactly."

"Did it go on a long time?"

"It seemed like a lifetime. But I think it was a few weeks, maybe even less."

"How did it stop?"

"I told Mum. She stopped it."

Matthew says this in a flat, emotionless voice. I know with absolute certainty he is telling me the truth.

"And then what happened?"

"Nothing much. It stopped, which was a good thing. Dad begged me to forgive him, tears flowing down his face. Of course I said yes."

"And do you?"

Matthew considers this as though it is the first time he has had to think of it. "I don't know. Sometimes I think I should. Mum said I should. To err is human, she says. To forgive is divine."

Bollocks. Fortunately, I do not say this out loud.

"Mum's always doing things for me," he says. "Giving me money. Bailing me out of trouble. I'm grateful to her but she's always in my face. She can't let go. I think she feels guilty about what happened. Well, I know she does."

"And you feel guilty too."

Matthew gives a barely perceptible nod. I want to tell him he shouldn't feel guilty but I do not. I know it would not make any difference. You cannot get rid of guilt by wishing it away.

"Thank you for telling me," I say after a short silence. "You were—you are—caught between your mother and father, aren't you? Difficult to be you."

"John, have you read *Paradise Lost*?"

"Parts of it. A long time ago."

"We did it at school. I identified with Lucifer. I liked him better than God. Milton did too. I see myself as God's fallen angel."

He smiles suddenly and in the brittle sadness of his smile I see Matthew's complicated state of mind. Half angel, half devil. Stuck in limbo between childhood and adulthood. Never able to be himself. I feel overwhelmingly sad. The revelation, when at last it came, proved not to be anything extraordinary, but more or less what I had expected. Sexual abuse. If Matthew has told me the whole truth, then it was on a small scale compared to what others have had to suffer. But that was not the point. Matthew felt betrayed. In more senses than one. His father had abused him but his mother had failed to protect him. The family had stayed together and *forgiveness* was their leitmotif from then on. His father desperate to be forgiven. His mother desperate that he should be. Matthew caught between them. This was the true Oedipal conflict, I felt, not Freud's elaborate unconscious fantasies of the child's sexual fears and desires, but the reality of being abused and having to live with it. Matthew's grandiosity was his way of coping with the pain. He created an illusion of specialness in order not to face up to the grubby ordinariness of being used by the people who should love you and look after you.

Matthew's disclosure did not bring his games playing to an end. For a short while he was more honest than he had been hitherto. He told me about his sexuality, his so-called perversion, and in doing so gained some release. We talked about our relationship. He said he had resolved from the beginning never to trust me, to treat me like a brick wall, not a person. He did not want to be betrayed again. He had trusted me at last but it was difficult for him to maintain the closeness. In the sessions that followed he once more resorted to jokes and jibes, to entertaining me with his stories or lapsing into silence. Whenever I tried to recapture the emotional closeness, he veered away. Time was running out. We had only a few sessions left. Tom suddenly reappeared and Matthew took up with him again. For a while he was gloriously happy until predictably there was a clash between them and he felt betrayed once more. My supervisor suggested that Matthew's falling into Tom's arms was his way of defending against the pain of ending his relationship with me. I was not so sure. I thought he genuinely cared for Tom and seized the opportunity. It could have had elements of both I suppose.

Psychotherapy was, according to Matthew, just a *talking shop*. It had made no difference to him, he claimed loftily. Although I did not really believe him, it had the desired effect of making me wonder how much good it had done. Matthew's attacks played acutely on my own uncertainties. I felt I could have done so much more. If only I had been more experienced. If I had seen him twice or three times a week. If we had had another year of therapy. If I had tackled his relationship with me earlier on. If I had been more active and challenged his defences aggressively. Thoughts that flitted restlessly through my mind as I realized my first attempt at psychodynamic psychotherapy was not going to end in a huge triumph. At the end of the last session we talked about what would happen if we met in the street. Oxford is after all a small place.

"Oh, I'll just give you a wave," Matthew said brightly.

Stevie Smith's poem came into my mind. Had Matthew been *too far out all his life*, like the swimmer in the poem, *not waving but drowning*?

CHAPTER EIGHTEEN

Getting personal

Matthew's lack of discernible improvement might have made me question the value of the psychodynamic approach. But it did not. By now I was experienced enough as a therapist to recognize that he would not have been easy to help whatever therapy I had tried. The sort of problems Matthew presented were categorized then, as they are now, under the diagnosis of *personality disorder*. I disliked the label not least because it conflated two incompatible ideas, the psychological term *personality* with reference to the general characteristics that people show to some degree, and the medical notion of *disorder* implying an illness or abnormality. This made no sense to me psychologically. I did not see how a personality could be anything other than a collection of general characteristics. To label some personalities as disordered was a value judgment and in the clinical case an example of medical hegemony, giving doctors (and others) unwarranted powers of control and influence. This is not to say that Matthew did not have serious problems; he clearly did. Nor that it is necessarily unhelpful to try to categorize his problems in order to understand them better. But the medical perspective implied in the word *disorder* took therapists down the wrong path. It implied a normality. There is no such thing as a *normal* personality although in people like Matthew various behaviours and attributes could coalesce to make life pretty difficult. The psychodynamic approach offered an explanation, or more accurately, a number of explanations for how Matthew came to his present state. These were encapsulated under the term *narcissism* and focussed on failures of early parenting, on the sexualization of relationships, and on Matthew's difficulties in identity and self-esteem. The year I spent with Matthew enabled me to understand him better. Or so I thought. I had hoped to use that understanding to guide him to a more adaptive and adult way of relating to the world. That had not happened. If there had been some change in Matthew, it was the merest glimmer, a spark of recognition that I worried would be all too easily snuffed out by events in his chaotic life.

Matthew may have learned little from therapy, but I had a learned a lot. *Oh that's good*, I imagined him saying, *the patient stays the same but the therapist improves. Is that what psychotherapy is all about? Making the therapist happy?* Not happy, more *a sadder and wiser man*. Amongst other things I had learned the value of sitting back, of *not* taking charge of the sessions, and of letting the patient tell his or her story. There was flexibility in not having a specific agenda or a precisely formulated blueprint to drive forward what I was doing. The trouble with both behavioural and cognitive therapies is that in each case the model dominated the discourse. Both therapist and patient are required to work assiduously within it to achieve pre-determined goals. Sometimes this worked fine. There were well-established techniques for reducing anxiety and, with the advent of cognitive therapy, others for changing depressed mood and modifying negative thinking. Jeremy, for example, was able to gain better control over his public-speaking anxiety by using the anxiety management techniques I had introduced him to. With depressed patients I found that the weekly Activity Schedule and Thought Record form enabled them to gain a more helpful perspective on their state of mind that often led to positive changes in mood. But these approaches were limited. I doubted if CBT techniques would have made much impact on Matthew. For one thing I did not think he would have used them. Later, as cognitive therapy went from strength to strength, practitioners extended the model to work with more difficult patients like Matthew, the so-called *personality disorders.* In doing this, they were forced to make significant changes to the approach. The length of treatment had to be extended sometimes to as long as two years of twice-weekly therapy. Considerable work had to be done to establish and maintain a treatment alliance without which the practical techniques would either not be used or be sabotaged. And among some practitioners, there was a growing awareness of the role of unconscious processes and the power of emotions in therapy. A few even began to incorporate aspects of the psychodynamic approach into CBT, notably paying attention to the transference.

To my mind the most important characteristic of my therapeutic work with Matthew was our relationship. Psychodynamic psychotherapy drew particular attention to the part played by unconscious elements, but the conscious aspects were also important. Matthew tested me with his jibes and sharp wit as well as by his frequent refusal to play the psychotherapy game (*just a talking shop*). I had to withstand these attacks and avoid getting drawn into a fruitless battle. Also in recognizing the hurt little boy beneath the angry young man, I tried hard not to repeat the pattern of wounding that he had come to expect and to some extent provoke. What made this easier was that I liked Matthew. I also relished the challenge. I drew on my own wit and humour in response to his. I admired his determined independence even if it got him into trouble. Perhaps I saw something of myself in him, something of the maverick quality that had made me, like him, resist orthodoxy. I had allowed these personal elements to be expressed in therapy. But I was always conscious that I had to maintain professional boundaries. I carefully refrained from self-disclosure. Interestingly, unlike some of the other difficult patients I went on to work with later, Matthew never tried to break those boundaries. I knew why. He felt protected by them, which he revealed when he told me he felt he had to treat me *like a brick wall.* This is what I took from my first experience of psychodynamic psychotherapy. The therapeutic relationship was not just an adjunct to therapy, not a non-specific factor as some had maintained, not merely to be identified with the treatment alliance or gaining rapport or being nice to patients, but the crucible in which change came about.

But Matthew had not changed. Or if he had, I could not show this in any clear way, not in any major changes he had made to his life. I could only hope the experience of a year's therapy had helped make him realize that he could trust some people to some degree sometimes. A rather limited gain admittedly. I hoped that by telling me about the *horrible things* he had done and were done to him, he had gained some relief from his shame and guilt. But I was acutely aware that Matthew's tendency towards impulsive and often self-destructive acts had not been tempered to any degree. I had achieved little or nothing in that regard. My memory of Matthew is tinged with a sense of regret and of opportunities lost, which in a way seemed apposite given that that was how I believed he felt deep down. He was my first proper psychodynamic psychotherapy case and I had put in a huge effort to help him. I wished I had been able to do more.

***

There was one omission from the Warneford course and that was the requirement to have personal therapy. It was a surprising omission since personal therapy in the form of a training analysis was a *sine qua non* of all psychoanalytic training. No one could train as a psychoanalyst without it and it was regarded by many as the most significant part of the training. The reason, I was to discover later, was financial. Sid Bloch and his team worried that the extra cost would put some people off. They did however encourage us to have personal therapy alongside the training. I resolved to do this, thinking that if the personal relationship is so important, then I could only benefit from the attention that would come from having therapy myself. I consulted Anthony Storr and he recommended a Freudian analyst, Theo Hawkes.[1]

Late spring in Oxford, 1988. I am driving slowly up the Woodstock Road past the almond and cherry trees resplendent in their pink and white blossom. I am going to meet Theo Hawkes for the first time. What I know about him is limited to the fact that he is a Freudian and that he trained as a psychoanalyst later on in life, having been a Church of England vicar for many years. Rather surprisingly,

---

[1] The name is a pseudonym. A few other details have also been changed although my account is accurate, at least as far as I remember it. I have done this for the same reason that I changed aspects of my patients' stories, that is, to preserve confidentiality, which is as important for the therapist as it is for the patient.

I have not attempted to find out anything more about him. This was before one could Google anyone at the touch of a computer keyboard, but even so I could have asked around or gone to the Bodleian and sought out any publications he might have had. But I did not. Perhaps I did not want to know more, wanting him to be the *tabula rasa*, the blank slate, against which I could project my own feelings and desires. Perhaps I am content to take Anthony Storr's recommendation as good enough. All I have done is have a brief phone conversation with Hawkes. My impression was of a friendly, courteous man, perhaps rather old-fashioned and formal. I found this reassuring. But it is curious nevertheless, this state of prelapsarian ignorance on my part.

I am getting near and slow the car down, peering for the house number, recalling Hawkes's advice that I should park my car in one of the side roads where there are usually spaces and walk back. I am ten minutes early and know better than to arrive before my appointed time. So once I have spotted his house, I sit in my car and wait. I am no longer a smoker and so I light an imaginary cigarette, take a deep drag and contemplate what I am letting myself in for. I have worked for over 20 years as a psychotherapist and never had any therapy myself. So it will be a new experience, I think fatuously, as though novelty is enough of a reason. It would be a good experience to be put in the patient role for a change. It should aid empathy and make me more aware of how difficult it can be to be on the receiving end of help. Doctors who become patients have sometimes found it a transformative experience. The neurologist, Oliver Sachs, was so incensed by the awful way he was treated after a severe leg injury that it changed his whole approach to medicine.

The house is a large, semi-detached Edwardian building in red brick set back from the road. I ring the bell and wait. I stare at the front door that has a fine stained-glass panel boasting floral patterns in wine red, dark green, and purple. Suddenly the door swings back and Theo Hawkes greets me, at the same time beckoning me warmly into the house. My first impression is of a vicar, probably because of what I know of his earlier profession and because he is dressed all in black. No dog collar though. That has been discarded. I catch a glimpse of the hallway—dark and slightly gloomy—before being ushered into the room on my right.

"Do sit down."

Hawkes points to an armchair. The chair is comfortable but firm. He sits in a similar chair opposite, a low dark wood table between us. A fine antique bookcase takes up most of one wall, the shelves crammed with books. A large cluttered old desk is in the bay window, a dark leather chair in front of it. There are gilt-framed pictures on the walls. A long couch covered by a neutral, beige throw runs along the wall to my right.

"I'm delighted you want to have analysis. I know about the new course at the Warneford. An excellent idea."

"I hope so."

"Essentially you're looking for the equivalent of a training analysis, aren't you?"

Automatically I agree though I have not thought about this at all. What would a training analysis consist of? Would it be any different from an ordinary analysis? But we move on before I have a chance to ask. We talk about what I know about psychoanalysis and my work as a psychotherapist and academic. Hawkes comes over in an avuncular way, friendly and relaxed. He is slightly portly and has grey thinning hair. My impression of him is of very much an Oxford man or maybe someone who has adopted this as his persona. We talk together more as colleagues rather than putative analyst and patient. I like this about him and it convinces me that I should go ahead though later I am to wonder if that was the best reason to embark on a course of psychoanalysis. We arrange the appointment times. Twice a week is the most I can manage with my work schedule. Hawkes stresses that I should be sure not to let anything else impinge on these times. Without my asking he tells me that he has his holidays at Easter for two weeks, in August for a month and a week at Christmas. I realize that I am being courteously told it would be best for me to do the same. I cannot help feeling this is a little precious, this insistence that the analytic appointments should dictate when I go on holiday. But I do not demur. The session comes to an end. It has gone more easily than I expected. As I leave I cast a quick glance at the couch, aware that next time I shall be lying on it, allowing my mind to wander wherever it will take me. There is something both exciting and disturbing about this prospect.

Should all psychotherapists have personal therapy? There is an argument that therapists need to have worked through their own hang-ups before setting out to help others. But not all therapists follow this line of thinking. Proponents of CBT for example have consistently rejected this view. For one thing, they argue, just as doctors do not need to become heroin addicts or psychotics to understand and treat people with these problems, so psychotherapists do not need to have been patients themselves to become proficient therapists. This is the *plumbers* analogy that I mentioned earlier. With the right bag of CBT tools, patients will be helped whatever psychological problems the therapist may have. Another objection to requiring personal therapy is that, through therapy, trainee therapists expose themselves to powerful figures in the chosen therapeutic school, ones who exercise considerable influence by virtue of their privileged knowledge of and power over the trainee. Personal therapy, rather than being a liberating experience, can become a force for conformity, a way of being indoctrinated into accepting the strictures of a particular school of therapy. The history of 20th century psychoanalysis gives considerable support to this view. Since Freud pioneered the psychoanalytical approach, various splits occurred in the movement. Freud himself threw several people out of his magic circle if they deviated too much from orthodoxy. The greatest split was with Jung, whom Freud had identified as his successor. Jung became interested in cultural and religious aspects of the unconscious and rejected what he saw as the narrow Freudian emphasis on *libido*. Analytical psychology was born. It developed into a rival school with its separate training programme that still exists today. There were other splits. In the UK the most protracted and painful was the development of the Kleinian or *object relations* school, following the influence of Melanie Klein and her work with young children. For many years the Kleinians and Freudians were at loggerheads, disagreeing not just about theory and practice, but also about training. Whom you trained with and, most importantly, who provided your personal therapy, your training analysis, became a major bone of contention. Indoctrination, even if not given that name, was undoubtedly a feature of psychoanalytical training in the 20th century.

To my mind the benefits of personal therapy outweighed the disadvantages. I dismissed the *plumbers* analogy as naïve and simplistic. I knew that there was more to therapy than a toolbox of techniques. So did most CBT therapists if they were being honest.

The personality of the therapist invariably came into play whatever methods were being used and a therapist who is more at ease with himself or herself, one who had worked through personal problems, would surely be a better bet than one who was struggling with them. Indoctrination was a more significant concern. But despite what Theo Hawkes said, I was not undergoing a training analysis. He would not report to a training course or have any influence on how I practised. My therapy would be entirely confidential; whatever went on in the consulting room should remain there. Or so I thought at the time though later I was to have doubts.

From my prone position on the couch I can see cracks in the ceiling. Like a tiny river with a myriad of tributaries. I cannot see Theo Hawkes but I am acutely aware of his presence behind me to my right. He has told me to say whatever is on my mind. This is the typical psychoanalytic injunction and I have discovered immediately it is far from easy to do. It is like someone telling you to relax. You cannot relax to order but somehow you must let go. Something like that is needed now, I tell myself. But the expectant silence makes it difficult. I run phrases through my head. Not what I should be doing. My body is tense, the muscles taut in my shoulders and back. I try to release tension but that too is difficult.

"It's hard at first but you will get used to it." His tone is sympathetic.

"I keep running things through my mind," I say apologetically.

"That's not uncommon."

And then I am off. Like a branch moved in a blocked dam allowing the water to flow through, I find I can talk. Not seeing Hawkes, not being able to gauge his reaction, means that I just continue talking, saying more or less what is on my mind. "More or less" because I know instantly that the notion of complete free association, of speaking without censoring or inhibiting what I am about to say, is a myth. Somewhere there is always a censor holding some things back. Of course psychoanalysts are aware of this and will attend to what is *not* said, to the omissions, the hesitations and the so-called Freudian slips. And I know this first session is bound to be difficult. As I get accustomed to the process I am sure I shall be more willing to talk uninhibitedly. At least I hope so.

It is hard for me now to recall what was said in that first session or indeed in any particular session of the two years I saw Theo

Hawkes. Except the very last, which is indelibly imprinted on my mind. I shall come to that later. Like most psychoanalysts Hawkes said very little. My generalized memory is him is of someone who was sympathetic, courteous, often curious, and given to occasional thoughtful interpretative comments that I would think about and comment on myself. There were no revelatory moments and with the exception of the last session, very little strong emotion. No doubt there were times when I was annoyed or elated by things that happened in my life. I would talk about these. I was on the Warneford psychodynamic training course at the time and I told him about my frustrations, about the difficulty of being a student again, about my colleagues on the course, about my patients, and about my feelings at working psychodynamically. He always listened sympathetically so that for the most part I felt supported. He therefore fulfilled one important function that all therapists need to provide, a neutral, non-judgmental person who is prepared to listen to the tales I wanted to tell. But the last session apart, there were no sparks and had that session not occurred, I would have regarded my first experience of psychoanalysis as a low-key, anodyne affair, surprisingly lacking in, if I may use the word in this context where words can have more than one meaning, penetration.

"I can't come next week, I'm afraid. That means our last session will be on 27th March."

By 27th March I will have been in analysis for just under two years. Hawkes makes no comment.

"I'm at the BPS conference next week." I say this by way of explanation. A couple of months ago I had said that I thought I should stop my analysis. We had agreed the final date.

"Is that okay?"

"Perfectly. We shall have one more meeting on the 27th and that will be our last."

"Good."

I only mean that it is good that we are clear about the ending, but I realize it may sound as though I am relieved to stop. Actually, I am. For the last few months I have not been looking forward to the sessions. I had been attending just once a week since the beginning of the year, no longer the twice-weekly sessions we had begun with. I rarely thought about my analysis between sessions. I had no idea what I might talk about until I was lying on the couch and then it was hard to find anything interesting or useful to say. Not that psychoanalysis requires preparatory thought. After all, the idea was to say whatever was on my mind. The trouble was that there was little on my mind. There were long silences and Hawkes did not seem to feel the need to do more than wait for me to talk. It irked me that he said nothing, but then for some while I had been feeling quite angry with him. I had discovered late on in my analysis that his wife was a psychiatrist in the Warneford's Department of Psychiatry where I was an honorary lecturer. On the couch I often talked about Professor Gelder, the then head of the department, and I had noticed that Hawkes always seemed interested in hearing gossip about him. I had put his interest down to simple human curiosity but when I learned of the connection, I felt he had been pumping me about the psychiatry department. I even wondered whether he was feeding this information back to his wife. Keenly aware that I might be just a touch paranoid, I did not disclose my thoughts to him. Maybe I should do it now, I think, as I lie silent staring at the familiar ceiling. But I know I will not. I am just looking forward to stopping the whole business. I think we have gone on for too long.

The final session at last! I am in a good mood. On the way here I wondered about getting Hawkes a present but I have done nothing about this, which tells me something. I know that usually psycho-analysts do not accept gifts though Hawkes might as it is the last session. I throw myself on the couch and chat freely, talking about the BPS conference I had attended last week, how I had given a talk and how it had been well received. After a while I fall silent. I do not feel impelled to say anything and I do not expect Hawkes to either. But to my surprise he does.

"Since it's the last session, I have a bill to give you at the end." He pauses. I am aware of the bill and wonder why he is mentioning it. "The thing is I have had to charge you for the sessions you missed in the last couple of months, including last week's. You understand, that's how it works."

"Actually, I don't."

I am seething with anger. He has never charged me for missed sessions before. As far as I can recall we have never discussed this. I know some psychotherapists insist on charging for all ses-sions, whether attended or not, even when the patient gives good notice of absence or is unexpectedly ill. But we have never had that arrangement. Abruptly I decide I am going to leave. I sit up, swing my feet on to the floor and sit on the couch. Hawkes veers into view. The expression on his face is a mixture of surprise and dismay.

"I think I should go. You've never charged me for missed sessions before. I don't remember ever discussing this with you."

"John, please. We seem to have got off on the wrong foot. I'll withdraw the bill and charge you just for the sessions you have had. It's my mistake. I'm truly sorry."

I hesitate. The impulse to leave is strong. I am aware of how childish this all is. And it is not the way to end almost two years of psychoanalysis. So eventually I agree to stay and lie back on the couch. We spend the remainder of the time talking in that artificial way that people do after a sudden eruption of emotion, each of us on our best behaviour, keen not to disturb the fragile peace. When it is over and I am about to leave, I thank him for all the work he has done for me. I say how helpful it has been and how grateful I am. Words, words, words. I do not feel anything of the sort. I am still angry with Theo Hawkes about trying to charge me for missed sessions. Is that the way to treat me after all this time we have had together?

In the week following the session a revised bill from Hawkes arrives together with a nicely written letter of apology. I feel somewhat mollified. In Blackwell's I buy Phyllis Grosskurth's *Melanie Klein. Her World and Her Work*, a recently published hardback book. Its cost is more or less the extra amount that Hawkes had wanted to charge me. I send the book off to him with a brief note and a cheque for the final bill. I receive a courteous letter back, thanking me for the present and wishing me well. That is it. Two years of psychoanalysis end with a sudden eruption of anger followed by a polite correspondence as though nothing untoward had happened. In the years that followed I would see Hawkes at occasional meetings and conferences. He was always amiable and friendly. He never referred to that last session or the therapy at all. Nor did I. Not surprising since it would not be *comme il faut* to talk about my analysis outside the consulting room. Yet it must have been clear to both of us that there was unfinished business, that right at the end the analysis had touched on something important, which, for whatever reason, neither of us had been willing or able to confront. What was going on?

There can be many reasons to embark on personal therapy. The commonest is to get help resolving a personal problem. I had not sought therapy for that reason, at least not consciously. Hawkes had described it as the equivalent of a training analysis, but on reflection that was misleading. A training analysis is undertaken so that the trainee can become aware of his or her neuroses, work through them using the psychoanalytic method and as a result become a better, more self-aware analyst. I was not training to be an analyst. I was curious about psychodynamic psychotherapy and wanted to see if I could learn something from that approach. This is an altogether more rational attitude. I wanted simply to experience what it would be like to be a client. But was that disingenuous? How could I truly experience that without the emotional turmoil that goes with the uncovering of personal problems? Otherwise I would be merely playing the part like an actor takes on a role. I did not *think* I was playing at being a patient but I did not need to think that to avoid getting too involved. My regular sessions on the couch had a useful function. I could talk about myself, recount the things that were going on in my life, while Hawkes listened. Therapy provided an outlet. I sought and got support from the sympathetic and always courteous Hawkes. I was initially impressed by the way he treated me as a colleague, an equal. It was what made me decide to go ahead with the analysis. On reflection, I realize that might have been a defence. It could be that unconsciously I wanted to ensure that our relationship did not lead to the sort of infantile regression that occurs in most psychoanalysis. I wanted to retain my adult state throughout. Some people might argue therefore that this was not really personal therapy at all. But I disagree. It was a form of personal therapy, one based on getting support and of having someone to tell one's story to, which are important in all therapies in my view. But as to its being *psychoanalysis*, it lacked the most significant feature of that way of working, the analysis itself.

What of the sudden eruption of anger in the last session? I thought about this in the immediate aftermath of the ending. Why was I so angry with Hawkes for his mistake, as I saw it, in attempting to charge me for the few missed sessions? The first thought I had was of my father who had been dead for nearly ten years. I had not been close to him though I had always wanted to be. Why should I have thought of him? My father had usually been very generous, enjoying taking the family out to expensive restaurants or taking us on swish holidays. Then a memory surfaced suddenly. It was the time my brother, who was living in Los Angeles, got married for the first time. His wife, Shirley, was a young black woman with three very young children and an ex-husband who was in jail. Quite a responsibility for him to take on. But that is another story. My parents, myself and my first wife flew out for the wedding. We travelled first class as my father was wont to do. I had understood that he would pay our flights too, a not inconsiderable amount of money. But after we got back, he had asked me for the cost of the flights. It irked me that he had unexpectedly wanted payment. It seemed my father cared more for the money than me. In therapy I had expected Theo Hawkes genuinely to care for me, but his action told me that he was only in it for the money. I had been let down just as my father had let me down. The moment I had the thought, my feeling of anger lessened. Rationally, I knew that Hawkes's income came from his psychoanalytic work. And I knew too that he could still be genuinely interested in me, or any other patient, while needing to be paid for his work. My intense emotional reaction was a sign of negative transference. The intensity of my feelings, my childish desire to leave, were clues to exactly the sort of unconscious process that psychoanalysis is all about.

But why had any of this not come out in the analysis? At first I thought it was my fault. I had not mentioned my increasing dissatisfaction with the analysis and my desire to end it all. Even at the very end I uttered false words of praise and gratitude instead of telling the truth. Yet should Hawkes not have picked up on my disaffection, on the significance of the missed sessions, on my desultory treatment of the therapy in the last few weeks? Was that not what a good psychoanalyst would have done? The more I thought about it, the stranger his behaviour in the last session seemed. Why did he suddenly charge for missed sessions when he had never done that before? And why did he immediately withdraw the bill if he had thought it was justified? Even his apology to me, however well-meant, hardly seemed good therapeutic practice for it immediately brought the matter to a close, not using the space for us to discuss what had happened. Had he not recognized the transferential elements or perhaps he had not wanted to face them? Had Theo Hawkes a problem dealing with anger? I shall never know if Hawkes was angry with me and unable to work with his feeling analytically, or had a problem in responding to others who were angry with him as I had been.

In his semi-autobiographical book, *Learning from Life*, the psycho-analyst, Patrick Casement, writes how he had to learn not to be too nice to his patients. Giving reassurance or providing support has a useful function but psychoanalysis needs to do more than this.

"I, like many others," he writes, "have wanted to be liked. It so happened that I had not been helped to get beyond this by my first therapist, who seemed to have the same problem. It was only when I got into analysis, with an analyst who did not have this problem, that I began to find my way beyond this."

Perhaps this is what happened between Theo Hawkes and me. We were both too nice to each other because neither of us wanted to risk showing our negative side. When anger erupted, it was perhaps no mistake that it occurred in the final session as that way it could safely be left behind and treated in that very English way through a polite and courteous exchange of letters.

SECTION IV

SO IT GOES

CHAPTER NINETEEN

Working under time pressure

For all my professional life, I had been a scientist. The letters after my name, MSc and PhD, attested to my credentials as such. But ever since 1964, when I ventured to write my first scientific essay on Tinbergen's *A Study of Instinct*, I had never felt like one. In the 20 years since I graduated I had adopted the *persona* of the scientist without being fully committed to it. I published articles in scientific journals. I spoke the language of hypothesis testing and experimental design. I was familiar with all the major statistical tests. I carried out both between-groups and single-case research studies. I had presented my work at scientific conferences. But in the consulting room, the place I felt most at home, the scientist persona slipped and in its place there was a person, a human being, eager to understand and to use whatever skills I had to help the patients out of the impasse they found themselves in.

It was a precept of both behaviour therapy and cognitive therapy that the therapist should be a scientist at all times, even in the consulting room. An idea about what was wrong with a patient was a hypothesis and therapy was a way of testing it experimentally. An agoraphobic is presumed to be anxious about leaving her home, a place of safety. The anxiety is never properly tested as the patient refuses to go out. If this hypothesis is correct, then taking the patient out should lead to an initial increase in anxiety and a subsequent decrease, which is what often happens. A depressed man is hypothesized to have irrational, distorted, and negative thinking that underpins his depressed mood. Using a thought record sheet, this hypothesis can be tested and the results confirm or disconfirm it. Where such thoughts exist, as they do in many depressed people, then changing the thinking should result in changing the mood. Again this often happens. This, it is argued by CBT therapists, is science in operation. But the more I thought about this, the less I was convinced. Suppose an agoraphobic patient is taken outside in a behavioural programme but despite repeated treatments, her anxiety fails to decrease. Does this once and for all disconfirm the hypothesis that exposure treatments will lead to anxiety reduction? No. The therapist looks for reasons. Perhaps the patient has developed an internal ritual, a phrase or mantra that enables her to switch off from the anxiety thereby not allowing the feelings to be properly processed. Or, like Mrs. Hewittson from the Dog Kennel Hill estate, she gains too much from her agoraphobic way of life to give it up. Or there is another factor in her anxiety that has thus far remained undetected, a global feeling of insecurity perhaps stemming from a highly anxious childhood that remains powerful whether or not she is away from home. There are too many variables in psychotherapy for it to be anything like a scientific experiment.

Human beings are complex and psychotherapy is equally so. Unlike in medicine where two or three hundred years of scientific knowledge have turned doctoring from quackery and mysticism into something far more respectable, something open to test and scrutiny, psychological knowledge remains uncertain, primitive, highly contentious, and constantly subject to the whims and fancies of theorists and pedagogues. The aspiration to have a scientific basis to psychotherapy is commendable. But the reality is that this cannot happen until psychology itself grows up scientifically and even then, the jump from knowledge to practice is a huge leap. I came to this conclusion during the training course although it had been germinating in my mind for years. I wrote one of my course essays on the topic, taking pride in the way I marshalled my arguments and drew upon my extensive knowledge of psychotherapy research.

To my chagrin the essay drew a low mark with the assessors' critical comments suggesting that my thesis had neither been fully understood nor particularly welcomed. My initial anger at this rebuff gave way to wry rationalization. *A prophet is without honour in his own country*, I opined loftily. Admittedly, I was hardly a prophet and my essay had an extremely limited audience (two assessors). Yet science has become such a prestigious and powerful influence that anything that seems to challenge that influence tends to be resisted. Psychoanalysts felt particularly vulnerable since critics had taken them to task because their methods failed to meet scientific standards. This led to a few bold attempts to show that key psychoanalytic theories could be substantiated empirically. I saw this as a retrograde step, an attempt to put a scientific veneer on what was not a scientific enterprise at all. I understood the pressures that led to this, in particular the way medicine has had to demonstrate that its procedures and treatments, many of which are costly and some potentially dangerous, were of proven worth. After all, we customers, as we are increasingly known, want to know that what the doctor recommends actually works and that we shall get better and without too much pain and risk. The problem with applying this medical model to psychoanalysis was that there was no objective sense of what "getting better" was. The very essence of psychoanalysis, the idea of a cunning, powerful, and distorting unconscious, undermines the notion of symptomatic or behavioural change as the main criterion of improvement. Nor were the methods capable of being laid down objectively in a treatment manual as had been attempted in other therapies, notably CBT.

Coming late as I did to psychoanalysis I saw the approach as refreshingly free from the constraints that other psychological therapies laboured under. Unfortunately, the zeitgeist had changed. Psychoanalysis was on the defensive. Because of its very virtues, the focus on exploration, uncertainty, meaning, on strong emotional undercurrents, on the flexibility and creativity of the therapist, on the tenuous and often fragile therapeutic relationship, it could no longer be justified in the competitive market of the modern health service. What was needed were short, sharp treatments with measurable goals and identikit methods. Like cognitive therapy. I had arrived at psychoanalysis in the twilight of its years. How much longer could this complex and unfashionable therapy survive? But,

I reasoned to myself, perhaps there was some way of synthesizing the subjectivity of psychoanalysis, its recognition of the part played by the therapeutic relationship and unconscious processes, into a more practical, short-term and therefore more applicable therapy, one the NHS could still keep under its increasingly crowded umbrella.

There is a form of psychodynamic therapy that seeks to do just this, known as brief or time-limited psychodynamic psychotherapy, in which all the work is done within clearly defined time limits, sometimes as short as three months. Many psychoanalysts, however, rejected this compromise, arguing that the essence of analysis is the open-ended nature of the experience; that what was needed above all was for both the patient and the analyst to feel free of any constraints. But the reality is that most psychotherapy is short-term (under six months), even when it begins with no specified end point. Moreover, except for a few people, long-term, three- or four-times-a-week therapy is completely impracticable. During my training I saw a patient, whom I shall call Laura, for a strictly controlled 12-session course of psychodynamic therapy. My experience with Laura showed me that it was possible to use psychodynamic methods within an allotted time period and that there were some advantages in having the rigour of a finite time to work in.

"I'm sorry I'm late," Laura says hurrying into the room. "Just so difficult to get away." My first impression is of someone who is always rushing from place to place.

"Why don't you have a seat?"

Laura looks startled as though I have surprised her by my suggestion. She sits, places the black briefcase she is carrying on her lap, then changes her mind and puts it on the floor. She rummages through it and takes out a handful of tissues. She looks up at me, smiles in a slightly self-deprecating way as though to say that she knows she's going to be upset and wants to be prepared for that eventuality. Laura is 38. She is married with three children, the oldest, Suzanne, being 11 years old. She is a physiotherapist. I know this from the assessment that was carried out in the Department of Psychotherapy. I also know that her mother died three years ago after a protracted illness and that Laura is suffering from a prolonged grief reaction experiencing intense feelings of guilt, sadness, anger, and self-blame.

Laura's grey-green eyes stare into mine and then look away. I take a note of her appearance. A smart black suit. Light brown straight hair, cut short so it frames her face. An air of business-like purpose in her appearance. I am about to make my opening remarks when Laura speaks.

"I'm a bit distracted. I found a lump on my breast. My doctor's booked me in for a scan next week."

I am startled by this portent of a possibly serious illness. I say nothing, wondering what to make of it.

"I don't know if I should be here at all. If this is the right time. For psychotherapy, I mean." She breaks off suddenly.

"Why don't we spend the session talking about that and other things? We have 50 minutes. Why don't you tell me what brings you here?"

A sigh. "Dr. Stainer asked me that too. You know, I can't remember anything we talked about. Isn't that strange?"

I am acutely conscious of Laura's ambivalence. Hard not to be. She arrived late and feels under pressure. She has questioned whether she should be here at all. She has told me about a lump on her breast, something tangible and potentially life threatening, putting psychotherapy in the shade. Yet for all that, I feel drawn to her. Her ambivalence sets up a sense of expectation in me, a desire to find out more, to help her. In fits and starts Laura tells me about her worries which mostly centre on Suzanne, who is having a difficult time at her new school. Her husband, Chris, has applied for promotion at his work, but he does not know whether he will get it. He is snappy and on edge at home. And Laura's work is hectic, she says. There's never any time. She has taken on the management of the physiotherapy practice, temporarily, as their manager is off sick. She tells me she has a vital contract to negotiate with a large company.

"Not much time for yourself with all these demands on you."

"Absolutely not. Which is why I don't know if I should get into psychotherapy now."

"Your mother's death and the awful grief you're feeling were what you talked to Dr. Stainer about. You haven't mentioned that here."

Laura says nothing. Then eventually she says, "I try not to think about it."

Because it's upsetting, I want to say. But I hold back. Let Laura tell me herself.

Another huge sigh. A long silence. A struggle is going on in her mind.

"Mum was ill. I didn't realize how serious it was. Well, I *did*, but I was so busy. We were moving house. I had started a new job. Chris was taking accountancy exams. So much stuff to do."

She stops. I wait.

"She'd been ill before. Many times ... I didn't think ... I was supposed to go to see her. I kept postponing it ... On the day she died, I was late ... Too late."

Suddenly, she is sobbing. She is saying something but I cannot hear what over the sobs. Gradually, she calms down, apologizes, wipes her face with the tissues, looks around for a wastepaper basket and, not finding one, stuffs the wad back in her briefcase. I sit quietly, waiting for her to continue. Slowly, punctuated with tears, she tells me the details of that traumatic day when her mother died. How she received a message on her answering machine that her mother had taken a turn for the worse. This had happened before and because she had several clients booked in, she did not leave until the late afternoon. Traffic was heavy and it took longer than she expected. On arrival at the hospital a nurse took her aside and told her that her mother had died an hour before. Laura was distraught. She recalled getting very angry with the nurses for their failure to make it clear that her mother was dying. But mostly, she felt guilty at not having been there for her mother at the time of death. She could have cancelled her clients and left earlier. She had let her mother down.

When the session ends, I raise the subject of psychotherapy. I say to Laura that her distress tells me that there is still unfinished business and that I think that psychotherapy could help her with this. What does she think? She agrees. I go on to say that I think that the therapy should focus on her relationship with her mother and we should use the time to understand why her grief and anger have persisted for so long. Was she prepared to do this? Again she agrees. Getting out our diaries we arrange 11 weekly sessions, booking each date into our diaries like business appointments. I say firmly that there will be no further sessions after that. The therapy would end at that point come what may. It feels strange to be so rigid about dates and especially the fixed ending, but it is what time-limited psychotherapy is about. Afterwards, I wonder if the time limit suits her. It means that psychotherapy is fitted neatly into her busy life and knowing it will not go on indefinitely could be a reassurance.

I had seen people with prolonged grief reactions before. Using CBT I had treated the emotions of grief and distress in a similar way to anxiety. I had got the patients to keep records of their feelings, plotting these in relation to their behaviour and the thoughts spinning through their minds. Together we worked out the key determinants of their grief, both external and internal. We went on to search for more adaptive and less destructive ways of mourning. Negative thoughts, which are often both highly prevalent and extreme in grief, were challenged, and guilt and self-blame reduced. In many cases the therapy had been successful. But this time I was not going to offer practical help. The psychodynamic approach had a different aim. We would work together and seek to understand why Laura's grief had persisted. We would try to find out if there were other emotions and traumas bound up with it. Above all, we would look for meaning. If that were successful, then Laura's grief should begin to lessen as she came to understand herself better.

Some people might think it reprehensible that I did not seek to get rid of Laura's intense, debilitating grief using CBT methods. After all, that was the problem. That was why she was seeking help. But a direct attack on her grief would deny Laura the opportunity to discover why she was stuck in this prolonged and harrowing bereavement reaction. Even if her grief could be assuaged, something would be lost in doing that. These two models—CBT and psychodynamic therapy—differ in their understanding of human emotion. On the one hand, grief, like anxiety and depression, is seen as a negative state of mind especially when intense and prolonged. Everything should be done to reduce its control and undermine its power. On the other hand, intense emotions contain within them a message about something important to the person suffering which, if properly understood, can be a revelation. It is important to take stock and seek to understand the reasons why someone should be so distressed, and not dismiss the feelings. CBT has the virtue of directness and power. Psychodynamic psychotherapy offers a sanctum, a place of safety, and the undivided attention of another, in the course of which a greater understanding can arise.

In truth, the difference between these two therapies is not as clear cut as it might first seem. In CBT the therapist draws up a formulation and in so doing explores the causes of the grief. This can be beneficial in itself, especially if the patient is given the opportunity to talk and the therapist sits back and listens. In short-term psychodynamic psychotherapy, the time pressure forces the therapist to take a more active role, seeking to get to underlying meaning quickly so that the patient may experience the benefit of greater understanding.

***

In the first few sessions Laura talked a great deal about her mother. I sat back and listened. I heard how ill and unhappy she had been throughout Laura's life. Her mother's ill health hung over the family like a dark cloud. There was a constant fear of her breaking down and even when well she could behave erratically, disappearing for several days without warning or shutting herself in her bedroom, the curtains drawn. As the oldest child, Laura was the mainstay of the family. Her father was often away on business. There was an aunt, her father's sister, but she was cold and harshly critical of Laura's mother. In the picture of family life that Laura sketched for me, I saw that she was, in one way, central, taking the role that her mother had not been able to take, the organizer of the family, and in another, peripheral because her own emotional needs were neglected. And when she talked about her life now, about her husband and her children, a similar picture emerged. Laura rushed from task to task, busy at work and even busier at home. There was no time for her to stop and attend to her own needs. As an adult she repeated what she had learned to do as a child, putting others first.

Time was a feature of our sessions. Laura would regularly complain that there was never enough time to do everything she needed to do, having to juggle the demands of work and home life. While there was a reality to this, a reality that many working mothers constantly experience, it was also a defence. By being busy, she could defend against being overwhelmed by the intense feelings of pain and loss that were straining to be expressed following her mother's death. And while Laura attended every session, she was often late, always with a reason to hand. The traffic was heavy. A client overran.

There was a meeting that went on too long. An urgent phone call to make. It was rarely more than a few minutes, but it was a sign of her ambivalence about being here at all. When I pointed it out, Laura got huffy and attacked the therapy as an intrusion on her life. She dreaded it, she said, more even than a visit to the dentist, capturing how painful it felt to her and how difficult it was (like pulling teeth).

"I had the most wonderful time in Scotland," Laura says excitedly.

We are just over halfway through our allotted sessions. She had been away on holiday with her family and unusually, for the final weekend she had stayed on her own in a religious retreat while Chris looked after the children.

"I talked for ages and ages to Giovanni. He's Italian, a brother at the monastery. He was so good at listening. I loved his deep voice and the way he put things. I haven't felt so good for years."

What do I make of this? I have a rival and someone who is *good at listening* (unlike me?), someone exotic and deep, vocally if not in anything else. He even has my name, the Italian version! I cannot help feeling that Brother Giovanni has stamped his size 14 boots onto my territory. I am not too pleased with him.

"I wish I could put him in a cupboard and take him out whenever I need him!"

Laura's comment dispels all my feelings of petulant annoyance. There is something so delightfully childish about it that it makes me smile. As Laura talks on about Giovanni, I take the opportunity to think. What Giovanni offered Laura was obvious at one level. Unconditional acceptance, a man who listened and talked to her, in the way that, she feels, nobody has ever done. A fantasy figure too in his monk's robes, foreign name and his different way of life. What was I to make of her desire to put him in a cupboard? The cupboard points to containment. Laura can keep him there and take him out when she needs him, thereby retaining control, something that she struggles with. It is also a metaphor for *internalization*, the psychoanalytic process whereby real figures become *internal objects*. Could she be saying, unconsciously, that she wants to internalize me (John/Giovanni)? The goal of psychoanalysis is, according to some theorists, to internalize the analyst as a way of retaining what has been learned after analysis has ended. Another possible meaning is she would have liked a father like Giovanni (who is close to being a "father" after all), someone who was there for her rather than the absent father she had?

"I understand how good it was for you to be really listened to, something that I hope goes on here too. You never had that from your mother or your father and I think you yearn for it. For you don't get that at home either, do you?"

I am about to say something more, something clever about her desperate need to keep her feelings contained as in a cupboard, but Laura's already speaking.

"On holiday we went to a beach. I got a picnic together, all the food the kids really liked, even 'bad stuff' like crisps and chocolate, and beer for Chris, and lots of games, umbrellas in case it rained, sun lotion in case it got too sunny, and a big rug so we could all spread out. Everybody had a great time. Chris was relaxed for once. He gave me a hug and said 'What would we do without you?' Then he went off to play with Suzanne. I watched them playing. I should have been happy but instead I felt terribly sad. Nobody cares about me, I thought. It wasn't true though. They care very much. But I felt really lonely, John. Isn't that awful?"

Tears are in her eyes. Intense sadness pervades the room. I feel a lump in my throat as I experience Laura's sense of loss as though it were mine too. I sense it is the voice of a small child speaking, the abandonment she felt as a child coming powerfully through to me now. I say this to her.

"But what can I do?" she pleads. "How do I manage these feelings?" The adult voice has returned.

"It's not so much about managing them, Laura, but recognizing them. Acknowledging them as part of you, how you really feel. You know, I keep thinking about your mother, and how she died, and how you got there late and how that's caused you so much pain. I'm thinking that it was also the other way round. Your mother got there too late for you. Throughout your life she could never give you the mothering you needed. Right to the end."

The words have sprung from my lips without conscious thought or preparation.

"I was so angry with the nurses, the hospital," Laura goes on. "I thought they'd let her die and not told me. But I think I was really angry with Mum. I didn't want to visit her. I couldn't bear it. I put it off. I know I did. That's why I feel so guilty."

"You did what you felt. All your life you'd looked after your mother but she didn't properly look after you. Hard for anyone not to feel ambivalent about visiting her."

"But I *should* have been there. I let her down."

"And she let you down."

I am increasingly uncertain where this is leading. I am trying to bolster Laura up. But I sense I have taken the wrong tack in doing this. There is a part of her that *wants* to punish herself. Her failure to be there at her mother's death epitomizes the bad girl, the one who felt angry and neglected by her mother. Yet because of her mother's illness Laura could not ever express or acknowledge it. The psycho-analyst and paediatrician, Donald Winnicott, wrote about children developing a *false self* in response to abuse or neglect. The self is that of a compliant and apparently capable, good child. All negative feelings are suppressed until the child loses all contact with how she truly feels, the *true self* as he calls it. Anger is unacceptable to the *false self* and so it is driven into the unconscious. When Laura experienced anger at her mother, she repressed it, turning it against herself. She was the bad person, the one at fault. This is an intellectual insight. Emotionally, I am experiencing a powerful closeness to Laura right now as she struggles with her mixed feelings. But, as she continues to insist upon her guilt and responsibility, I also feel a stirring of impatience with her. Could this be a projection? Laura placing the anger she cannot express into me? If I act on it, it would confirm her as the guilty party. I decide to backtrack.

"It's very hard for you," I say quietly. "Hard to lose your mother anyway. On top of that, you've lost any chance of reparation, for the two of you to be emotionally close as you always hoped would happen but never did."

Laura begins to cry, not huge sobs but a steady outpouring of misery. I sense this is true feeling, uncontaminated by desperate, conflicted thought. I say nothing further. At the end of the session, there is a quiet between us. I am hopeful that something has happened, that Laura will begin to move on now in her grief.

In the next session Laura told me she did not want to talk about the painful feelings of the previous week. In fact, she could not really remember them. It was all rather fuzzy, she said. I was not totally surprised at the way her defences had been reactivated though I felt a keen disappointment. My fantasy was that Laura would begin to face her true feelings, that together we would help her get through her prolonged grief and she would be grateful to me for my excellent support and help. The wonderful Brother Giovanni would have been relegated to a bit part. I pointed out how her failure to recall her feelings was a defence, but although Laura could see this intellectually, there was no emotion in her response. The session passed in a desultory fashion. I wondered what had gone wrong. Perhaps nothing had. Laura's coping strategies were just too powerful to be shaken by one emotional experience. But I brooded on what felt like a failure.

"I had this strange dream. I don't know if I should tell you about it."

We are near the end of the final session. In the past few weeks Laura has been feeling better, less troubled by feelings of grief and less depressed. She had revisited the hospital in which her mother died and talked to the nurses. She had found it reassuring to hear that her mother had not been in pain and that her last moments had been peaceful. I thought she was seeing her mother as she had really been, not the fantasy figure she had created, someone desperately waiting for her daughter to appear so that she could tell her how much she really loved her.

"I was driving my car. It was an alien landscape like you see in sci-fi films, derelict buildings, deserted streets. A futuristic time. I didn't know what I was doing there or where I was going. There was an old man sitting on his own outside a block of flats. All alone. I felt terribly sad. But I didn't stop. I just drove on. That's it."

She stops and looks at me brightly, waiting for me to comment. The dream makes me think of Laura's father and her sadness at not ever getting close to him. But it also feels like it represents her own loneliness as though the old man is part of herself, the part she has to leave behind as she drives on into the future.

"The loneliness seems important," I say, trying to be noncommittal. "It's what you feel a lot of the time."

"Yes. But I feel less lonely now. I've talked to Chris. He says that I blame myself too much, that I did a lot for my mother. I think that's true."

I swallow my pride at being usurped again. In one way or another I had been saying this all along to Laura but she has heard it only when Chris has said it.

"And you drive on. In the dream I mean."

She looks uncertain for a moment. "Oh, you mean I can move on now."

"Can you?"

She nods her head. "I think I can." She looks at me again, this time as though she is seeing me for the first time. "Odd how I have spent all this time talking about myself to a stranger. I never thought I'd do that. I know nothing about you, John. But maybe that helped me to open up."

"It might well have done. And how do you feel now?"

"Sad that it has come to an end. In some ways it feels like we've just started."

"I'm sad too, but pleased that you've at last begun to move on."

We sit for a moment in silence and then Laura leaves. It is a fitting way to end. Despite the ups and downs I sense that something real has happened though it would be hard to describe exactly what. But perhaps that is how it should be. Not everything needs to be spelled out.

CHAPTER TWENTY

Thinking and feeling

A t the end of 1989 I qualified as a psychodynamic psycho-therapist. Was this going to be the final chapter of my long journey in psychotherapy? Could I now put aside my doubts and hesitancies and settle down to a way of working that I could fully identify with? And what did being a psychody-namic psychotherapist mean in practice? I was not a psychoanalyst. To achieve this rarefied title I would have had to train for several years at one of the major analytic schools and undergo a training analysis that lasted at least three years. What was the difference? I had read widely in psychoanalysis. I had had almost two years of analysis with Theo Hawkes. I was becoming adept at attending to the swirling undercurrents of the unconscious as it expressed itself in the therapeutic relationship. I had learned the value of saying less, sometimes saying nothing at all, and of listening carefully to the meanings hidden in the patient's narrative. I was beginning to accept that psychotherapy was at heart a delicate personal relation-ship. A gossamer thread. It was not always possible, and indeed not always desirable, to know in advance what I was going to say or do. This was a far cry from my behaviour therapy days when I bossed my patients around and played it by the Book of Science. Or from cognitive therapy with its firm belief in rationality and the value of changing people's thinking, like an electrical charge, from negative to positive. Psychoanalysis, with its own rituals and observances, with its lengthy and costly induction and training, with its esoteric language and ideas, with its demand for commitment to many years of therapy, felt to me like another way of distancing the therapist from the patient, making him or her seem like a superior being, a god-like figure who *knows the truth*. The analytic method, the pure gold of psychoanalysis, meant that the analyst and patient were closely intertwined, meeting three or four times a week, as the weeks, months, and years pass. There was no doubt this elevated the analyst into a position of enormous significance in the patient's life. I had heard of patients who had moved house to follow their analyst. The doctrinal aspects of psychoanalysis, the sense that there was a right way to go about Freud's work just as there is with God's work if you are religious, did not appeal to me. And as in religion, there were splits and divisions so that there was not just *the* right way, but several right ways to do things depending on whether you were a Freudian, Kleinian, Jungian, Adlerian, Sullivanian etc., Orthodoxy was something I had always baulked at. I still did.

Being a qualified psychodynamic psychotherapist meant I could incorporate psychoanalytic ideas into the way I worked. But exactly what had I learned? What was I doing that was different from two years before? Laura's case was instructive. Laura had presented with a clear problem, unresolved grief about her mother's death. We had agreed to work on that. Yet I did not assume I knew why her grief persisted or that I could tell her what was the best thing to do to rid herself of it. From the start my strategy was to try to make sense of what was happening and to work with Laura to do the same. This was a *search for meaning* above everything else. Once the problem was understood, or at least partially understood for all understanding is only ever partial, Laura could move on. She could leave her loneliness behind and drive on into the future as her dream had presaged. The focus of therapy was not so much on solving problems, on getting the patient better, but on sharing an understanding of what was happening. Was this enough? After all, indirectly I was being paid to make Laura better and when I went on to work in private practice, I entered into a contract to do that in one way or another. No, the search for meaning, I decided, was not enough in itself. There had to be a sense of movement, of change. Psychoanalysis, in its pure form, saw these two aspects coalescing in the intense and lengthy relationship that allowed meaning to emerge slowly and change to occur gradually. But only the most dedicated, or perhaps the most dependent, person would tolerate years and years of therapy in order to change. Later, when I went into private practice, I came to understand that some people entered therapy not to change but to stay themselves.

What I valued most about the psychodynamic approach was having the time to listen. This was true even for the time-limited psychotherapy I did with Laura. I had never properly listened to patients before or at least not in that way. I had wanted information, which is very different. The information was often about what form the person's anxiety or depression took (the so-called *symptoms*) and what factors provoked and maintained it (*antecedents, beliefs, consequents*). It might also include aspects of the person's personality, family history, and early experience so that I could construct a formulation, a way of conceptualizing the problem in CBT terms with clear implications for therapy. My listening was designed to elicit the information I had already anticipated finding. It was as though I put on a set of filters such as opticians use in eye tests in order to bring some things clearly into focus, leaving the rest of the visual field blurred. I did not have an open mind. I did not sit back and wait. I jumped in. I thought back to people I had treated. What difference would it have made had I sat back and waited? Take Angie, for example, with her intense anxiety about harming her children. If I had said something like, *why don't we just talk for a while, see what comes out of it,* would the therapy have turned out very differently? An impossible question of course. But if for the moment I ran with it, what might I have learned? She might have told me how unhappy she was, that she felt trapped as a young mother and dependent wife when she wanted something more, something for herself. She might have talked about her childhood and perhaps recalled an upbringing in which she had felt her mother had neglected her or her father terrified her, or where the birth of a younger sister was experienced as an intrusion. There might have been a long suppressed memory of harming her sister that her own children's sibling rivalry had stirred up. A deeply buried, unconscious memory. All this was pure speculation. I did not know how Angie's parents had treated her.

I did not even know if she had a younger sister. I did not know if she felt trapped as a young mother. But that was the point. I did not know because I had not bothered to find out.

But, I argued with myself, my treatment of Angie had been a success. I had helped her get over her anxiety. She had got better. Moreover, she had *wanted* to get rid of her frightening anxiety. Nowhere did she say she wanted to talk to someone or explore what her fear was about. But then I had not offered her that option. If I had, might she not have taken it? I would never know. I did not want to impose my beliefs on my patients. I did not want to insist that they talked about what their problems might mean, putting the idea of immediate symptomatic relief on the back-burner. But on the other hand, if I did not give my patients the opportunity to talk, and me to listen, might I not miss crucial clues to the wider meaning of their problems? Peter, my very first therapy patient, came to mind. He had presented with a specific problem, not being able to use public toilets, and I had taken that problem at face value. He went through a behavioural treatment, systematic desensitization, and even if that made very little impact on his problem, it did show that I treated the problem and him seriously. In the course of therapy, and in the naïve way I chatted to him as just another guy, someone like me, we established a good relationship. Peter talked. I listened. He came to a decision about his life and took a chance: he left his studies and went to India. I now think his anxiety about using public loos stood for a wider anxiety about being himself and escaping the restrictive influence of his upbringing. Was that not the way forward, I thought with some excitement? I would continue to treat the problems the patient presented and at the same time listen for clues to the wider meaning, bringing that into therapy if and when it seemed appropriate. It was not an either-or issue. If I could integrate psychodynamic and cognitive-behavioural methods, then perhaps I would have the best of both worlds. It was not to be as simple as that, as I was to discover. Nor was I the first person to set a course to this particular reading. There were already integrationist therapies of various sorts, some of which explicitly linked psychodynamic and cognitive approaches. But it felt right and as I was increasingly realizing, what feels right can be as important as anything science could demonstrate.

CHAPTER TWENTY ONE

"I've been told you're an expert in anxiety management"

The pretty young girl sitting in the armchair opposite me radiates bonhomie and good health. To say this is unusual in a prospective psychotherapy patient is a massive understatement. Most clients are intensely nervous when they first arrive and many show the signs of distress and tension that brought them here. But Cordelia looks calm and poised. *She is in the bloom of youth.* The phrase jumps into my mind. Maybe it is the floral dress she is wearing—large red flowers on a bright canary yellow background—that made me think of blooming. Or that she seems very young, even younger than her 23 years. And she is strikingly beautiful, her lush black hair framing a perfectly formed oval face with a soft, creamy complexion that most women would die for. Her dark brown eyes, so dark they are almost black, sparkle as they search mine out. In her look there is a mixture of curiosity and something else. Playfulness is the nearest I can get to it.

"Where would you like to begin?"

"The panic attack. Three months ago I panicked in an exam. It was so bad I had to leave. The invigilator wanted to stop me but I was desperate for the loo."

She looks at me and grimaces. "Stupid really."

There is a pause. A frown passes over her face. She runs her hand through her hair. A tiny, barely perceptible sigh.

"The first thing I noticed was my hand was trembling. I couldn't hold the pen. Then I felt hot. Like a hot flush, I suppose, though I'm a bit young for that." She laughs gaily. "Then I thought 'I can't breathe!' and that made me really panic. And on top of that I suddenly had to go for a pee."

"And you left?"

"Yes. There was about an hour to go but after I'd gone to the loo, I went back to my room. I just lay down on the bed and tried to relax. I thought I'd flunked the exam but actually I got 65%, would you believe? So it was okay in the end."

Again I wait for Cordelia to go on. This time she is silent. It seems only a minor problem but, over the phone when she had made the appointment, she had implied that the problem was getting worse.

"And since then?"

"Now I think it's going to happen again. Not just in exams but in classes and seminars. Even when I'm out with friends. It's ridiculous."

Cordelia tells me she has started the second year of a master's course. She doesn't know what she's going to do after that. She also says that she's never experienced anything like this before. She's worried it will become a habit. She anticipates becoming anxious and then of course does. It is a pattern I am very familiar with.

"So what do you think is going on?"

"I don't know. Aren't you supposed to tell me?"

I smile at this disarmingly direct riposte. Cordelia smiles back.

"Perhaps when I know a bit more," I say. "But I want to know what you make of it."

"Okay," she says, with sudden decision. "It's an anxiety attack. I looked up the symptoms on the internet. Also my friend, Carlos, says it's classic anxiety. He's worked in a hostel for the mentally ill. He says he's seen lots of anxiety attacks. They're just like that."

"It sounds like anxiety. But why might it have happened? Were you poorly prepared for the exam?"

"No! I'd worked bloody hard and I knew it all. I could have done much, much better."

"'What about any other stresses or worries?"

"I have a boyfriend, Jake. I met him last term. He's lovely." She stops. "He wants to marry me. But I don't know."

"You're not sure?"

"No, I'm sure. I love him to bits. Maybe we should wait a bit. He's doing a PhD. We haven't got any money or anything really. Maybe I was worrying about that."

It does not sound terribly worrying and certainly far from unusual in someone her age. But it could be that she is more conflicted than she has let on.

"Anything else?"

"Not really. That's it." She leans forward in the chair so that her black hair falls over the sides of her face. Her arms are resting on her lap. She turns both hands upwards like a supplicant and says with disarming directness, "I need professional help to stop the panicking, Dr. Marzillier. That's why I've come to you. I've been told you're an expert in anxiety management."

I am an expert in anxiety management. I have done enough of it over the years. It is 1996 and I have left the NHS, left my job as head of the Oxford Clinical Psychology Training Course. I have set myself up in private practice, working from a room in my house in north Oxford. My study is now my consulting room. Cordelia is one of my clients. She got my name from a list that her GP gave her of private therapists in the Oxford area. On the list I am described as a cognitive-behavioural therapist. Of course, that is true. I am and, over the years, many of the people I see are referred to me precisely for that reason. Cognitive therapy has gone from strength to strength and GPs and others are on the look-out for therapists, clinical psychologists in particular, who can treat depressed, anxious, and stressed-out patients with this new and highly effective treatment. But I am also a psychodynamic psychotherapist and for the last few years I have developed a way of working that combines elements of both approaches. My first and most important rule-of-thumb is that I never assume I know what the problem is. Not even when, as in Cordelia's case, she describes a quite specific and recognizable problem. If I have learned one thing over the last 25 years, it is that things are often not what they seem.

I take a general history. Cordelia's parents separated many years ago when she was nine years old. Her father remarried and she and her younger brother, Anthony, were shunted between the two families. Her mother never remarried. I ask if she remembers the period leading up to her parents' separation. She tells me of shouting matches and how terrified she felt at her father's anger. She was protective of her mother though when she tells me this, I sense something else and make a mental note to follow it up. The picture of marital disharmony, while distressing when it happened, was soon over. Cordelia's adolescence was unexceptional. But one thing stands out. She was extremely bright, achieving four A grades at A level, going on to get a first class degree and was now on track for further success at post-graduate level. Until the panic three months ago exams never worried her. She breezed through them. So what had changed to make her panic? Perhaps, I think, this is an unconscious rebellion against academia, something that, because it cannot be admitted consciously, is acted out indirectly. But I have no evidence for this theory. And plenty of young people realize that they have had enough of the academic treadmill and just step off it. Why would Cordelia need to go through such a distressing and convoluted way of sabotaging her academic success?

"Shall I tell you the really worst thing about it?" she says, looking at me with a frank, open gaze that I am becoming familiar with. "I worry that I need to pee and of course then I start to feel the urge. So if I'm in a seminar, I have the thought, 'Oh God, I'll have to leave in the middle to go to the loo.' And then all I can think of is getting out and going to the loo. And now even before the seminar starts, I worry that I'll have that thought and get myself into a state about that! On the net, I read it's called anxiety about the anxiety. Is that right?"

"That's right."

"And you can help me get over it?"

"I think so." I outline a simple anxiety management programme. Cordelia listens eagerly, drinking in my every word. I give her a booklet and suggest she reads it through to see what she thinks about it. I ask her to keep a detailed record of any time she feels a panic coming on so that we can analyse it next time.

"Cool," she says. "Just what I need."

We leave it there. Cordelia goes off clutching the anxiety management booklet, happy to have found a treatment to help her. I sit back and reflect on Cordelia and her problem. I recall Peter, my first case,

who also had a problem about peeing, which turned out to be a way
into therapy for his general worries about his career and himself.
Cordelia is the same age and in a similar position. But if Cordelia's
problem masks a disturbance or uncertainty about herself, she has
not given any evidence of it. She comes across as a bright, confident and successful person who for some unexplained reason has
become anxious.

"Dr. M, I have to tell you, this anxiety management programme is
great. I've been using the breathing exercises to control the anxiety. It
works! I moved on to challenging my negative thinking. If I have the
thought *I need to go to the loo,* I tell myself that's my anxiety speaking.
I say *I've just been to the loo so I'm okay.* Just relax. I do the breathing
and I'm fine. Yesterday I got through a whole seminar without any
anxiety at all. Isn't that terrific?"

This is Cordelia's opening remark at our second session a week
later. I am startled at her sudden and dramatic improvement and
at the way she has devoured the treatment in one sitting. I cannot
remember ever encountering this before.

"The idea was," I say slowly, "that you read the booklet and kept
a record of your panics. I didn't expect you to carry out the whole
programme in one week."

"But it's so easy and it works. I'm feeling really confident again.
Thanks a bunch, Dr. M."

I half expect her to get up, shake my hand and leave. Cured in
one session.

"I'm impressed. You have done well."

"Haven't I just?" she says, giving me a coquettish look. She is
flirting with me, this very pretty young girl and I am not sure what
to make of it.

"But I'm puzzled," I say. "Up to last term you were absolutely fine.
Then you come back to university to take the exam and suddenly
you have a panic attack. The anxiety generalizes, gets worse. You
seek help and then, hey presto, in one short week you're better."

"Too good to be true? Is that what you mean?"

"I suppose it is."

"Does it matter?"

I say nothing, holding her look. After a few seconds she looks
away. I do not know if it matters or not. What is it that's keeping me

from accepting that Cordelia is a bright girl with a simple problem that she has quickly overcome with minimum help from me? This is CBT's strength: simple, direct, and effective. Some of my colleagues have even developed computerized treatment programmes that people can use without a therapist's help at all. Psychodynamic psychotherapists tend to be suspicious of sudden, dramatic improvements. The term they use is *flight into health*. The thinking is that patients get scared about what the therapy has begun to uncover and so escape further intrusion by suddenly getting better. But Cordelia has not had any therapy other than the booklet I gave her.

"I wonder if we might go back a bit to when the problem started. You'd completed the first year of the course and you were fine. No anxiety at all?"

Cordelia nods.

"Then the summer break and you return, take the exam and for the first time experience panic, leave the exam, go to the loo and collapse on your bed."

Cordelia is watching me intently as I rehearse the details of her case.

"How did you spend the summer break?"

"I was at home."

"Did anything happen? Anything that might have upset you or stressed you?" It is a question I should have asked last week.

Cordelia sits absolutely still. I watch her face as, quite unexpectedly, a tear appears in one eye and runs down her cheek and then a tear in the other eye, and another and another. She is crying silently, this bright and confident young girl. The transformation is as swift as it is unexpected. I hand her a tissue. She takes it and wipes her face. She looks at me, her eyes still glistening.

"When I was at home, I slept with my ex-boyfriend, which was stupid. I got pregnant. Dr. Marzillier, I had an abortion."

The existentialist therapist, Irving Yalom, stated that every good therapist seeks *to create a new therapy for each patient*. Rather than start with a preconceived idea and apply a set of established methods, the therapist remains open to a number of possibilities. What does this person want? Why does she need help? Why is she coming to see me now? What is she like? What is her personal history? Can I help her? And if so, what is the best way I can do this? These are the sorts of questions that would run through my mind when I saw someone new. I was after understanding. I wanted to avoid rushing to a premature assessment, knowing that people needed time, that a relationship of trust needed to be built up before some things could be disclosed. And from my psychodynamic training I came to realize that there was another level, one that is summed up by that much disputed and maligned term, *the unconscious*. Sometimes, and perhaps it is more often than not, people do not consciously know what is making them unhappy. We are very capable of hiding the truth, deceiving ourselves into thinking our problem is something totally different from what it is. Intense emotions like guilt and shame can drive self-knowledge underground. We do not *want* to know some things and so we manage to put them out of our minds, forgetting, repressing, denying, transforming them into something else. Strip away the Freudian language and what is revealed is something quite simple. The conscious mind is only the surface. Much of what governs our mental life is unconscious.

My training as a psychodynamic psychotherapist attuned me to pay attention to what lies beneath. I learned to listen attentively and to hold several possibilities in my mind without having to assert that any one of them must be right. I was willing, in a way that I had not been before, to accept uncertainty, not to know what is going on at least for the time being. In fact, I particularly enjoyed this aspect of my work. It satisfied my curiosity about people, what brought me to psychology in the first place over three decades ago. I believed it made me better at my job. But I was also aware that the vast majority of people who came to see me wanted to be relieved of their distress. In the medical terminology I was increasingly moving away from, they wanted to *get better*. Cordelia wanted to be rid of her anxiety and panic. I understood that and suggested a treatment programme that might help her and it did. The strength of the behavioural and cognitive therapies lay in their practical, straightforward, and well-established methods for dealing with certain problems. Problems like phobias, obsessions, anxiety, panic, and depression, the most common reasons why people seek psychological help. Since I had graduated from my psychodynamic psychotherapy course, I had sought to integrate the strengths of both therapeutic approaches into my private practice.

It is interesting to note that when therapists are asked about their preferred therapeutic orientation, most say their approach is *eclectic*.

The minority of psychotherapists stick rigidly to a single school of therapy; most branch out into others as I did. "Eclectic" can mean many things. It can mean that the therapist picks and mixes techniques from different therapies, rather like one goes through a display of brightly coloured sweets and takes what one fancies from the different boxes. Psychotherapists do not especially like to see themselves in this way. It suggests that psychotherapy is a bit haphazard. Try relaxation. Try hypnosis. Make an interpretation. What about prolonged exposure? EMDR? In other words, if you keep trying different techniques, something may work. The founding fathers and mothers of the various therapeutic schools deeply object to this magpie tendency as you might expect. They go to great lengths to protect what they regard as their own methods, insisting that therapists need to be properly trained in them, which usually involves attending a costly and often lengthy course and being accredited as a *bona fide* practitioner. This is despite the decades of research that has failed to show that specific treatments are the major determinant of therapeutic improvement.

Research reviews have shown that the therapeutic relationship is as important as specific techniques in producing therapeutic improvement. It is also what many patients say matters to them most. The dichotomy between techniques and the relationship is misleading as psychotherapy inevitably entails both. It is unfortunate that many research psychologists have focussed their work primarily on techniques and largely ignored the importance of the therapeutic relationship.

Eclecticism can also mean seeking rapprochement between well-known and apparently opposed schools of therapy. One of the earliest attempts to do this was by Paul Wachtel, in the late 1970s, who argued for an improbable liaison between psychoanalysis and behaviour therapy. A more recent example is Tony Ryle's cognitive-analytic therapy (or CAT), which links cognitive therapy and psychoanalysis. Psychotherapists tend to regard this as a more respectable form of eclecticism since the rapprochement is theoretical as well as practical. It is not just a question of dabbling with different techniques but resolving apparent theoretical anomalies. In CAT, Ryle takes the psychoanalytic idea of intrapsychic conflict and grafts it onto modern cognitive theory, resulting in a combined cognitive and dynamic formulation for problems. The treatment that follows mixes the practicalities of attending to and changing negative thoughts with a focus on transference and countertransference in the therapeutic relationship. It sounds very good. But one drawback, as I discovered when I embarked on a CAT training course, is that a new school is created with its own language, rules, and procedures. If you fall foul of one or more rules, then the trainers of this newly minted therapeutic school want to put you right. In other words, another orthodoxy has been created.

My approach to integration was essentially pragmatic. I largely took my cue from the patient. If someone came for help with a defined problem, as Cordelia did, I focussed on the problem. Above all, it is the respectful thing. That was why the person had come to see me. Moreover, there were many occasions when a practical, CBT approach proved beneficial without the need to do anything further. Sometimes, as my psychotherapeutic practice developed, people would seek me out specifically for exploratory psychodynamic psychotherapy, wanting a period of time to reflect and work on themselves. Often they were involved in some capacity in mental health. Over the years I saw a fair number of counsellors, psychiatrists, psychologists, and psychotherapists, using predominantly a psychodynamic approach. As the years passed, I found that some people returned having had a period of successful, problem-focussed therapy. Occasionally, like Jeremy, my patient with public-speaking anxiety, it was because the problem had come back. Some wanted a brief refresher course, a few sessions to help them through a particular difficulty. And then a few returned because they wanted help with other, more general problems, *problems of living* as they are sometimes called, or painful experiences from their past that had never been dealt with. They knew me and trusted me. We would embark on some explorative psychotherapy, sometimes setting a time limit, sometimes not.

Cordelia's disclosure about her abortion provided an explanation for her unexpected anxiety on returning to university. Her panic had not come out of the blue. She had been through a highly traumatic experience in the summer vacation. She had slept with her ex-boyfriend, which would have been bad enough given that she was in love with Jake. It had been a careless, drink-fuelled act at the end of a long party. If she had not become pregnant, she might have put it behind her. She would have had a difficult decision to make, whether or not to tell Jake. That alone could have triggered her anxiety and we could have talked about the experience, exploring why it had happened, and what she might do in relation to Jake. But she got pregnant. If her intention had been to forget about the act, now she could not. Then she had had an abortion. How had that been decided? And what had happened? I decide to ask her.

Haltingly at first and then with increasing fluency as her feelings of distress and anger spill out, Cordelia tells me how she had confided in her mother who then took over. Through a doctor friend, her mother had arranged for the abortion to be carried out quickly.

"Did you and your mother discuss it?"

"How do you mean?"

"Whether to have the abortion or to go ahead with the pregnancy?"

"No. My mother is very conservative in many ways but she is not against abortion. She's very pro-choice. A woman's right and all that. I was in the clinic and it was all over ten days after I'd told her."

"What about counselling?"

"There wasn't any. Well, the doctor talked to me, said it was perfectly safe, I wouldn't feel a thing, which was *wrong* by the way. It was terribly painful afterwards. And when I was at home, I felt so bad. Guilty, awfully ashamed. I had been so stupid. Mum said I was not to tell a soul, certainly not Jake, but I did. I couldn't keep it from him. It wouldn't have been right and anyway he knew something was wrong."

"How did Jake react?"

"He went very quiet. I understood. It was a huge shock and I'd betrayed him. But then he was magnificent. He's really supported me. He's my rock."

There are tears in her eyes as she tells me this. *Good on you, Jake,* I am thinking. Many men would have behaved quite differently. Still, it must have affected their relationship, but this is not the time to get into that.

"You say your mother is conservative but also pro-choice. An unusual combination." I am fishing, wanting to get Cordelia's reaction to her mother's determined action, her taking over and sorting out her daughter's predicament. While her mother might be pro-choice, it did not appear that Cordelia was doing the choosing.

"My mother has always been very strong-minded," Cordelia says looking directly at me. "I know what you're getting at. You think she railroaded me into the abortion. It's not that simple though. I was desperate. I was grateful she took over."

"'And now?"

"I'm angry with her. I know I am. Not for that so much but for ..." She stops, hesitating. "'Well ... for everything."

I am at one of those decision points where therapy resembles a game of chess in which there are several possible moves and whichever one one takes will irrevocably shift the game in one direction rather than another. I could follow up this hesitant disclosure about her mother. I could simply echo, *for everything*, hoping for more disclosure. Or I could ask directly what she means by it. It chimes with my earlier sense that there was something difficult about her relationship with her mother. But this would take us away from the trauma of the abortion and I feel the need to know more about that, about how Cordelia felt and how she now feels. Is there a sense of loss? Does she regret it? I am no expert on post-abortion counselling but I know enough to realize that there are often powerful physical and psychological consequences to it and that some people become very distressed. I am also aware of the form Cordelia's anxiety took; she felt a powerful urge to go to the loo. Was this an unconscious re-enactment of the abortion, one evacuation standing for another? Or it might be something physical. I am acutely aware of my ignorance about the physical effects of a termination on a woman, whether there might be a change in her sensitivity to micturition as a result of the procedure.

"Looking back, what do you think of the abortion?"

"I deeply regret it. I know rationally it's for the best. I couldn't cope with having a baby, certainly as it's not Jake's baby. But I can't help thinking I've done something terrible. I've killed a potential life."

Cordelia is crying, visibly and audibly very upset.

"Do you think about it? Is it on your mind a lot?"

Cordelia nods.

"What sort of thoughts? Can you describe them to me?"

"'I think I've ruined my life. I've spoiled everything. I was doing so well. I was good at my work and I had Jake and at last I'd got away from my mother. Now it's all gone to pieces. And it's because

I was a stupid, stupid girl who couldn't resist having a fling with my ex and got myself pregnant. Now it's payback time. I'll never put it right."

You do not have to be a cognitive therapist to recognize the stream of powerful, self-destructive, negative thoughts.

I have my own views on abortion. Like Cordelia's mother I am on the pro-choice side. But I will never be in Cordelia's position. I do not know what it is like to go through an elective operation, the purpose of which is to stop a life from developing. I do not know how I would feel. Intellectually, I can understand I might feel an emptiness, an acute sense of loss. I might worry about having done the wrong thing. This seems to be what Cordelia is feeling. And the content of her negative thoughts alerts me to two other things, her perfectionism, now punctured by the experience of the abortion, and that for some reason, as yet unexplained, she felt the need to get away from her mother.

Cordelia and I met for a further eight sessions, making ten sessions of therapy in all. In the early stages we talked about the abortion and she got some respite from her distress about it. We did not do any formal cognitive therapy for her negative thinking. We might have done but we did not get round to it. Instead, Cordelia talked about her distress and her life. She talked about her mother and some significant details emerged about her childhood, indicating that it was far from the cosy picture she had first painted. I listened and occasionally interjected my comments, all the while thinking that what she needed was a safe space to explore these matters. She would have occasional bouts of panic but for the most part she remained anxiety-free. I was happy to work with Cordelia in this way but for one thing, her continued flirtation with me, which became both more obvious and more intense. In one session she told me how she and Jake were experimenting with sado-masochistic sex. With an air of apparent innocence, she asked me if this was normal. Another time she brought in Anthony Storr's book, *The Art of Psychotherapy*, and said how impressed she'd been by it, so much so she was going to become a clinical psychologist and psychotherapist like me. I was being seduced by Cordelia, by her mixture of intelligence, charm, and likeability, by her intermittent bouts of anxiety that needed my expertise, and by her challenging, enjoyable flirtatiousness.

I was not sure why she was doing this. I did not know if she was conscious of it. But I knew it needed addressing and that it must have a significance beyond our relationship.

When I pointed out what was happening between us, saying that I thought we should examine this together, Cordelia reacted first with surprise and then with hurt disappointment. The next session she was in a rage. She told me firmly that she'd decided to end the treatment, that it wasn't doing any good anyway. Moreover, I was quite wrong about her. She was not a flirt. I held my ground and we weathered the storm. The flirtation all but disappeared. At a natural break, I decided that we had reached a point where the therapy had to have a clearer direction and purpose. Cordelia no longer needed just a safe space to talk. I suggested that she might spend some time exploring what had happened in terms of herself and her family life. My hunch was that Cordelia's missing father was implicated in the dynamics of her relationships with men and in her flirtation with me. What about taking six months of weekly sessions to look at these issues?

Cordelia took some time to think about my proposal and eventually decided against it. There was a financial issue as she had no money. Her mother was paying for the sessions. But over and above that she felt that the time wasn't right to do this. She wanted to get on with her life, finish her course, marry Jake and work out what her career should be. An escape from what might be a difficult and painful voyage of self-discovery or a realistic appraisal of her options? I did not know, but in the end the decision had to be hers. We parted on the same amicable terms that we had met on. She is one of the people I think about from time to time and wonder how she is getting on and if she ever went into therapy, and if she had been right not to take up my offer, and if she did in the end marry Jake and if the relationship held true. One of the frustrations of being a psychotherapist is that you rarely know what happens to the people in the long run, though some might argue that may not always be a bad thing.

CHAPTER TWENTY TWO

Getting too personal

D *r. M ushers me into his consulting room. He seems relaxed and friendly, courteous in an old-fashioned way. A certain reserve too, suitable for a psychotherapist who has just come to the end of a long and distinguished career. I imagine him doing this, week in week out, year after year, politely ushering his clients into the room, another hour-long session about to begin. I like the room immediately. It has touches of elegance in the Persian rug on the floor and the antique pedestal desk against the wall. Evidence of a working life too. The Apple Mac and printer seated on a modern beech table to my left. The bookshelves in the alcoves. A set of in-trays on a three-door filing cabinet. It feels safe here. A secure space, to use Bowlby's terminology. Very suitable for baring one's soul. Only I am not here to bare my soul. I must remember that.*

A large rectangular picture on the wall over the pedestal desk catches my eye. A print in dark browns and russets of a small, mediaeval town. Italian, I guess, Tuscan or Umbrian. The square is odd-shaped, like a large horseshoe. I know where it is! Siena, and it is the Palio, the festival that takes place every year. Horsemen race furiously around the square in a colourful pageant of flags and costumes and blaring trumpets. I am ridiculously pleased to have recognized it. Then I wonder, is this a metaphor for psychotherapy? An interminable ride around an odd-looking square? Or am I looking for meanings that are not there?

"Please take a chair. Whichever you wish." Dr. M gestures at two identical, voluminous, burgundy leather armchairs facing each other across a low table. They are alongside the large sash windows that look down on the typically long rectangle of a north Oxford garden – trees and shrubs, a well-kept lawn, mature flower-beds, all bordered by old redbrick walls. I have a vague notion that C.S. Lewis or Tolkien could have lived in such a house.

"Is this a test?" I ask with a nervous laugh. "Which chair I prefer?"

"No test." A brief shake of his head, a half-smile on his face. "Just your choice."

I opt for the chair on my left and find myself gazing up at an alcove of shelves crammed to the ceiling with books, a powerful display of the knowledge people come here to seek. Some titles leap out at me. Surviving Trauma. The Origins of Love and Hate. The Gift of Therapy. *I am relieved to find ones I recognize. Bowlby's trilogy,* Attachment, Separation, Loss, *only they are in the wrong order. I must stop trying to see significance in every little thing.*

Dr. M is seated opposite me. He smiles, an open smile which then unexpectedly turns into a frown. "I haven't offered you coffee or tea. A glass of water maybe? Old habits die hard, I'm afraid. Patients never got offered anything," he explains apologetically. "Except once, when someone was choking, and I got her some water."

"I'm fine," I say.

"Good. Then where would you like to begin?"

This is the opening to a book I planned to write, a fictional version of this memoir, in which a retired psychotherapist is interviewed by a young female post-graduate student about his life and work. I wrote 25,000 words of it before I abandoned the experiment and took up the memoir instead. I include it here because I based the description of Dr. M's consulting room on my own. This is what my prospective patients would see when they first arrived at my house. I put myself in the mind of the young interviewer and included her thoughts and concerns, which my prospective patients must also have had when first they were ushered into my consulting room. But what people see and what they do not varies enormously. Some patients, I suspect, saw nothing, so deeply caught up were they in their own concerns, or, to put it differently, they may not have consciously registered the details although at an unconscious level they certainly would have done. My home is a tall Victorian house in a desirable part of north Oxford, on a quiet, tree-lined road that ends in a cul-de-sac at the back of Lady Margaret Hall. Before a patient so much as crossed the threshold, she or he would know that I was a reasonably wealthy person to be living here, which may have given rise to all sorts of thoughts and feelings, envy perhaps in some or, in others, the hopeful belief that the outward trappings of success meant that I would be good at the job. Another feature was that my practice was in my home. I had meant this as a temporary state of affairs, thinking that it might prove, literally, too close to home. The necessary boundary between my personal life and professional work could be threatened. I thought I might eventually rent a consulting room somewhere else or even put up a small building, a sort of shed or summerhouse, in the garden, so that people did not come into the house. But I never did. I never felt the need. In fact, very few people commented on this being my home and then it was always positive, to say how lovely the garden was or how relaxed they found it being there. Whenever direct personal questions were asked, usually at the beginning, I deflected them, pointing out that I kept my private life and professional work separate. Nevertheless, seeing a patient in one's own home inevitably brings personal elements into view. The dark blue of the front door is the colour my wife and I chose. The door opens into a glass-roofed porch in which, because it was warm and sheltered, seed trays occasionally lay impassively on the floor. As my patients stepped over the threshold into the house proper, they saw a dark wooden settle in the small hall above which hung a brightly coloured Hockney print of a bowl of tulips. Beside it was a stand for a bundle of umbrellas, walking sticks and tennis rackets. To the right, if the door was not closed, my patients had a brief glimpse of the large, airy sitting room before they stepped into my consulting room and the door closed behind them. Even in the isolation of my professional sanctum the house was not completely shut off. Occasionally, other voices would be vaguely heard, the drone of the vacuum cleaner, the phone ringing and being answered, children's laughter, the blurred sound of the radio or TV. All hints, however vague, to a domestic life going on around us. Although I had carefully set up the room as a psychotherapist's consulting room, the furniture and decorations reflected my personal taste. Hence the items my hypothetical young interviewer noticed, the Edwardian antique desk, the Apple Mac computer on the modern beech wood table, the books on the shelves, the picture of Siena on one wall. This was my environment after all, where I spent the large part of the working day. I wanted to enjoy being there. But I displayed no family photographs, and no personal papers were left visible for prying eyes to see. Any writing I was doing had to be put away before the first person arrived. Novels or newspapers did not lie carelessly around to be observed or commented on. The room had to be first and foremost a professional space. One unforeseen consequence of this was that I finally acquired the habit of tidiness though, as my wife would testify, this did not seem to stretch much beyond the consulting room.

In the strict psychoanalytic tradition the therapist should be a blank slate onto which the patient's fantasies can be projected. This is despite the fact no one could have been more personal than Freud in his analytic work. A visit to his consulting room in Maresfield Gardens in North London, the one he occupied in the last year of his life, reveals this all too clearly, from his display of archaeological artefacts to the lush rugs and furnishings that make the room so welcoming. The notion of the invisible therapist is itself a sort of fantasy, one that psychoanalysts vainly hope to achieve as though they could cast off their personality like a set of clothes. Over the years I have seen inside several Oxford psychoanalysts' consulting rooms, some as a colleague and others as a patient. How different they were. I remember a small terraced house off the Botley Road with dingy, sparsely furnished rooms that were rented by the analyst whom I saw for a few months, a Kleinian who was more than usually cold and distant. I do not know how I stuck it out for so long given that each visit was as welcome as going to the dentist. In contrast, another analyst had lovingly built a wooden chalet in her garden with high-class mod cons and all creature comforts. Occasionally, her cat would stroll in and curl up on one of the thick rugs on the floor, a testament to its homeliness. Once, in search of a Jungian psychoanalyst, I found myself in a small suburban house on the outskirts of Oxford. I was taken upstairs by the friendly woman therapist and into a spare bedroom that served as her consulting room. I spent an uncomfortable hour there, unable to relax in this ambiguous setting. The way the consulting room is set up is important as the style reflects how the therapist views herself and her job. But the therapist's personality is more significant. The analyst I eventually found, who proved to be the most helpful therapist I ever saw, worked in a single-story converted garage to the side of the driveway that led to her large house. The decorations were limited and the room could be cold so a small electric heater was placed on the floor near the couch. Personal touches had been kept to a minimum but the warmth of my analyst's personality, her kindness and concern, transcended the unpromising environment. Curiously, the procedure on arrival was for the patient to go past the garage/consulting room and ring the doorbell of her home and then immediately retreat to the consulting room and await her imminent appearance. I do not know if she ever considered the symbolic aspects of this, the way we poor patients rang at her front door but were never let in. Once she was held up in London and her husband answered my ring, the door held open briefly as he courteously explained the delay, giving me a glimpse of her hallway. But that is the nearest I got.

The balance between the personal and professional is not just to do with the furnishings of the consulting room. Psychotherapists deceive themselves if they imagine they can hide their personal feelings however professional they strive to be. When I opened my diary on a given day and saw the names of my day's patients, there were some who occasioned silent (sometimes not so silent) groans. Other patients I eagerly looked forward to. Between weekly sessions a few would come into my mind as I went about my business. Some I worried about. Others I thought of fondly. One or two would make me despair. It was not a question of whether these personal feelings should or should not happen. They just do. Liking a patient does not mean that you are better at helping them. I have done good professional work with people I did not especially care for or whose way of life and values I could not remotely share. Some behaved in ways that I did not approve of. I doubt, however, if I would have taken on the fictional mafia boss, Tony Soprano, as the psychiatrist, Dr. Melfi, did in the TV series, *The Sopranos*. Apart from anything else he would have scared me to death. A therapist has to be comfortable with the people he or she sees. The intimacy of the work makes it difficult otherwise. There is of course the danger of getting too comfortable and some therapists can get far too close to their clients. When a therapist and his female patient find themselves lying stark naked facing each other on the rug in front of the fireplace, I suggest that there's been a slight slippage in the boundaries. It did not happen to me, I hasten to say, but it did to a well-known counsellor who, bravely or foolishly, wrote about it in a book on psychotherapy.

The first time that I was sexually attracted to a patient was in my behaviour therapy days. The woman was not particularly beautiful, nor did she flirt with me in the sessions. I recall her lying stretched out on the couch in the room I was using as I was teaching her to relax, languid and sensual like a cat. In my mind's eye I undressed her and fantasized frantic coupling as we fell into each other's arms. It shocked me, made me pause. There was no one to talk to about it for in my behaviour therapy days, relationships were not what mattered. I had similar sexual thoughts the next time I saw her. There was something about her, her vulnerability perhaps, or some very basic sensuality, that acted as a stimulus, and of course something in me responded to this. I solved this conundrum by inviting her husband to attend the next session. A tense and antagonistic man, he angrily told me how men flirted with his wife and, as he politely put it, he *would tear the head off anyone* who tried to get off with her. I was suitably chastened. For a long time the sexual attraction psychotherapists felt for their patients was never mentioned. The converse was, of course. At the drop of a hat, patients were presumed to fall for their therapists. In the famous case of "Anna O" that started off psychoanalysis, Freud's colleague, the distinguished Viennese physician, Josef Breuer, was the therapist and Freud the junior colleague. Anna showed her burgeoning desire for Breuer by developing a phantom pregnancy. Horrified, he withdrew from the case and dashed off on a second honeymoon with his wife. Freud, as the story goes, was intrigued and analysed what had happened in terms of a displaced reaction from her unconscious feelings for her recently deceased father. The psychoanalytic notion of transference was born.

It is no surprise that psychotherapists become sexually attracted to their patients. Theirs is a relationship of intimacy. One person is highly vulnerable and the other highly powerful. Dependency is always a risk and with dependency, other feelings may easily follow. It is gratifying for therapists to be trusted with personal confidences. It feeds a sense of omnipotence and self-importance. Many patients and, it might be surmized, not a few therapists, are sexually frustrated. Intimacy could easily spill over to flirtation and then more. It is hard to get accurate figures on how many therapeutic relationships develop into sexual ones. Rightly, the sexualization of therapy is seen as an abuse of power, akin in seriousness, some believe, to the sexual abuse of children by a parent or other member of the family. For several years I sat on the Investigatory Committee of the British Psychological Society whose job was to investigate all complaints made against members. Only a small minority of the complaints was to do with sexual abuse, but I strongly suspect that many more never reached us. Therapists are unlikely to own up to it and patients often feel too ashamed and vulnerable to report it. Even if they do, they are likely not to be believed since, the theory goes, it is the patients who develop erotic fantasies, not the therapist. In groundbreaking research, the psychologist Ken Pope reported that, in an anonymous survey of American psychotherapists, 87% of therapists admitted having been sexually attracted to at least one patient in their careers. As Pope caustically remarked, *one suspects the other 13% were lying or repressing*. There is no one pattern as other research has shown. Therapists who have a sexual relationship with their patients range from a one-off fall from grace by a therapist going through a personal crisis to sexual predators who deliberately enter the profession to abuse prospective clients. It is not just male therapists abusing young, female patients, although that is the commonest pattern. A number of women therapists have also abused their patients, both male and female, and male therapists abused male patients. It is possible that there are some sexually rapacious patients who throw themselves at the poor unsuspecting therapist and force him or her to gratify their desires, but I am less than convinced. Given the way the power is stacked in the therapist's favour, this is unlikely and should be easily resisted were it to take place. In almost 40 years of psychotherapy, I have never encountered a sexually rapacious patient. The nearest I got to it was when a female patient asked me for a hug, which I refused. It may not have been sexually motivated but it could have easily developed into something more. She got her way right at the end of therapy when she determinedly thanked me for my help with a hug.

Whatever the wrongs of psychotherapy developing into a sexual or romantic relationship, and research shows that these relationships rarely last, we should not be blind to the intimacy of psychotherapy and what therapists gain from it. Even if the therapist ensures that the relationship is carefully and professionally boundaried, seduction can creep in, clouding the therapist's judgment, resulting in the therapy going off the rails. Once I took on a woman for therapy who had spent two years in intense twice-weekly psychoanalysis with a female therapist I happened to know. Her account of their relationship, coupled with the therapist's own neurotic problems, indicated that this had developed into a *folie-a-deux*, in which both parties became hooked into an elaborate and intellectual game of deeper and deeper interpretations that seemed to gratify something in both of them, but was in the end quite unhelpful. Seduction is not just about sexual desire. In essence, it is when the therapist and patient cultivate an illusion of their own importance to each other, distancing themselves from the ordinary reality of therapy. The ordinary reality is that the patient has come to seek professional help. The therapist is there to provide that help. The therapist has other patients to see. The patient has a life outside therapy as does the therapist. The relationship will end at some point. Anything more, any elevation of the relationship into a higher plane, is something else altogether. Yet, the personal element of the therapeutic relationship cannot be ignored. With some patients, therapists will develop a special attachment quite simply because we are all human beings. The question for the therapist is how it is handled. Early on in my career I learned this the hard way.

Tracey and I are walking in the extensive grounds of the Bethlem Royal Hospital. Tracey is 28. She is small and wiry, her black hair cut short to her head like a boy's. There is something boyish about her altogether. She wears black jeans and a tight-fitting black T-shirt which has a lurid skull-and-crossbones on the front and *Death to the Enemy!* emblazoned on the back. She is never still. Even sitting down her body moves about in little jerks. There is a slight tremor in her right hand that she tries to disguise. Normally I would attribute these odd movements to her medication—amongst other things she is on haloperidol, a powerful anti-psychotic drug with nasty side effects—except that she has told me she is not taking any of the cocktail of drugs the psychiatrists have given her. "Don't tell the docs," she whispered to me. Tracey is not psychotic and the haloperidol is to keep her calm, a way of coping with her sudden outbursts of rage. She has wrecked the ward twice already in her short stay. Tracey's diagnosis is antisocial personality disorder. As a summary of her chaotic life, it is a starkly realistic label. She was brought up in care. She had run with a feral gang of girls, terrorizing the part of Peckham she grew up in. She escaped prison by a hair's breadth and joined the army. The five years she spent in the army was the one period of stability in her life. She loved it all, she told me, the marching, the manoeuvres, the pride in the uniform, the sense of purpose, the camaraderie. It channelled her aggression into something acceptable, at least for a while. She also met Maggs and they had an intense, if short-lived, sexual relationship. For reasons she will not tell me she and Maggs fell out. The ensuing physical fight left Maggs disabled, a badly broken leg that forced her premature discharge from the army. Tracey, contrite and despairing, also left. It was shortly afterwards that she had made her first serious suicide attempt.

It is 1971, early in my behaviour therapy days. Tracey's psychiatrist has asked me if I could help her control her anger by behavioural methods. This is before anger management was invented, but my plan is to do something like that, find out what triggers Tracey's rages and teach her alternative strategies. I am also thinking of a system of rewards and punishments following the success of ward-based behavioural programmes in the States, known as "token economies". I have not broached this with Tracey yet. I wonder how she might react to, say, only allowing her access to the ward TV if she goes a day without attacking someone or throwing furniture around. I have a feeling that she might not be too happy with this.[1] We are walking in the grounds because Tracey is claustrophobic and cannot bear to be stuck in a small office. It is not easy trying to get the therapy done outdoors. Apart from anything else Tracey never stops talking. For several days I have found myself listening to her amazingly

---

[1] I tried just such an approach with a highly aggressive psychotic man on the locked ward at the hospital. I told him that watching the ward TV was contingent on his behaving peacefully, which the nurses would keep a check on. Any aggressive act would automatically debar him from the TV room. The next day the nurses told me he'd picked up the TV and smashed it to pieces. First (and only) round to the patient.

chaotic, yet exciting life. In the short time we have been doing this, I have come to like Tracey. She is an intelligent, quick-witted, and sparky young woman who has had few in the way of breaks in her life. A fierce rebel too and, maybe because I like rebels, I admire her for it. She seems to like me too. She tells me things she can't tell anyone else, she says, because she knows she can trust me.

Suddenly, Tracey stops and I stop too. She puts her hand on my arm and leans into me.

"John. I want to tell you something. But you got to promise not to tell the docs. Or anyone. Will you?"

I hesitate, not sure what to do. It is early in my career but even so I am aware that I could get caught between Tracey's trust in me and the treatment she is supposed to be having.

"Okay," I say slowly, wanting above all to keep Tracey's trust.

"I'm leaving, skedaddling. I'm discharging myself from this loony bin. Can't take any more of the shit. It's total crap. No offence, John. But it's not what I need, know what I mean? You won't tell the docs, will you?"

She looks at me pleadingly like a young kid with a secret, which in some ways is exactly what she is.

"It's your decision," I say breezily. "You're not sectioned. So you can go whenever you like. It's a free world."

Tracey leaps in the air. "I knew it. You're the one person I can trust. Thanks, John." For a moment I think she's going to kiss me.

Tracey left the hospital that afternoon. My uneasiness about keeping her decision secret from the psychiatric team vanished with Tracey. But a few weeks later I am in my office conducting a tutorial with two of my students when my phone rings.

"John?" The voice is languid but unmistakably Tracey's. "I'm calling to say goodbye and thanks and all that."

"I'm in the middle of something, Tracey," I say with growing unease.

"S'okay. I'm feeling really warm. Never knew blood was warm, did you?"

"Tracey!"

"S'okay. Just the pills kicking in. Bit sort of sleepy. Time to say bye-bye ..."

My heart leaps into frenetic action. The two students look at me with curiosity. I avoid their gaze.

"Tracey," I say urgently, "where are you? Tell me your address."

She mumbles something I cannot make out. I press her again. Her voice comes and goes. I am panicking. There is no other word for it. "Tracey!" I shout. "You must tell me your address!"

Eventually she spills out where she is, a bed-sit in Peckham. I tell her to hold on and that I'll send an ambulance right away. I put the phone down and meet the curious gaze of my students.

"We'd better postpone the tutorial," I say with a nonchalance I do not remotely feel. "Something's come up."

There is a clear difference between doing your best for a patient you happen to like and doing your best as a professional. With Tracey I had let my personal feelings for her override professional considerations. I should have told her I was part of the psychiatric team helping her and therefore had to tell them about her plans to leave. I should have recommended if she were really intent on leaving, she do this responsibly by informing the doctors and nurses, packing her bags and exiting through the front door. Not disappearing suddenly without telling anyone. Apart from anything else this will have caused anxiety in the staff who wasted time scouring the hospital for her. I had been stupid, naïve, self-centred. Tracey's dramatic phone call directly resulted from my *laissez-faire* attitude. She was testing me again, seeing whether I would leap to her aid, drive down and rescue her. I did not. I sent an ambulance. It was my first lesson in professional responsibility. I never forgot it. It was also my first experience of knowing a patient who makes a serious suicide attempt. My moral position on suicide at the time was simple: people had the right to take their own lives. We live, as I had airily told Tracey, in a free country. I soon came to realize that things were not that simple.

CHAPTER TWENTY THREE

Unanswerable questions

L ate morning. My work phone rings. I answer it in my usual way, expecting a conversation with a client or a colleague, unsuspecting, innocent as we are at moments like this, the time before everything changes.

"Ken Forsyth here." A GP who sends me referrals from time to time. "It's about Leone Knight," he says without any further preliminaries. "I'm sorry to tell you she's topped herself."

The shock is physical, a jolt through my body. The phrase, *topped herself*, reverberates, telling me something incontrovertible, that Leone is dead. Simultaneously, I think that Dr. Forsyth could have used a more sensitive phrase. Why do doctors talk like this? Too much experience of death perhaps. But still. He talks on and I manage to register the basic facts. It happened late last night. She had taken a lethal dose of pills. Forsyth says something about it being an impulsive act. Then he is gone and I am left to my own thoughts.

I sit still for what seems a long time. The house is quiet. Mary is at work. I am not expecting anyone until the afternoon. Despite knowing that Leone is dead, I somehow do not quite believe it. A part of my mind thinks that she will walk into the room as she has done many times before, a half smile on her face, and put down the collection of shopping bags or whatever she is carrying, and curl herself into the chair like a cat, ready for the session. "It will never happen." I say this out loud. "She's dead." As though saying it will dispel the memory. I get up and walk to the window and look out unseeing on to the garden. "Stupid, stupid girl," I say, though Leone is, or rather was, a 39-year-old woman, with a husband, two children, several ex-lovers, many friends, and a father and mother whom she both loved and hated. I am suddenly very angry with her. *Why? Why did you do this? Why? Why did you not call someone? Why not call me?* And then other thoughts crowd in, selfish and ignoble thoughts that I am ashamed to be thinking but I am. *When did I last see her? Did I miss something? Will I be held accountable? I was her therapist even if she only came to see me monthly now. What will her family think of me? Will someone sue me?* I get up to put an end to this stream of self-serving thoughts.

"Leone is dead," I say out loud in the empty room. "That's a fact. I will never see her again." Tears spring into my eyes. *Oh Leone, why did you do it? Why leave us all bereft? What could have driven you to this awful, irrevocable act?*

Leone was part of my private psychotherapy practice that had been up and running for five years. Working from my home I had got into a rhythm, a way of working that I liked and seemed to suit the clientele. I would generally spend up to an hour and a half at the first meeting. This gave me the chance to get to know the person and the problems they brought. I did not take notes during the assessment but wrote detailed notes afterwards together with a summary of my impressions. As long as I did it immediately I could recall most of the important information. It was rare for me to start therapy right away. I might give my patients a task to do, a leaflet to read, a diary to keep just as I did with Cordelia, who started therapy anyway off her own bat. But I usually suggested that we take three or four sessions to explore the problems further before deciding whether to go on and, if so, what the therapy might be. I had reached this way of working for two reasons. It enabled me to base my assessment on a better knowledge of the person and their problems. And I believed it was the right thing to do ethically. I had written and lectured on the ethics of psychotherapy, including the notion of *informed consent*. I argued that most patients, desperate for help at the end of what was often an emotionally charged first session, were likely to agree to whatever a sympathetic and authoritative therapist might suggest. One session was not enough. Informed consent would be more likely after several sessions when the patient's emotions had generally become less intense, when he or she had more information to base a considered judgment on, when there had been an opportunity to ask questions, to read around the therapy, and consult friends or family. Then the patient could decide whether to continue and we could both agree what the parameters of the therapy would be. I felt comfortable with this way of working. It seemed civilized and appropriate.

I was experimenting with a technique that I had picked up during my training as a cognitive-analytic therapist. This was to construct a preliminary formulation at the end of the assessment period and present it to the patient. I did this as a written letter, sometimes combined with a diagram illustrating how I understood the fundamental psychological problem, what I thought had led up to it both immediately and historically, what prevented the person from sorting the problem out themselves and how therapy might provide a way forward (i.e., what the therapy would consist of). Something similar occurred in CBT in the form of a cognitive-behavioural formulation that was drawn diagrammatically with the patient, becoming the blueprint for the active treatment. The difference with the CAT formulation was that it combined psychoanalytical ideas with cognitive ones. My formulation took into account early family history, hypothetical unconscious conflicts both in the past and the present, transferential aspects of the therapist-patient relationship and other relationships as well as dysfunctional cognitions and ineffective patterns of behaviour. A tall order to do this after only four sessions but I discovered it could be done if the formulation was seen as preliminary and not set in stone. Psychodynamic therapists might object that the process was artificial. It could lead to a premature fixation on certain features, the ones that appeared in the early sessions, and prevent further exploration, which was at the heart of the analytic method. There was some truth in this. But it was counterbalanced by the value of bringing the patient into the decision-making process, clarifying to some degree what treatment would be about, thereby ensuring that the person's consent was informed as much as could be reasonably expected. For short-term therapies, by far the majority for most therapists outside classical psychoanalysis, I believed this was a necessary step to take. It also had the virtue of forcing me to clarify my thoughts, sharpening up my subsequent work in therapy. And I found the patients liked it. It was a gift, something tangible that I had produced for them, and even where I had got something wrong, that could be easily rectified. This was the approach I had adopted with Leone four years ago when she had first come to see me. Why had it all gone wrong?

The doorbell rings. A short burst. A pause. Then another longer one. Opening the door I find a small, auburn-haired, smartly dressed, thirty-something woman. In her hands she holds three very large white shopping bags, two in one hand, one in the other. *Monsoon. Whistles. Jaeger.* The best designer clothes shops. A smart leather handbag, almost as large as a shopping bag, hangs from her right shoulder.

"Leone?"

"Hi." She pulls a wry face. "Can't shake hands. Been on a shopping spree as you can see. I thought while I was in Oxford I'd ..." She leaves the sentence unfinished.

"Combine business with pleasure?"

"Spot on." A lovely smile transforms her face.

"Come in," I say, stepping aside as Leone and her shopping bags slip into the house. I am already aware of something different from normal. A frisson that has passed between us that is more to do with a man and a woman than therapist and patient.

Leone was referred to me by her GP, Dr. Forsyth. He mentioned depression and marital problems. She had been in therapy before. She and her husband, Philip, had had a few sessions at Relate, what used to be called the Marriage Guidance Council. *She would like some help of her own* is what Dr. Forsyth had written.

Leone places the bags on the floor next to the chair. She looks at me enquiringly. "Do you mind if I take off my boots? They're really too tight."

"Fine," I say without thinking though it is an unusual request, certainly in the first session. I watch as she unzips each black leather boot, exposing the curve of her calf. It is an intimate act and, frankly, erotic. When finished, she curls her feet up under her in the chair, looks up at me again and says, with an air of innocence, "What happens now?"

"You tell me what's brought you here." My tone is different from normal. There's a playful element to it. Flirtatious even.

"Oh, yes." A sigh. "Where do I begin? It's so difficult this business. You must get bored listening to neurotic women telling you their problems."

"It's what I do though I wouldn't put it quite like that."

"No, I'm sure you wouldn't. You probably have clever words to describe it all. The Oedipus complex. Stuff like that."

I note the undercurrent of anger. I suspect that this is about men and how they treat women, how Leone has been treated.

"Dr. Forsyth said you are the best in the business."

I hardly know Dr. Forsyth. I have seen at most two patients he has sent me. How could he know that? Would he say it?

"But then I think, Dr. Marzillier—or can I call you John?— ..."

"John is fine."

"... that I'm wasting your time and Philip's money coming here."

"That you should just pull yourself together and get on with life?"

Leone laughs. "Spot on. The truth is, John, I don't know what I want. But I'm not happy. I know that. But then who is?"

Her eyes stare into mine. They are large and round, a light shade of green, carefully highlighted by the application of mascara to her eyelashes and the soft tones of make-up below the eyes. There is no escaping the sexual overtones to her look. I am drawn to her for that reason, no doubt like many other men. How easy it is to be seduced, to flirt with this attractive yet vulnerable woman, as I have already found myself doing? But I have a professional job to do. I need to keep that in mind. It is not often that I have to warn myself about this as I am doing now. Leone is going to be a challenge for I am pretty sure that the flirtation will continue, that it is her way of engaging with men, of bending them to her will. Until, that is, they disappoint her or let her down, which is when all her fierce anger will come out, the claws unsheathed and ready to scratch. You may think it is not believable to reach this conclusion from such a very brief exchange. But I can assure you it happens. First impressions are hugely significant. The thoughts are not always articulated but they are there, often unconscious and, as they were in my case, expressed by a change in the way I would normally behave. I had learned the value of attending to these signs.

After four assessment sessions with Leone I understood her better, well enough to write out a preliminary formulation together with a diagrammatic flow-chart and present it to her in the CAT style that I had recently learned. She had talked at length about her family background and I had discovered, though in truth it was not difficult to find, her powerful and intense ambivalence about her father, a highly successful lawyer who, she claimed, openly disparaged women as second-class. She was envious of her older brother who held a prominent job in his local community. She was angry with men in general yet strongly attracted to them. In her early years she had gone in for whirlwind affairs, often with men who were attached to other women. It was how she met and married Philip. Holding on to a relationship was far more difficult though and her marriage was under strain. At a fundamental level Leone believed that she was always second best, having assimilated this originally from her father. She fought against it, sometimes by seeking to be very masculine, that is, challenging and awkward and confrontational, even wearing men's clothes like a business suit. Alternatively, she emphasized her femininity, curling up in the chair like a cat, flirting with men as she had with me, what has been called in old-fashioned language, *putting on feminine wiles*. Both strategies failed to make her happy. Clashes with men occurred—one was happening at the time at her work—and she usually withdrew in the end, berating herself as a coward, feeling empty and worthless, the anger turned against herself in a spiralling depression. Her flirtation with me continued. It may just have been a long-established habit, but I thought it was also an unconscious attempt to undermine whatever good might come out of therapy so that, perversely, she might retain her core worthlessness, confirming herself as fundamentally bad. This was similar to the self-defeating pattern Dorothy Rowe had described in some depressives. In my formulation I suggested that the way forward was to move away from these old, ineffective patterns and, using the space and neutrality that therapy provided, to explore how she might find a different way of relating to herself and the world, men in particular, one that was less driven by envy and competitiveness than by what she herself truly wanted. Leone eagerly accepted and we agreed to meet once weekly for a three months course of therapy. I had no inkling at the time that three months would turn into four years, during which time Leone ended and resumed therapy twice, nor that our work together would end on a final and tragic note.

Why do people commit suicide? There is no simple answer to this question of course. As with any other act the reasons can be varied depending on the individual and the circumstances. There is a great difference between an older person with a painful, terminal illness choosing to end her life and an adolescent boy, in despair after the end of a relationship, throwing himself off a high building. Of the many psychological theories that have been proposed to explain suicide, those that focus on the individual's state of mind have most resonance to the ordinary practitioner. Impulsivity is a common feature. In moments of extreme despair people can impulsively swallow a large number of pills or throw themselves under a train. Hours later, if the act is interrupted or unsuccessful for whatever reason, the impulse can vanish. Suicide is no longer seen as the only possible option. Consuming alcohol or taking drugs act as potent disinhibitors. Research has shown that the risk of a suicide attempt succeeding is greatly increased for those who have taken drugs or alcohol. Leone killed herself only hours after meeting friends. It is possible she was drinking though I never discovered that. What was clear was that no one had the remotest idea that she was contemplating suicide. If she had been planning it for some time, she had kept it to herself.

A month before she killed herself Leone had come to see me. She was depressed and unhappy. Though her mood was very low, I had not picked up on any suicidal thoughts. But I did not ask her directly for I would have made a specific note if I had. I had reassured her that her depression would lift at some point as it had many times before. We made another appointment in a month's time. I had said to her, as I often do when people are low, to contact me if things got worse and we could arrange an earlier appointment. Leone killed herself just two days before she was due to see me again. Had I missed something? It was the question I asked myself repeatedly in the days after her death. Had her depression deepened so much that she had been plunged into a powerful black mood that had tipped the balance between life and death? Those who have studied suicide have commented how intense despair takes over, mentally constricting all options to two, to live or to die. It is as though a dark filter comes down cutting out all other possibilities. To my mind the best portrayal of the suicidal state of mind occurs towards the end of Tolstoy's *Anna Karenina* when Anna is being driven to the station where she will throw herself under a train. The remarkable stream of consciousness that Tolstoy recreated shows Anna's pervasive negativity, her hatred of the world and particularly of herself, her sense of hopelessness and despair punctuated by the occasional fleeting but illusory hope, the way her thoughts have shrunk to a small point so that nothing outside her awful purpose has any impact and, above all, the ceaseless drive of her own despairing, depressive thinking. Her eventual suicide is entirely understandable.

The suicidal state of mind however should not be seen in isolation. Just as Anna Karenina's whole life led her to that very point, so, for many who commit suicide, there has been a long process leading up to it. The psychologist, Mark Williams, has highlighted how initial anger and protest at the world give way to depression, recriminations, repeated failure, leading to resignation and death. As I struggled to make sense of what happened to Leone, I realized that there could well have been such a pattern, over the past few months, perhaps even years, that brought her to this desperate state of mind one lonely night. Of course it is possible to see all sorts of things with the benefit of hindsight. And we all have an understandable desire to impose a pattern on the apparently inexplicable, to make sense of something that puzzles us.

In the three months after Leone first came to see me, she went through a series of crises, of dramatic ups and downs in her life that dominated the sessions. She had ferocious rows with Philip and threatened to leave him. Her battle with her boss at work ended with her walking out. Within a few weeks she applied for and got another job. She clashed violently with both her parents. While some therapeutic work was done on the theme we had identified, of her being second best to men, the maelstrom that was Leone's life ran ferociously through our sessions, impossible to ignore. At the end of three months with the therapy due to end, she was exhausted, struggling to keep her head above water, her life as turbulent as ever. She asked for more sessions to provide her with some stability and to work through what was happening to her. We contracted to carry on, this time on an open-ended basis, and for the next 18 months Leone came to see me once a week, using the therapy as a way of touching base. No longer were we focussing on the specific theme though it was always there in the background. Therapy had turned into something else. I had become an anchor, a support, and therapy a *secure base*, to use Bowlby's phrase, to help Leone chart her way through her chaotic life. Because psychotherapists are so concerned with treating people and problems, the supportive element is ignored or underplayed. Yet for some people, this has a vital function. In my own analysis I had brought my life problems to my therapist, using the sessions to work things out. Leone did much the same. Starting her new job. A financial crisis. Unwisely getting embroiled again with an old flame. And, all the time, the continuing, seemingly never-ending battles between her and Philip. The theme of being second best ran through these experiences and I always kept it in mind as I tried to help her sort out her life. But in truth many sessions were about containment, holding Leone metaphorically, like a good parent would, giving her unconditional support. Psychotherapy is after all a form of attachment. But it is not a lifetime's attachment. At some point an endpoint had to be reached. As often happens, this occurred after a natural break (Christmas). In the first three months of the following year, Leone and I brought the therapy to an end. It turned out to be no more than a temporary reprise. A few months later she contacted me again and another long period of therapy was undertaken before a change of her work—she took a job in London—made it impossible for her to see me regularly and we stopped for what I thought might be the last time. But then another call came.

"I have been very stupid, haven't I?" Leone looks at me quizzically, a pleading look in her eyes as though she wants me to contradict her. It is six months since I last saw her. She looks different. Her face is thinner and there is a hollowness under her eyes. Her hair is cropped very short. She is wearing an expensive designer suit, black with a muted grey stripe. A mauve silk tie hangs casually around her neck over a crisp white blouse. The whole ensemble is a parody of the male businessman.

"Is that what you think?"

She turns away, disappointment written on her face. "Why don't you shrinks ever answer questions? It pisses me off."

I wait. Leone is still not looking at me. After careful consideration, I say, "I think *you* think it's stupid. It's certainly added a complication to your life." Leone has told me she's started an affair with her husband's best friend, his business partner. It was why she rang and asked to see me again.

Tears are in her eyes as she turns back to face me. "I love Michael," she says simply. "I know it's stupid and Philip will forever hate me if he finds out."

So Philip does not know.

"But I can't live without him and he feels the same." She stops abruptly. "I ought to tell Philip. It's the decent thing to do."

"How do things stand between you and Philip?" When therapy had ended a year ago, she and Philip had agreed to separate. The plan was to sell the large house they had bought near Charlbury 15 years before and move into separate accommodation.

"We're still living at 'Wycherley'. In the end we couldn't face selling the house and the kids like it so much. But we sleep in separate rooms. To a large extent, we lead totally separate lives. We don't have sex any more, haven't done so for months. Because I work in London now, I stay over two or three nights a week. In Michael's flat." She raises her eyebrows. Ironically, knowingly. "Philip knows that I stay in the flat but not about me and Michael."

It is a mess, but far from uncommon. I wonder if Philip suspects or maybe even knows. Leone has never been good at keeping things secret. I am also wondering why she has made contact with me again but just then she tells me.

"I wanted to spend a few sessions talking it through, John. What I should do. Michael and I have talked about taking off together. He has a permanent job offer in New York, which he can take up at any time. But there's Bea to consider. She'd be devastated. And of course both our families."

It's even more of a mess. "You want to go but you don't want to go?"

"Exactly. I feel deep down it's my only chance of happiness. I love Michael. He's my soul mate. I think I have always loved him and he me. But neither of us said anything until now. I know we could be truly happy, John."

This is one of the times when I wish I had not become a psychotherapist, when I wish I had trained as a lawyer so that I could fall back on something tangible, like a statute or a judgment, so that I could give advice solidly based on reason and fact. Leone's profession of her deep, undying love for Michael, and his for her, strike me as an adolescent fantasy. I think that it will all go badly wrong. But what do I base this on? Is this simply prejudice? Am I taking the conservative position because of my own values? Those who have studied passionate love dispassionately, psychologists and others, point out that it is the archetypal narcissistic illusion, a projection of what is missing in oneself into the other person, who then acts out those projections, what Kleinians call *projective identification*. The other takes on a magical, superhuman quality. Friends and family see only an ordinary person with certain virtues and certain failings. But to the lover he or she is a god. Once passionate love is over, the illusion punctured, the relationship takes on a different, more ordinary quality. To sustain it something else is needed. This is more to do with caring and compassion and hard work. What Leone is describing is the heady experience of a passionate, all-embracing fantasy. I see it as a defence against the dissatisfactions and disappointments she has felt throughout her life. Hence, the desire to take off to New York. How many of us want to believe that in a different place, a different country, everything will be completely transformed including oneself?

All this was very well but what do I say? Is it my job to deflate the balloon? To bring Leone down to earth? I decide it is not, though I wondered later if this was cowardice on my part, an unwillingness to disappoint her, to take away her happiness however illusory or fleeting it might be. Telling myself it is the job of the therapist to be neutral, I encourage her to talk, to explore the options, without giving away what I think, and in doing this, she works her way round to giving herself permission to pursue the affair, to seize her chance of happiness. She and Michael will bring it out into the open and accept the consequences.

What happened next was sadly predictable. Once the illusion touched reality it almost immediately dissipated. Michael began to back pedal. He could not leave Bea and the family. The New York job was not financially secure. It was not even salaried. He had to bring in enough money to support himself and more. Then he would have alimony and child care payments to make. Moreover, the business he and Philip had started was booming. He could lose out on some huge bonuses over the next few years. Interestingly, Philip wanted Michael to stay. Despite the affair, he did not want his long-term business partner and close friend to leave. He was too important. He said he could forgive the transgression as long as it had definitely ended. Leone was like that, he told Michael, a temptress, a minx. He would be a fool to give up everything, his work, Bea, his family, for her. I heard all this from a dejected and tearful Leone. Once again she was second best. She was now not only losing the illusion of ultimate happiness but her friendship with Michael and Bea. It felt to her that she was in danger of losing everything.

These were the events that were eventually to lead up to Leone's sad death. It was a long drawn-out business as she and Michael could not completely bring their affair to an end. Leone was alternately furious and depressed. She railed against everyone, Philip and Michael in particular for ganging up against her. Curiously, I thought that she did some good therapeutic work during this time. It was as though she finally realized that she had to take charge of things herself. She could not any longer look to a man to give her happiness. I encouraged her to build a new life round her work. And gradually Leone seemed to achieve something of an equilibrium after the crises of the past three years. She stopped coming to see me every week. We switched to a monthly meeting simply for the purpose of touching base. But it was during this time that another crisis arose. This involved yet another man who had let her down. She was plunged into depression again and all her old negative feelings resurfaced. In the session I sought to help her reduce the impact of her depression, pointing out that this was a crisis and that she had got through similar crises in the past. I suggested seeing her GP and taking time off work. The one thing I did not do was to arrange to see her again earlier than the monthly follow-up although I did say she should contact me if she needed to see me. Had I misjudged the intensity of her depression? Would she have still been alive if I had insisted on her seeing me the following week? I would never know. It is this sort of question many people ask when something tragic and unexpected happens to someone they are close to. What if I had done something differently? Could I have prevented it? One woman I saw, whose husband died one evening of a sudden heart attack, berated herself for bringing him a brandy. If only she hadn't, she thought, then he might not have had the attack and still be alive. This is a sort of magical thinking.

Taking on culpability as though the clock could be turned back and the inevitable prevented.

But I was Leone's psychotherapist. It was my job to pick up the signs. I had a professional responsibility for her well-being. Was I not then culpable in not having done more than I did? Did I mess up? If I had suspected she was actively suicidal, I might have arranged to see her the following day and insisted that she promise to call me, day or night, if the impulse to kill herself became strong. I might have got her admitted, even arranged to have her sectioned if she had refused. A few years later I did get a highly suicidal patient admitted into psychiatric care. However, a couple of days later she absconded and threw herself under a train. Sometimes when people are determined, nothing will stand in their way. In her book, *Night Falls Fast*, the psychiatrist Kay Redfield Jamieson, herself a survivor of more than one suicide attempt, recounts how she and a close friend, someone who was also prone to suicide, made a solemn pact that if either felt the urge to kill themselves, they would call the other, arrange to meet and spend a week together to talk it through. Wherever they were. Whatever time of day or night. They would make the call. This was to be their failsafe option. Many years later her friend killed himself. He made no attempt to call her.

Might I have done more? Might Leone be alive now had I done so? Or was the impulse too strong, the outcome unpreventable? Unanswerable questions. Psychotherapists want answers but sometimes there are none. I am left instead with the memory of an intelligent, attractive, challenging, unhappy, and bright person whom I was privileged to know for a short period in her chaotic, intense, and often exciting life.

CHAPTER TWENTY FOUR

So it goes

A psychologist should not pretend to understand what he does not understand. Moreover, a psychologist should not convey the impression that he understands what no one understands. We shall not play the charlatan and we will declare frankly that nothing is clear in this world. Only fools and charlatans know and understand everything.

(Janet Malcolm. *Reading Chekhov*. Granta, 2004)

These words were not written by a psychologist but by the playwright and writer, Anton Chekhov, in a letter to his friend and fellow writer Ivan Shcheglov. Chekhov, one of the greatest short story writers, wrote what we would perhaps call psychological stories, tales of real people in difficult but very human situations. Few who have read *Ward Number Six* will forget Dr. Andrew Yefimovich Ragin, the laissez-faire doctor, who ended up as a patient in the terrible psychiatric hospital he was working at. Or the way that the philanderer Dimitri Gurov is strangely unable to put the young Anna Sergeyevna out of his mind, the lady with the dog, in the story of that name. Or the sad tale of failed love and ambition that is the essence of the story, *Dr. Startsev*. Chekhov was a brilliant psychologist and writer. He knew enough to realize that no one could really understand everything about people. Not psychologists. Not even writers.

Chekhov's words seem an apposite way of ending this memoir about my life as a psychologist. I started off believing that knowledge, scientific knowledge, was the key to understanding and helping people. Eventually, I came to realize that science could not provide the answers I wanted. Even later, I realized I was asking the wrong questions. I was expecting too much from psychology too soon. This realization came through my experience of working as a psychotherapist, from my patients. The grand aim of behaviour therapy, that the therapist should base his or her methods on scientific knowledge and principles, crumbled when facing the realities of people like Mrs. Hewittson, Gillian, Peter and many others whom I saw. People have a way of bringing one down to earth. But I would not want readers of this book to think that I reject science as irrelevant to the study and understanding of the mind. The discipline of psychology has changed enormously over my lifetime. Behaviourism is long gone, regarded by all but a very few as an embarrassing hiccup in the development of scientific psychology. The advent of cognitive psychology freed up academics to study mental processes and in doing so has brought psychology into the world of thought and emotion, of thinking and feeling, not in the way Freud and his followers had envisaged and not as distinct from it as many psychologists like to believe. Cognitive psychologists know that a large part of the way we behave is governed by processes of which we are entirely unconscious. Freud's ideas about how the unconscious worked are, unsurprisingly, out of date, but the importance he gave to the operation of the irrational, unconscious mind remains significant to this day.

Psychology as an academic discipline is no longer hidebound by simplistic notions of science (or perhaps I should say by *my* simplistic notions of science). And science itself has significantly changed. The scientific world has expanded, literally as new technology has taken probes to Mars, Saturn, and beyond, and metaphorically in areas that I can scarcely comprehend such as the notion of parallel universes in quantum physics. (Frankly, my one attempt to read about quantum physics ended when I finished a chapter of David

Deutsch's book, *The Fabric of Reality*, and, attempting to write down what I had learned, I ended up staring at a blank page). In the last decade and a half there have been some truly exciting scientific advances, perhaps the most striking being the first sequencing of the human genome. In the closely related discipline to psychology, neurology, the technology of functional magnetic resonance imaging is allowing scientists more precise ideas about the location and functioning of specific areas of the brain. Psychology plays a significant part in this advance. The neuroscientists need to have accurate assessments of psychological functions in order to link brain activity to human experience. There are implications for clinical practice too, as greater understanding can lead to new methods of intervention for those with brain injury whether neurological, psychological, or a combination of the two. And new and challenging theories have arisen. The work of the neurologist, Antonio Damasio, for example, presents a radical revision of the way emotion is implicated in the development of thought and language. Today, any student lucky enough to study psychology at university is going to find a broad, vibrant, entertaining, and challenging discipline with tentacles that stretch into many diverse areas of human experience.

Psychotherapy and psychology have the same prefix but they are in many ways worlds apart. Psychotherapy is about helping people, which, as you will have gathered from this book, is a messy, complicated, and uncertain business. Psychology is about understanding people scientifically. It is a rigorous academic discipline which, through experimentation, observation and theoretical analysis, seeks to describe and explain the many different facets of human and animal behaviour. Psychotherapists have existed in one form or another for centuries, ever since people sought help for mysterious malaises or difficulties in living with their fellow human beings. Henri Ellenberger's sociological account, *The Discovery of the Unconscious*, takes us back to the shamans and their rituals. In the 18th century the Austrian Franz Mesmer invoked the notion of action-at-a-distance to provoke and cure young women of their hysterical illnesses, anticipating what Charcot and Freud did by a century. Priests and clergymen have always listened to members of their congregation's psychological problems and, within the rubric of their religious doctrine, sought to relieve unnecessary suffering. I once came across an American study that compared the effectiveness of local barbers to trained counsellors which found that the barbers did just as good a job as the counsellors at a fraction of the price (and you get your hair cut too). For some reason the study did not get a lot of publicity among counsellors. There are aspects of psychotherapy that have nothing to do with academic psychology. They are more to do with the human condition and the problems we all have in coming to terms with ourselves, our families, our friends, and the world we live in.

As the end of the first decade of the 21st century approaches, what should we expect from psychotherapy and psychotherapists? If Peter, my first patient, were to seek help today, would his experience be very different from 40 years ago? Okay, he would be unlikely to be seeing a therapist in a pub and talking about the latest films, but that apart. It is an impossible question for the context would be different. Before he made his first, tentative request for help, he could well have read one of the thousands of self-help books on psychotherapy. Or he might have consulted the school counsellor. He could have searched the net and worked things out for himself and perhaps even joined a forum for people with similar problems to his. He would have seen psychologists and psychotherapists on television in fictional programmes like *The Sopranos* or commenting on real life events such as the effects of the July 2005 London bombings. He might even have gleaned something from the psychologists' expert analyses of the vagaries of young people's behaviour when sealed off in a house somewhere in Hertfordshire and made to carry out senseless tasks by unscrupulous TV producers. (*Big Brother* is regarded by some academic psychologists as the best, long-term experiment on human behaviour ever, one that no ethics committee would ever allow them to do.) That is the problem with hypothetical questions. They are just that, hypothetical.

One change however is clear. There are more psychotherapists in all their guises than there were 40 years ago. Many GP practices have counsellors attached who offer practical, short-term help for people who are depressed or anxious or have other psychological problems. GPs are now more psychologically minded partly due to the increasing input of psychology in their training. There are many more and varied applied psychologists too. As well as clinical psychologists, there are counselling psychologists, health psychologists, educational psychologists, child psychologists, forensic psychologists, occupational psychologists, coaching psychologists and sports psychologists. I even read an article about a travel psychologist though he was not, as I fondly imagined, employed to give counselling on inter-city trains but an academic studying how psychology impinges on the roads.

What expert knowledge should a good therapist have? I started my career believing that therapy should be based on the scientific understanding of human behaviour. This was the credo of the behaviour therapy movement. When behaviour therapy morphed into cognitive therapy, or CBT as it became known, the belief in science persisted. Therapies should be subject to scientific research to test out competing theories and to evaluate whether or not the treatments work. I had strongly believed this in the early part of my career. But over the years my naïve optimism in science has been tempered by the realities of clinical experience. I realized that reducing therapy to a set of techniques to be delivered by people trained in a particular school distorted the way therapy worked. Superficially, it looks good to claim that research has shown that 90% of people with panic disorder will benefit from a short-term CBT intervention. It is what the funders of therapy, the NHS, the insurance companies, want to hear. What is missed out is why a person might panic and what that panic means to the person and the people around them. The individual is lost in the statistic. But it is the individual that matters. A very different therapy is needed for someone like Cordelia whose panic arose out of a specific trauma, and someone who has an anxious temperament brought about by insecure attachments and a highly anxious childhood.

My journey through various therapy schools brought me to the realization that the personal qualities of the therapist play a much larger part than has been credited in the research literature. It is a curious omission since what could be more psychological than the person? Yet many psychologists shied away from studying the therapist's personal attributes in favour of techniques. Therapy schools do not help since they enshrine the notion that there are specific techniques to be learned, often on lengthy and costly training programmes. The drive to show that therapy works has also privileged technique over the person in the vain hope that research will show definitively that a particular method, whether CBT or something else, is effective. This quasi-medical model has dominated therapy research to the detriment of a proper understanding of what psychotherapy is truly about. But if therapist qualities are important, what makes a good therapist? I can only give you my personal view, reflecting my own experience, my background and prejudices, but at least by now you will have a good idea of what those are. I am aware too that the qualities needed to work, say, in a young offenders' institution, a home for people with learning difficulties, or an adolescent psychiatric unit are very different from a private practice in a house in leafy north Oxford or a GP practice in Oxfordshire. Yet there are some characteristics I would hope to see in any therapist. Curiosity, empathy, a willingness to listen, flexibility of mind, sensitivity, open-mindedness, and patience. I also think that all therapists need a degree of healthy professional detachment, the ability to switch off from the job and the capacity to draw back from getting over-involved.

I worked for 12 years single-handedly as a private therapist. I cannot know for certain what my patients got from seeing me. Many expressed their thanks. Some may have done that even if they did not mean it. Excessive politeness is after all a very English disease. But I believe that I helped people, some of whom desperately needed help, and that is a powerful reward. And if people had not shown some benefit, I doubt if I would have persisted. I know that nothing definite can be concluded from single cases as my strictly scientific colleagues might remark. The patients may have got better anyway. Through my rose-tinted spectacles I may be seeing what I want to see. But I do not discount this different sort of knowledge, which is personal, tacit, and grounded in feeling. Along the way there were those I did not help or helped very little. Kevin who told me that I just spouted the guff all psychologists spout. Oliver who drank two bottles of wine a day and did so while holding down an admittedly undemanding job. Leone who killed herself. In between the evident failures and the successes there are those who fall into that shadow world where nothing is quite that clear. I saw several people who continued to attend, week in, week out, sometimes for one, two or more years, whose depression, or whatever the original problem was, remained relatively untouched by the therapy. Yet they continued to come to see me and not because I encouraged them to do so, offering them a slim hope of eventual recovery, but because they got something else out of it. Psychotherapy is not only about getting better. For some people the regular support, the opportunity to unburden themselves in a place of safety, the *secure base* that Bowlby wrote about, the chance to think about their lives, both past and present, is just as important, perhaps more so.

As they grow older, some people become more negative and sceptical, even cynical, putting down the enthusiasm of the young as hopelessly naïve. Even Freud, toward the end of his life, became pessimistic about the ability to help people through analysis. I do not think that way about psychotherapy or anything else. I am no longer the callow youth who rushed in, all guns blazing, seeking to make people better. It would be strange if I were! At the end of my career I was a different sort of therapist, more reflective, more willing to listen, focussed as much on the person as on techniques, more tolerant of foibles and failure, less driven. My approach to psychotherapy was balanced between the search for meaning that I believe is universal in humans and the desire to give succour, to provide relief from unhappiness and from life's vagaries and problems. A good psychotherapist should be able to do both.

I am standing by the door of my consulting room. I look into the room as I have done thousands of times. The two burgundy leather armchairs face each other across the familiar low table. Empty. Silent. It could be any other day but it is not. My last patient left five minutes ago. There will not be another. I hesitate, then go over and sit in one of the chairs. I look up at the alcoves of books, my psychotherapy library, the external manifestation of my professional persona. I catch sight of *Attachment, Separation, Loss*. The Bowlby trilogy. "I guess I'm on *Loss* now," I say out loud. Ironically, with a knowing half-smile. Irony, that defence against uncomfortable feeling. I do not actually feel very much of anything. Though I know I shall never see another patient for psychotherapy, I feel no triumph, no sadness or relief. No satisfaction at a long career concluded. No regret at my decision to end. It is just like the end of another working day. Maybe, I think, this is what death will feel like. Just the end of another day. Night falls and another morning expected, though there won't be one. I frown. An unnecessarily morbid thought. *You're not facing death but a transition into something else*, I tell myself. *No need to be sentimental about this, John*. I recognize the tone of voice. My mother was never one to be sentimental. I heave myself out of the chair and go to the desk. I dutifully write a few lines of notes on the last session, close the file and put it away in the filing cabinet. Before I leave I again look round the room. I will change it, rearrange the furniture, but not yet. Let the room stay as it is for a while. Let the memories of all those sessions gradually fade until there is only the merest echo of all the words and feelings, the desires and hopes, the moments of happiness and those of despair, that the room has witnessed over the last 12 years of my career as a psychotherapist.

Forty-four years ago I gazed out of the window at the top of my parents' house on the Berkshire-Surrey borders, moodily waiting, unsure of what lay ahead, but anxious to get going, to discover what the world had in store and what I might give to the world. I chose psychology. I became a psychotherapist. That time has gone. In the phrase Kurt Vonnegut made his own, *so it goes*.

ACKNOWLEDGMENTS

Of the hundreds of patients I met in my career, a few of whom appear on these pages in heavily disguised form, many taught me about what is possible and what is fanciful in psychotherapy. I am grateful to them for insights that no textbook or workshop could provide.

Many colleagues—therapists, students, teachers, supervisors—have inadvertently contributed to this book simply because our paths crossed and they shaped the psychotherapist I came to be. They bear no responsibility for anything I have written but without them this book could not have existed.

Several writers and friends read earlier drafts of my manuscript and provided much needed critiques. I am grateful in particular to Anne Church Bigelow, Jenny Stanton, Peter Adamson, Gabrielle Townsend, Thierry Morel, Damian Gardner, Chris Allen, Christine Cox and Tim Sheehy.

I owe a particular debt to my wife, Mary, and my two daughters, Kate and Sarah, who provided unfailing encouragement together with sage advice about how to make my book entertaining and informative to a reading public. Their support, love and wisdom have been invaluable over the years.